Wolfgang Schneider, Lebogang L. Nawa (eds.)
Theatre in Transformation

WOLFGANG SCHNEIDER, LEBOGANG L. NAWA (EDS.)

Theatre in Transformation

Artistic Processes and Cultural Policy in South Africa

[transcript]

Based on the conference "Theatre in Transformation" held in Pretoria and Soweto, South Africa from 11-13 March 2016, supported by

Bibliographic information published by the Deutsche Nationalbibliothek
The Deutsche Nationalbibliothek lists this publication in the Deutsche Nationalbibliografie; detailed bibliographic data are available in the Internet at http://dnb.d-nb.de

© 2019 transcript Verlag, Bielefeld

Cover layout: Maria Arndt, Bielefeld
Cover illustration: Animal Farm by ShakeXperience, Durban 2015. Photo: Val Adamson © Nobulali Productions
Editing: Johanna Kraft
Typeset: Francisco Bragança, Bielefeld
Print: Majuskel Medienproduktion GmbH, Wetzlar
Print-ISBN 978-3-8376-4682-5
PDF-ISBN 978-3-8394-4682-9
https://doi.org/10.14361/9783839446829

Inhalt

THEATRE FOR YOUNG AUDIENCES.
THE ART OF EDUCATION

FREEDOM OF EXPRESSION.
PERSPECTIVES ON THE PERFORMING ARTS

Theatre in Transformation

Foreword of the editors

Wolfgang Schneider and Lebogang L. Nawa

In comparative political science, transformation is called a process of fundamental change in a political system and if necessary also in a social order.

Cultural policy research is also concerned with transformation processes, in particular through observations, analyses and reflections on the social role of art and culture. The publication is based on a research atelier in South Africa which assumes the following hypothesis: The inner and exterior condition of a theatre can be a mirror for the political condition of a whole country; serving as seismographs of a society and as their change agents.

The central questions are: What is the effect of a social transformation for the major arts theatres in South Africa? Where is the process apparent in the theatres, who are its agents, what are the underlying concepts? What does the idea of "transformation" mean for theatre? What were the working structures of the theatres in the 1970s and 80s? How did they change post-1994? What were the short-term and long- term consequences of the social changes for theatre? Which kind of political tendencies or statements emerged from the theatre before and after the liberation struggle against colonialism and apartheid – on stage and beyond the stage? Where could one perceive the transformation of the theatre (both, within the institution and in the exterior image)? In what format? How did the programming change? What changed, what became possible, what is completely ordinary today that was impossible before the liberation struggle? Who were or are – perhaps until today – the cultural political vectors of such a transformation within or exterior to the theatre: Theatre directors? Cultural politicians on the level of municipalities, regions or the state? Workers unions? Theatre staff? Actors' companies? The theatre scene surrounding the theatre? The media? If yes, which media? Press? Radio? TV? Theatre specialised media? Visitors' organisations? International organisations? Foundations? Were there or are there any concepts for the transformation of a theatre? If yes: Who is its author and what was it or is it about? What is eventually the stadium of its realisation?

How did the attitude or even the concept for a transformation change during the time – within the board but as well within the theatre staff? Were there clear or even outspoken ideas about the process? How far and how fast did the cultural political requests or demands of the subsidising bodies change? What are the cultural political guidelines today and how do they differ between the theatres? Was the position of the Market Theatre (Johannesburg) or the Baxter Theatre (Cape Town), the State Theatre (Pretoria) or the Soweto Theatre – a better one since it had this history of an anti-apartheid-theatre? What were the expectations of the public after liberation? What are the expectations of the theatre scene? Which coherence do you see between those transformations and the cultural political requirements or guidelines of the Republic of South Africa? Are those transformations its result? Or did those processes influence the development of the local, regional or national cultural policies agenda? What was or is finally and accordingly the understanding the role of theatres in the South African transformation society?

Theatre has always been a key art for South Africans. It was one of the struggle grounds of the oppositions against apartheid in the seventies and eighties. But the theatre has lost most of its old audiences during the last twenty years and the struggle for new audiences is ongoing and is far from being won. That means that today, the leading theatres are friendly "colleagues" and some-times strategic partners.

"During Apartheid, they represented different countries in terms of ideolo-gies, audiences and programming", said leading South African critic Adrienne Sichel about the two Gauteng theatres. The Market Theatre was founded in Johannesburg in 1976 by a group of idealistic artists. They chose Johannes-burg's old Indian Fruit Market – built in 1913 – to host their venue which was conceived to be accessible by people of all races and skin colour, just as the old market which had provided food for everybody. That was the reason why the area was exempted from the strict access regulations of the era which hardly allowed people to mix with each other. But as soon as the Market started to work properly, it became internationally renowned as South Africa's leading anti-apartheid theatre with shows like *Woza Albert!, Asinamali, Sophiatown, Born in the RSA* and many of Athol Fugard's plays.

Similarly, the National State Theatre in Pretoria was built on the site of the former fruit and vegetable market place. But while the Market Theatre used the old historic buildings and refurbished them, the monolithic building of the State Theatre complex was built in 1981 on the old market site after its demo-lition. It was the former province of Transvaal which funded and constructed the complex with its originally five theatres, rehearsal rooms, workshops and administration offices for its Performing Arts Council of the Transvaal (PACT); an umbrella for opera, ballet and the English and Afrikaans drama companies which were working according to central European repertory theatre traditions, although the international culture boycott at this time prevented South African theatre companies from playing international contemporary plays.

Cape Town's Baxter Theatre was founded in August 1977 as the theatre of the University of Cape Town. From its very first days, it was an alternative to the publicly subsidised Nico Malan Theatre Centre (today called Artscape Theatre Centre). While Nico Malan was under the influence of the government which was able to influence its programme and prevent critical or challenging works, the Baxter was much less under control since it was protected to a certain degree by the university's academic freedom, though it did not have the same challenging profile as the openly oppositional Market Theatre.

Theatres were among the first places to be opened for all the races as far as it was possible in 1977, which means that the State Theatre buildings were since its opening in 1981 accessible for all audiences. In the late eighties, several Black actors, dancers and singers were being employed by the different PACT companies. After the first democratic elections in 1994, the four regional performing arts councils and their companies were dissolved and transformed into 'receiving houses', which continued to be state funded – a matter which is quarried in the book. From 2005 onwards, the Windybrow Theatre in Hillbrow, Johannesburg as well the Market Theatre became state funded. The State Theatre underwent a severe crisis when the whole institution was shut down by the Ministry of Culture after revelations about corruption and budgetary deficits and was only reopened two years later.

In 2002, that the young Aubrey Sekhabi was appointed as new artistic director of the State Theatre. Together with his associated director, Mpumeleleo Paul Grootboom, they transformed the institution to one of the powerhouses of theatre on the African continent. The Market Theatre was led by the charismatic director Malcolm Purkey from 2004 to 2013. He was succeeded by James Ngcobo; actor and director who had already been working for most of the time with the Market Theatre during the Purkey era. He is now the very first Black director of South Africa's legendary "theatre of struggle". Since the Baxter Theatre was founded in a period of a beginning opening of the South African society, the theatre is proud to issue a statement, as it should, in its current website, to the effect that: "Even through the difficult years of racial segregation its doors remained open to everyone and it thrived, drawing on indigenous talent and creating a uniquely South African theatre tradition." (Baxter Theatre Centre)

The research atelier aims to describe – from different perspectives – the transformation process of the leading, publicly funded South African theatres from the time of apartheid until today: From inside the theatre, through the eyes of the theatre directors as well as of the employees, and from outside, through the eyes of political responsible persons, the accompanying observers of the theatre landscape.

The editors are proud to present a collection of different researches and cultural-political positions, which proclaim the diversity of the theatre landscape in South Africa, which mark divergent development and all of them document the relevance of the performing arts in processes of transformation. In this aspect the publication is also a contribution in the discourse on art, art education and their role in the society, South Africa; an example and model for a vibrant cultural policy that is indeed supported and promoted by the artists and the civil society alike. Unless otherwise specifically stated, the views expressed by the authors in the book do not necessarily reflect those of the editors.

The significance of this process, particularly the three-days symposia held from 11 to 13 March 2016 around which this book is compiled, was best captured by Aubrey Sekhabi during his welcome address on Friday 11 March 2016 at the State Theatre. Sekhabi acknowledged that it was seldom that South African Black Theatre practitioners in particular met to exchange views on the State of Theatre in South Africa at certain intervals. Consequently, their views were often misrepresented by their White counterparts who happen to possess the means of production and dissemination of information, including in publications. This statement became a refrain throughout the three days. Thus Sekhabi saw the gathering, and by extension the book, as golden opportunities to reverse the trend.

Indeed, the gathering as well as this book became rare platforms for convergence of intergenerational mix and intersectoral or intersectional pollination of multi-perspectives far broader than the anti-apartheid struggle mainly focused on race dynamics. It brought to the surface, in full measure or force, new faces and voices with images and lexicons different if not disturbing to conservative ears and eyes in themes around patriarchy, femicide, homophobia, xenophobia and other social ills concealed during apartheid and not given prominence as part of the struggle against socio-economic and political injustices. The unfamiliarity of new ethos thus sets apart this book from its recent predecessors as it broadens the scope of the definition of transformation far beyond mere changes in systems and structures. They probe the plausibilities and validities of the philosophies informing them against authentic versatile African cultural grid not wired to prescriptive universal idioms not conducive or relevant to real local conditions. Hence, theatre practitioners across the country have gone out on their own to create alternative theatre spaces than government-commissioned Soweto Theatre, for instance.

Against this backdrop, the occasion also brought to spin with ironic twists or paradox impressions of theatre from perspectives inside and outside the country. For instance, in "The ideal of a Rainbow Nation: What theatre arts and cultural policy in Europe can learn from South Africa?" Julius Heinicke writes that "some of these ideas from South Africa could be taken up in Germany as a way of facing up to some of today's challenges" and that "these innovative techniques in theatre may give important impulses for the European context". It is curious whether the irony of the article is or is not lost to the fact that some of the innovations reflected in several articles by Heinicke's South African counterparts are inspired by German philosophers like Martin Heidegger of the earlier times of the 1920s and later followed by Bertolt Brecht? In South Africa, Heidegger's tenure represents the transition from colonialism to apartheid while Brecht captures the struggle against the fascist twins of Nazism and apartheid. Indeed, this implies that knowledge generation and dissemination spans across space and time as attested by the selection of panellists as well as article contributors across South Africa's geo-political demographics.

The other theme to emerge throughout the three legs of the research atelier is that 'a one size fits all cultural policy promotes imbalances' in the arts landscape with drastic consequences. Indeed, as if by prophecy or prediction, Sefako Mohlomi cautioned in his article, "Theatre Development and Cultural Policy in Rural Areas: A grassroots perspective from North West Province, South Africa", that cultural policy imposed on people as it is its provisions like infrastructure construction can be met by violent retaliation from the people it is supposed to serve. Indeed, in the month of April 2018 after this article, sustained violent protests in the North West province against political maladministration and lack of service culminated in the iconic Mmabana Arts Centre been vandalised and torched by angry residents. This, in short, is one of the prices to pay for lack or slow pace of transformation in South Africa.

Similarly, "The Art must burn", the title of an article in the "Culture Review" magazine Spring 2016 edition refers. It drew attention to the student protests in South Africa that took place at the same time as the team of the Hildesheim UNESCO-Chair in Cultural Policy for the Arts met South African cultural practitioners at the research atelier in Pretoria and Soweto. Matjamela Motloung concludes with these remarks shared by the editors:

"It is good that art is burning because art is supposed to provoke a position and for far too long South African artists particularly Black artists have been comfortable with receiving funding and responding to its needs. It's time we bring back the artist that recognises their position in society and probe, and make the art that disturbs the status quo." (Motloung 2016)

The editors are grateful to the facilitators of the research atelier: Rolf C. Hemke und Daniel Gad from the University of Hildesheim. Thanks to the hosts of the venues where the discourse took place, namely: Aubrey Sekhabi from the State Theatre; Patrick Ebewo from the Tshwane University of Technology; and Mongane W. Serote from the Jo'burg Theatres under which Soweto Theatre falls. Thanks to all the lecturers, panellists, facilitators and the audience who took part of all the colloquiums. Thanks to all artists and academics for their insightful contributions to the publication through their articles afterwards as postscripts to the gatherings. And lastly, thanks to the publishing house Theater der Zeit in Berlin for allowing us to reprint some texts from the magazine "Down in a land of cages. New Theatre in South Africa" (2009).

Black, White and, Coloured written with a capital letter indicate that it is not a 'white', 'coloured' or 'black skin colour', but a constructed social category for the designation of persons.

Bibliography

Baxter Theatre Centre. Available: http://www.baxter.co.za/general-informati on/, Last Access: 14/7/2018.

Motloung, Matjamela: Art must burn. In: Culture Review 2016. Available: www.culture-review.co.za/art-must-burn.

Prologue: Time to take stock?

The Role of Theatre in Transformation

Rolf C. Hemke

The South African theatre scene has a unique position on the continent. No other country has so many state-subsidised theatres, such quality and breadth of theatre education, so many large, well-frequented festivals, along with serious theatre critics who are known to the wider public. So South Africa must be in a good position? Not really. Because the theatre scene that has produced internationally renowned artists such as Athol Fugard and William Kentridge, along with a younger generation that includes Brett Bailey and Mpumelelo Paul Grootboom, has found itself in a state of permanent crisis ever since the end of apartheid. However, the economic situation has never been better for most theatre makers who currently shape the Anglophone theatre scene, as those who were already active in 1994 were involved in the anti-apartheid theatre movement. This meant that they never received any public subsidies. But in terms of content, no other theme has been able to replace the one great 'enemy' that was alluded to and protested against at that time, a theme that united audiences and theatre makers alike...

Hybrid identities

Today, the country's eleven official national languages and even more numerous – often hybrid – cultural identities are a key factor. It therefore requires a certain pragmatism and robustness to even attempt to outline some basic categories of theatre. Yet this is probably essential for making such an essay on the transformation of a theatre system easier to comprehend. Hauptfleisch refers to "the lines of categories such as 'White theatre in English', 'White theatre in Afrikaans', 'Black theatre in English', and 'Black theatre in vernacular'". (Hauptfleisch 1997: 6). He also points out that such kinds of categories are "symptomatic of the self-consciousness created in all cultural discourse in South Africa by a cultivated and imposed racist ideology", but at the same time admits that he has no other pragmatic solution other than "working with the parameters of these cultural classifications." Of course there are certain projects that now involve actors with different skin colours, but such projects remain very much the exception and can fail miserably, such as in the famous case of Mpumelelo Paul Grootboom's *Interracial* (cf. Grootboom's 2010, 199 ff./ 202 ff.; ibid., Carp, S. 206 ff.).

The general economic crisis that South Africa seems unable to shake off also serves to ensure the persistence of existing social structures; a situation that continues to fuel ethnic divisions throughout society – even without apartheid laws. This is also reflected in the country's theatre. The partly commercial theatre scene in the Cape is predominantly White, and productions are in Afrikaans. Its financial situation is still different from that of the English-speaking, mainly Black scene, which is concentrated in Gauteng – so Johannesburg and Pretoria. English-speaking theatres in and around Cape Town – such as the famous, university-supported Baxter Theatre under White director Lara Foot – also suffer from lack of funding, but they enjoy worldwide artistic renown. When considering this situation, the key word remains the same: 'transformation'.

A prerequisite for writing about transformation is writing about the process of transformation: "One transforms a piece of clay into a sculpture, transforms noise into something called music, before the eyes of an audience a rather ordinary looking fellow may be transformed into a king," writes Rob Baum (2013: 19). But when it comes to the transformation process of South African theatre from apartheid through the phase of peaceful revolution to the 'new', democratic South Africa of today, it is better to approach the term from a political standpoint: "In South Africa 'transformation' is a political term denoting contemporary social and economic reforms." (Ibid: 18)

But this throws up new questions, as Aubrey Sekhabi, Director of the State Theatre in Pretoria since 2002, highlighted in his introduction to the *Theatre in Transformation* conference that was held in Pretoria on 11 March 2016: "One can't help but ask a few questions when talking about transformation – what are we talking about? Are we talking about the transformation of the leadership of the institutions, are we talking about the transformation of the media or the transformation of the content. [...] What has really transformed? [...]".

Faltering transformation

The location of the first day of this 2016 conference, the huge State Theatre, is one of the most symbolic places for such a debate, as was pointed out by Adrienne Sichel, renowned theatre critic for the Johannesburg *Star*. The huge concrete block with its six stages of varying sizes in the centre of Pretoria was inaugurated in 1980 as a demonstration of the power of White colonial culture – at a time when the country's political system had long since begun to crumble. In June 2000, the culture minister closed the theatre due to massive budget overruns and corruption. This opened up the possibility of dissolving the theatre, dance and opera companies that were still based there, remnants of the end of apartheid. Since Aubrey Sekhabi reopened the theatre in 2002, the complex has primarily functioned as a receiving house, a guest performance venue that has no artistic budget but receives funding solely for building management and technical staff. Aubrey Sekhabi eloquently explained how this presented a huge problem, as funding for artistic projects had to be applied for on an individual basis, and this applied to all five state theatres, including the Johannesburg Market Theatre.

On the following days, the other two conference venues proved symbolic of the upheavals caused by this faltering transformation. For a long time, the organisers were unsure whether the University Theatre of Tshwane would be available because academic activities were being disrupted by massive student strikes, while the chic Soweto Theatre received them in an atmosphere of protest. Young cultural activists had gathered to urge them: "don't talk, act". At the time of the conference, the magnificent, colourful, newly erected building, which was fenced off from its poor surroundings, was at a standstill as the director's contract had run out the previous year. Despite much toing and froing, a successor had still not been appointed and all the funding had been used up, so the theatre was no longer able to present an artistic programme. It took almost a year, until 2017, before a new director was appointed. When – and the question has something sibylline about it – will it be possible to say that the South African theatre system has completed its transformation?

Black Protest Theatre

During the apartheid era positions were clear – at least as far as South Africa's Black majority was concerned. One the one side there was 'White' theatre – well funded because it was subsidised or commercially successful – and on the other side there was 'Black' Protest Theatre. Author and activist Mike van Graan has studied this style of theatre, saying: "'Protest Theatre' is not unique to South Africa. [...] 'Protest Theatre' is a genre of theatre that manifests itself in many situations of political conflict and social oppression, and unashamedly calls itself by this name." (Van Graan 2006: 278) White South Africans who opposed apartheid had their own particular reasons for attending such performances, as van Graan states with a touch of irony: "Watching Protest Theatre was like going to confession for their collective sin as beneficiaries of apartheid." He goes on: "[...] there is a sense that 'Protest Theatre' was regarded as inferior theatre, theatre that wouldn't stand the tests of 'good theatre'" (ibid.: 279). This may be due to a circumstance that Zakes Mda describes as follows: "Theatre was a mobilisational force, and for many a practitioner, supported by an audience eager to be rallied to action, it was fulfilment enough that the theatre effectively served that function." (Mda 2002: 283)

Van Graan then attempts to describe the features and characteristics that distinguished South African Protest Theatre in the anti-apartheid struggle. His criteria can be summed up as follows: the focus was on the message, which was conveyed to the audience in a very straightforward storytelling style, often by addressing the audience directly. Each actor usually played a number of roles, while costumes, props and set design – if they even existed – were kept to a minimum, for budgetary reasons and for the sake of greater mobility. Actors mostly had little or no training, and the characters they played often looked more like caricatures or clichés of types than dramaturgically developed characters. Many performances also involved music and dance. The performances originated and mainly took place in township community centres, and were based on a democratically organised workshop system without any real author or director (cf. van Graan 2006: 278).

The 'White side' of Protest Theatre

However, we should not ignore the fact that the protagonists of Protest Theatre also included some well-known White theatre makers, such as Barney Simon and Athol Fugard. As part of the Protest Theatre movement, they were among the small band of artists who originally drew attention to the South African Protest Theatre style through their productions, for example at the Market Theatre, and at a time when there was a 'cultural ban' on taking South African art and culture abroad, they were able to attract international support for the anti-apartheid movement (cf. van Graan 2006: 281f.).

Against this backdrop, it is also worth mentioning the little-known fact that perhaps the two best-known Protest Theatres in the anti-apartheid struggle, at least among those that were also supported by Whites, had the benefit of at least some indirect financial support from the apartheid government. Although the Market Theatre deliberately rejected any form of direct state aid, it had signed a lease agreement with the City Council of Johannesburg for the theatre premises in the former vegetable market in Johannesburg at a price well below the market price. The Baxter Theatre in Cape Town, on the other hand, was and remains largely supported by the University of Cape Town, which, like all other universities, received government grants during the apartheid era (cf. Hauptfleisch 1997: 166).

Theatre that goes beyond good and evil

At the heart of the institutionalised 'White' theatre scene of the apartheid era were the four fully subsidised Performing Arts Councils (PAC) in the country's four provinces of that time. They provided a Eurocentric audience in the metropolitan areas with culture (cf. van Herden 2011: 85f.) and – similar to German repertory theatres – worked with their own theatre, opera and dance companies. From the early 1990s, South African society found itself on a path to a change that, as it gradually became clear, would be irreversible. "It was a time of huge conjecture, replete with wildly oscillating emotional responses to the equally tumultuous daily events in what has on occasion rather aptly been referred to as 'pre-post-apartheid' South Africa." (Hauptfleisch 1997: 160) Perhaps the most famous anti-apartheid writer of his time, Athol Fugard, described how deeply shaken he felt: "After the democratic transition, I had a sense that I had outlived my time and become redundant, because I was a voice that plugged into the energy and the conflicts of the old South Africa. [...] Those conflicts [...] were a very energizing factor in my writing." (Mda 2002: 282) Here, Zakes Mda adds that many other, less gifted, authors could not have accompanied the transition from apartheid to democracy in their writings, simply because the South African reality during apartheid was such an absurdity that an accurate, realistic retelling of everyday events on stage would have seemed like a piece of absurd theatre – a recipe that simply did not work after the end of apartheid. The clear narrative of good and evil was at an end: "We are now faced with complexities and ambiguities that we need to interpret." (Ibid.: 282)

During this period, Hauptfleisch identified four categories of artistic reactions, which he describes in detail. While the "return" – as he calls it – to classical material and the increased focus on commercial entertainment theatre are not the subject of this essay, categories one and four deserve closer consideration. This reveals that his first category actually includes two different forms of theatre. He describes the first of these as:

"[...] highly emboldened avantgarde, obscene, politically aggressive and other previously banned forms of theatre. Thematically the topics in this kind of theatre range widely, with continued interest in issues of intolerance, violence, feminism, gay life, euthanasia, aids, religion, Afrikanerdom, and a variety of cultural rituals" (Hauptfleisch 1997: 160).

This brings Hauptfleisch to the possibility of producing theatre that has greater social relevance and developing new forms of applied theatre, which he finally classifies as a development of the Protest Theatre of the anti-apartheid movement: "[...] the concept of 'theatre as a weapon in the struggle' has been replaced by notions of 'theatre for healing' and 'theatre as bridge builder' in the public forums of cultural debate and in the companies being set up" (ibid.).

He describes the fourth category as the "creation of an 'African' or South African theatre, taking the classical forms and styles of the pre-colonial era, blending them with the best of the 'struggle period', in a new hybrid. This 'crossover' movement is extremely far developed in the music arena [...]" (ibid.: 162). These words strongly remind me of what *Sarafina* composer Mbogeni Ngema said to me in an interview during a guest performance of one of his productions at the Ruhrfestspiele Recklinghausen in spring 1998: "We must all pay allegiance to Africa, know that we are African whether we are Black or white [...] that is the job that we need to work on in South Africa as artists, together, collectively, to produce African work." (Hemke 2000: 27) According to Hauptfleisch, readers of the theatre magazine *Scenaria* during the apartheid era were faced with a different view of these developments in theatre: "[...] they fear that it will become totally 'Africanized' (i.e. gum-boot dancing, naked girls, drums and incoherent shouts, replacing the epic poetry of Shakespeare) [...]. It is a paranoia graphically expressed in virtually every issue of journals such as *Scenaria* for the past five years." (Hauptfleisch 1997: 164)

Transformation processes through theatre festivals

However, changes to the traditional structures began immediately with the first free elections in 1994, when the new ANC government redivided the country into nine provinces. In 1996, the *White Paper on Arts, Culture and Heritage* was adopted, which became the basis for a structural reform of public subsidies for the arts. The PACs' budgets were slashed and subsequently converted into venues for co-productions and guest performances, without resident companies. From then on, the PACs and independent theatre producers and groups had to apply to the newly formed National Arts Council (NAC) for funding for artistic productions (cf. van Herden 2011: 86). The PACs were dissolved in 2000 and the building complexes were gradually placed under new – mostly Black – management. Indeed, the State Theatre in Pretoria only reopened after two years (cf. Sichel 2010: 170; 172). Many (predominantly White) artists whose livelihoods were previously secure suddenly found themselves economically marginalised and in need of new sources of income (cf. van Herden 2011: 93f.).

As a result, over the years that followed a kind of festival scene developed in South Africa. This particularly served to exploit smaller, but artistically more or less advanced productions (which could not be commercially exploited in the urban centres for runs of several weeks) and repositioned the role and importance of such events in South Africa. A key role in this new wave was played by the concerted efforts of numerous arts organisations to uphold and support the Boer language, Afrikaans. Therefore, in the second half of the 1990s there were two factors that came together and led to the establishment of a number of festivals (cf. ibid.: 90f.). The movement gained particular momentum with the founding of the Stigtingvir Afrikaans, the Foundation for the Afrikaans Language, which was tasked with generating funding and spending it on the promotion of Afrikaans (cf. Hauptfleisch 1997: 165). This led to the foundation of the KKNK, the Little Karoo National Arts Festival, in Oudtshoorn in 1995, followed by the Aardklop Nasionale Kunstefees (Earth-Beat National Arts Festival) in Potchefstroom, the Afrikaanse Woordfees (Afrikaans Word Festival) in Stellenbosch and many more. However, these festivals tended to attract mainly White South Africans, and particularly Afrikaans-speaking Boers. This was noted by Mokong Simon Mapadimeng in 2013, when he wrote: "Arts festivals too still occur largely on racial lines which in turn limits opportunities for interracial dialogue. They remain largely racially divided and less integrated as the predominantly white Afrikaans festivals [...]; the predominantly Black African festivals [...]." (Mapadimeng 2013: 69; 79) He mentions the traditional National Arts Festival of Grahamstown and the Cape Town International Jazz Festival as being some of the few festivals that attract mixed audiences. "These festivals are elite in nature as they are not easily accessible to economically marginalised ordinary South Africans." (Ibid.) But he fails to explain why these particular 'elite festivals' tend to attract a more mixed audience.

Rainbow audiences?

My own observations during repeated visits over several days to Grahamstown suggest that the audience structure of the individual events depends very much on what is on offer. The audience at the huge Fringe and Community Theatre Festival, which takes place in Grahamstown alongside the actual, interdisciplinary main programme, is usually not mixed. This festival runs along the same lines as the Edinburgh Fringe. In principle, anyone can rent a venue and perform whatever they want. So the programme is anything but elitist, and the audience acts in a strictly affirmative way along racial lines.

The situation is different with the relatively limited selection of events on offer in the official programme of the National Arts Festival. Here, too, it can be seen that a Black director and author's theatre performance with a company of this kind tends to be more popular with a coloured audience than a ballet performance by the Cape Town City Ballet, for example. Nevertheless, the proportion of people with a 'different' skin colour is significantly higher, which may actually be due to the fact that these are hand-picked, prominent artists or companies that are perceived as relevant by an educated White, Coloured and Black audience that can afford the ticket prices.

The reasons for this audience behaviour have little to do with the theatre, but more with the overall social context. Mapadimeng also mentions this, citing general legislation such as the Employment Equity Act and the Skills Development Act, which, however, have had limited results. He goes on to explain that: "[...] the economy still remains by and large white owned and controlled. [...] [R]ace remains not only the aspect of identity but also the key marker of socio-economic and political inequality" (Mapadimeng 2013: 69 f.).

The fact that the composition of the audience is also affected by this comes down to economic reasons, as Mapadimeng explains. Since the end of apartheid, residential areas have remained divided along racial lines, particularly because many Blacks cannot afford to move away from their traditional residential districts. Mapadimeng adds: "In places where black Africans reside, the infrastructure for cultural and artistic activities such as community theatres, dance studios and company arts centres are underdeveloped" (ibid.: 69; 75) – apart from a few rare exceptions. This concerns both the infrastructure for professional or semi-professional artistic activities and the access of large sections of the Black population to art. The change in the balance of power in theatre management and in the management of the major theatres is also progressing so slowly (even to this day) that at the prestigious Naledi Awards ceremony in 2008 (South Africa's 'theatre Oscars'), *Lion King* composer Lebo M. Morakewent on the attack, calling the theatre industry "untransformed" and dominated by Whites (cf. ibid.: 69; 77). This stirred up a great deal of controversy, but little changed.

Changing the system

If theatres are to attract audiences, they have to respond to their needs – this is one of the guiding principles of the State Theatre in Pretoria. Its long-time director Aubrey Sekhabi cites the example of how the theatre regularly schedules matinée performances (not only for school classes), because for many Black residents of distant townships, access to culture is limited to the city centres. Poor or non-existent local public transport connections in the evenings and high crime rates mean that it is important for many Black audience members to be able to travel home in daylight, as their journeys often take two hours or more.

"What has really changed?" asked Aubrey Sekhabi in his aforementioned opening speech at the *Theatre in Transformation* conference: "A lot has changed. Today you come to the theatre and you can see that from 10 o'clock there has been activity." He went on to mention four shows being held at the State Theatre at different times for different target audiences on that day, Friday 11th March 2016, including two school performances for some 1,200 schoolchildren. "That is the theatre that is really working. [...] How many people are writing about it? And why has nothing been written about it?" Here, Sekhabi highlights the need to take stock of a slow process that may be taken for granted by those who work within these structures. This is precisely the starting point for this discourse – taking a step back and taking stock, almost 25 years after the first free, secret and equal elections in South Africa. What has changed in South African theatre since then? How have its structures developed? Have things actually moved on more than many people realise? Or is the South African theatre scene still lagging behind the development of society as a whole, as some commentators suggested after the controversy stirred up at the Naledi Awards in June 2008?

Translated into English by Gill McKay.

Unless otherwise referenced, quotes are taken from panel discussions at the *Theatre in Transformation* conference held in Pretoria form 11 – 13 March 2016.

Bibliography

Baum, Rob (2013): Transforming the social body through arts praxis. In: Patrick Ebewo, Ingrid Stevens und Mzo Sirayi (eds.): Africa and beyond. Arts and sustainable development. Online. Newcastle upon Tyne, United Kingdom: Cambridge Scholars Publishing, p. 17-29.

Ebewo, Patrick; Stevens, Ingrid; Sirayi, Mzo (ed.) (2013): Africa and beyond. Arts and sustainable development. Arts, Society and Sustainable Development Conference. Online. Newcastle upon Tyne, United Kingdom: Cambridge Scholars Publishing.

Grootboom, Mpumelelo Paul (2010): ZUM TEUFEL MIT DEN WEISSEN! Fuck white people! In: Rolf C. Hemke (ed.): Theater südlich der Sahara. Theatre in Sub-Saharan Africa. Berlin: Theater der Zeit (Research, 77), p. 199-205.

Hauptfleisch, Temple (1997): Theatre and society in South Africa. Some reflections in a fractured mirror. 1st ed. Hatfield, Pretoria: J.L. van Schaik Academic.

Hemke, Rolf C. (2000): Identité et apartheid: parfum pour un chien mort. In: *UBU Scènes d'Europes*, (16/17), p. 27.

Hemke, Rolf C. (ed.) (2010): Theater südlich der Sahara. Theatre in Sub-Saharan Africa. Berlin: Theater der Zeit (Research, 77).

Mapadimeng, Mokong Simom (2013): Chapter Five. The Arts and Interracial Dialogue in Post-Apartheid South Africa: Towards Non-Racialism? In: Patrick Ebewo, Ingrid Stevens und Mzo Sirayi (ed.): Africa and beyond. Arts and sustainable development. Online. Newcastle upon Tyne, United Kingdom: Cambridge Scholars Publishing, p. 69-83.

Mda, Zakes (2002): South African theatre in an era of reconciliation. In: Frances Harding (ed.): Performance Arts in Africa. A Reader. First Edition: Routledge, p. 279-289.

Sichel, Adrienne (2010): Die ungleichen Brüder. In: Rolf C. Hemke (ed.): Theater südlich der Sahara. Theatre in Sub-Saharan Africa. Berlin: Theater der Zeit (Recherchen, 77), p. 170-180.

Van Graan, Mike (2006): From Protest Theatre to the Theatre of Conformity? In: *South African Theatre Journal* 20 (1), p. 276-288.

van Heerden, Johann (2011): Beyond the Miracle: Trends in South African Theatre and Performance after 1994. In: Kenechukwu Igweonu (ed.): Trends in twenty-first century African theatre and performance. Amsterdam, New York: Rodopi (Themes in theatre, 6), p. 85-111.

Theatre in Transformation. The history

Arts and Culture in South Africa
Taking Centre Stage on the Globe from Colonialism, Fascism, Apartheid and Beyond

Mongane W. Serote

The first fight against colonial rule in South Africa started in 1492 when the Khoi and the San fought against the mighty Portuguese who attempted to settle by force of arms in the South Western shore of our country. Armed with bow and arrows, spears and *knob-kerrie*[1] and using cattle trained for warfare as artillery, the Khoi and the San defeated the mighty Portuguese army which scuttled back to Portugal.

It can be claimed that in the 21st century, those Khoi and San warriors were then fighting for our current sovereignty, independence, democracy and the African Renaissance. So also did the AmaZulu at the Battle of Isandlwana in 1879 when they defeated the mighty British army which scuttled, tail between its legs, licking its wounds.

Today, we are still in the same trenches as the Khoi and the San, AmaZulu, and the various warriors from different language groups throughout the length and breadth of our country, who laid their lives down for the freedom of our country, fighting against forced European settlers with the objective to colonise our people – a scourge which lasted for over five centuries when eventually, through the liberation struggles, the apartheid system disintegrate at the feet of the Mass Democratic Movement (MDM) – led by the African National Congress (ANC) together with other liberation movements like the Pan Africanist Congress (PAC) and the Black Consciousness Movement (BCM). Even as we have negated tribalism, racialism, apartheid and colonialism relentlessly with unprecedented courage as a people, with unflinching commitment and conviction that, if we are not free, and if others are not free in this world, no one is free, still, we are aware that the human spirit is not free. In 1994, South Africa joined Africa and the countries of the world – as a politically free country.

---

1 | Knob-Kerrie is an Afrikaans phrase for hand-baton or stick used as weapon alongside a spear and shield.

It must be stated without any contradiction whatsoever that imperialism, a scourge of the world in the 21st century, is a crime against humanity. All we need to do is to understand why things are as they are in Libya, Iraq, the Sahel, Syria, Mali, Ivory Coast, Zimbabwe, Venezuela, Brazil, and in some Asian and Latin American countries where what the people there had built for themselves is being or has been torn apart. As Africans, if we claim our continent and the African Diaspora and state that in the international world, the so-called Globe, we belong to the South; we will note that what defines us as such, besides our geographical positions, and the fact of our being endowed by nature with immeasurable resources, is the fact that we bear the deep wounds inflicted upon us by imperialism during the decades of the cold war, as we pitted our struggles against imperialist countries supported by the Soviet Union and Cuba, and now we find ourselves in a unipolar globe. The direct result from that system of imperialism is the emergence of terrorism which has rendered the whole world as an unsafe terrain of bloodletting; which must in our minds translate to "An injury to one is an injury to all..."

From Apartheid to Liberation

For us as South Africans, we come from a not so long ago past when apartheid, as a system, was like a full blown cancer devouring organs and organism with impunity from the South African national body, disregarding anything which tried to stop it. Then, all of us as cultural workers in our country took centre stage. We were inspired by the spirit of commitment and sacrifice of the masses of our country and of the world which did not only express their outrage against the apartheid system, but committed to fight against it and to destroy it.

In 1982, we declared in Gaborone, Botswana, while, anchoring the arts and culture struggle on the foundations which were there already in South Africa, on the continent, and in the world, through a program called "Çulture and Resistance" which primed more Arts and Culture events to assert and confirm, that Arts and Culture is part and parcel of the liberation struggle. We did not end there.

We took centre stage in Europe, America, the Soviet Union, Asia, Latin America, through musicals, theatre, poetry readings, photography, film, music, plastic arts and dance, to emancipate and liberate the African voice. And as we did so, we formed allies with ordinary people in the world, and they formed allies with us so as to liberate the voices of the oppressed throughout the world also. We could do so because there was the liberation movement, the ANC and the MDM and other liberation organisations like the PAC and BCM, and there was the anti-apartheid Movement. We contributed to the emergence of a culture of a people to people democracy which would have known no boarders. We can claim that those efforts contributed to the African consciousness which had been planted on the continent by the African political giants, collaborating with other political giants in the diaspora, and Asia before and after the Bandung conference; all of which unleashed the spirit of Pan Africanism, African Renaissance and the call for the freedoms of people of the world. The Non-aligned Movement (NAM) emerged and as also the Organisation of African Unity (OAU) emerged.

We must remind ourselves that it is against this impeccable and long standing backdrop of struggle, nationally and internationally, that the discussions between the Jo'burg Theatres, represented by myself as its Chairperson, as well as some of its Board members in the names of Messrs Ishmael Mkhabela and Mabutho "Kid" Sithole, and some South African theatre and cultural personalities and the German theatre and cultural academics from Tshwane University of Technology and the University of Hildesheim respectively, were held at the Soweto Theatre in Soweto on 13 March 2016. The partnership being explored gives both sides a perfect opportunity to enter into similar partnerships with other cultural workers and groups in Europe and our continent, and other peoples of the world to mount the global centre stage and regain what is still fresh in the minds of the peoples of the world; a promising time of optimism and hope!

The Arts flourish within the Human Spirit

Mollowa Ditshomo rendered a moving performance piece before the partnership discussions that brought back the memories of the struggle when there was a slogan that stated: "When one comrade falls, other comrades must pick up his or her spear and fight on..." This group is based at one of the art centres of our country – the Funda Community College – which was part and parcel of the South African tapestry portraying the cultural expressions of our Nation.

About three or four weeks before the partnership discussions at the Soweto Theatre, we had the opportunity to spend time with the creative people who are based there including, *Mollo,* and others who were involved in other different art forms under the auspices of the Department of Arts and Culture (DAC) program called the *Living Legends Legacy Project* (LLLP). We heard about how Funda has been invaded by a group of hooligans who have occupied the centre to rent it out to churches so that they can make money. These hooligans claim that they were freedom fighters and that because of that; they are entitled to live by all means necessary. The creative people, including *Mollo* who have countered that hooliganism, are currently reclaiming the space as it should be; a place where the arts are nurtured.

Historically, Funda produced many outstanding cultural workers: writers, actors, dancers, musicians, plastic artists, etc. It was most moving to experience how *Mollo* and others, led by Mme[2] Dikeledi Molatoli, were determined to reclaim that space to lift it up almost bare-handed and with the tips of their fingers, to find a manner to give it life again. During the struggle, Funda was an oasis of arts and culture which contributed to a culture of resistance not only in South Africa, but as said, in the world as well. How can it then be a place of hooligans in the period when non-racialism, non- sexism and democracy are being nurtured? The arts flourish within a cultural context where the human spirit claims freedoms and overruns barriers. If one knew of Funda during its days of being part and parcel of the struggle for freedom in our country, looking at it now, one can say Funda is done. It is broken. It is a shameful skeleton of what it was which is now standing. It smells like a deserted toilet and has to be rescued by the people of Soweto; the young, who, in its name and history, must be ready to find the manner to ensure that it reclaims its past. Mme Molatoli and her group have picked up the spear of those people who, not so long ago, fought against the apartheid system and built Funda. This does not augur well. When you plant flowers and instead of them blooming, they rot; when you try to plant vegetables and worms emerge and eat up the plants; when the claim about prosperity is pronounced yet squatter areas and poverty are glaring; when those who were freedom fighters become hooligans who threaten the population. It is time to ponder; to introspect and to understand that things have gone terribly wrong. It is not only what we see which is an expression of things gone wrong, it is also what we hear. When the songs of struggle distort and ridicule the struggle, when instead of the diversity of the nation being the inspiration and strength of individuals and collectives, threatens the being of individuals, and tears collectives apart, indeed, things have gone terribly wrong.

Funda is a small symptom of a very large ailing body. The many art centres which had sprouted in rural, urban and suburbs of our country during the struggle have become derelict. It is not only what we see or hear which expresses the being of the body and the mind, it is when what we cannot see or hear or even touch, succumbs quietly to render us blind and deaf and unfeeling when we perpetually become weary that we must discover in us, the feel and understanding that, the spirit never gives in, nor does it die-it cannot be broken. A prolific and renowned German theatre icon and poet Bertolt Brecht and the outstanding African poet, David Mandessi Diop, have nurtured and contributed a narrative and discourse in Europe and the world, on the continent and the world respectively, which does not only claim politics as lives of people expressed and determined to make sense of why we are here in the world, but which is also as a creative narrative and discourse of the being and the spirit of the human race.

---

2 | Mme is affectionate reference to a woman in African sense rather than the common Western Ms. or Mrs.

Act for a future with quality of life for all

It is our responsibility, those of us who are alive to remember that symptoms are hazard lights alerting those who are watching that something is not in place for harmony. When a place where people are present releases a stench of a toilet, as the sermon ripples in the space, competing for position with the stench – it is a sign that even the people themselves deny the image they see in the mirror whether they are passing by the mirror or they are face to face with the image on the mirror. When it is like that it is indeed a time for introspection. The arts are moments to prime introspection; they are also a symbiotic process which must feed the spirit, the mind and the body because, as stated in Bertolt Brecht's play, *The Good Person of Szechwan*: "No one can be good for long if goodness is not in demand".

We are at that stage in the world when "goodness" must be in demand. Besides this having to be done so that we can make sense of why we are here in the world, which must be complemented by the priming of the spirit and feelings, as David Mandessi Diop asks in the poem, *Africa*:

"Africa tell me Africa
Is this you this back that is bent
This back that breaks under the weight of humiliation..." (*Africa*, a poem by D.M. Diop)

These nudge our spirit to read the writings on the wall, which must prime our spirituality and feelings to remind us that we are here so that life must be lived and lived so in living. We are experiencing protracted moments of assault by acts which contradict and negate the science and spirit of our revolution. We even feel us regress as if into the past where powers of tyranny hold reigns. All of us want a way out and that we must not lose the gains of the revolution. At the same time, the moment demands from us that we must understand what it is we must do and we must be to absolutely commit, and as we do so, to act for a future which must ensure quality of life for all and for a liveable world for us in the present and for coming generations.

Are these not moments of the arts, the inspiration of the mind and the heart which, after expression, must commit us to action where the goodness of the human-spirit resides? Both of us, South Africans and Germans, have been in pasts interspaced by the most horrible deeds by human beings – the brutal system of apartheid and the inhuman ideology of Fascism, respectively. Both our nations have inherited those pasts, as also we know that they came to pass through great effort, sacrifice, commitment and conviction which our people pitted against those systems.

I recall that there was, or there still is, a giant of theatre in Germany which commemorates Bertolt Brecht. It is called the Bertolt Brecht Ensemble. I reiterate that: "No one can be good for long if goodness is not in demand" of this giant of theatre and poetry who was taught by life and the life of political strug‐gle, not only in Germany, but also by the struggles of the people of world has stated. He was so taught and he taught the life of the arts to be a myriad of voices which become lullabies which must say to those who are in slumber that even in deep slumber dreams must know and be informed by actions. Brecht has also said that: "intelligence is not to make no mistakes, but quickly to see how to make them good" (Brecht 1965 p. 87) .This, the German poet reminds us South Africans and his country-men and women of an old time which came and went, that we in a new time with its swift speed, which is becoming one county – the globe, must not forget that the arts are pregnant with life expe‐riences that will outlive the human race and politics and become, according to Amilcar Cabral, a culture which determines history, whether positively or negatively (cf.Cabral 1970).What must we do when that history is negative?

We can do a simple thing. We can hold hands and create a song because we know that it is stated in *The Good Person of Szechwan* that: "No one can be good for long if goodness is not in demand." We can hold hands as we march and sing inspired by and anchoring on the souls of the old, the poor...as Diop through words repeats:

"Africa tell me Africa
Is this you this back that breaks under the weight of humiliation
This back with trembling scars
And saying yes to the whip under the midday sun" (*Africa*, a poem by D.M. Diop)

The poor of the world who have faced canons and automatic rifles chose to live than exist in death. They gave us a culture of holding hands together and sin‐ging. So did the June 16 1976 students in Soweto who instinctively knew that, as Brecht's play indicates: "No one will improve your lot if you do not yourself" say there is a vision, which appears, as if it were mist or in the mist, which portrays the history of our country and ties us together with the history of Ger‐many – as if we walk hand in hand in song marching. It is not a coincidence that the Jo'burg Theatres and the people who come from the Bertolt Brecht En‐semble country must sit and negotiate to work together in theatre and the arts. It is time to go home, to seek peace.

Praise Poetries, Night Songs and Ritual Dances as part of Theatre History

I am reminding us here in South Africa that as we had convened that way, we come from a history of theatre which was on stage earlier than the 40s, 50s, 60s, 70s, 80s – a span of over seven decades going far back even before *Dipha‐*

la, *Scathamiya*, *Mohobelo*, and many other indigenous theatres and art forms which not only entertained but also educated and pondered over the drastic changes which were taking place in the lives of Black people in our country. We go back to the time of praise poetry and story-telling, to the time of rituals and dances for the ancestors before the theatre of the church.

Theatre in South Africa has been an extremely important art form. The night songs in the dark under the stars and the moon; the dances and the praise poetries moments and sessions; the ululations whether for joy or sadness, the men and women, young and old in the different languages of the people of this country, in their wisdom and education, created consciousness, awareness of different forms of life understanding that, consciousness must be expressed in order that it must become action which shapes and develops people. Theatre or the arts in general as those rural masses understood, and as Bertolt has expressed, cannot be for its sake only. Our ancestors understood that.

One of the legends of our country, Gibson Kente, "The Father of South African Theatre" in the townships, is a person who, when the actor, Mr. Mabutho "Kid" Sithole, talks about and makes him become part of the myriad drama which one must take with after being exposed to the tour of the heritage sites of Soweto. Most South Africans, and one must add, because of the apartheid system – especially Black people in the townships – know the many theatre productions which Kente produced in this country. But also we must note that the many Black people he mentored as actors, producers, directors and so on have occupied the centre stage of this dramatic art and have incubated fresh ideas by being innovative with this art form. They have been most creative in laying bare the beauty, the beasts, the contradictions, the pain and the joy – the collective being of the South African nation.

Kente and his peers, Barney Simon, Athol Fugard, Sam Mhangwane and others, have not only been prolific drama creators, but they have also, many times, caught the unique but so tragic life experiences of South Africans and weaved in the South African consciousness, as also they have never hesitated to ask through theatre: is this what we came here for, is this what we were created for as human beings?

The Soweto Theatre, the first of its kind which is not an improvised derelict for theatre, but which was built during the democratic dispensation in Soweto for a population of 4 million people and hopefully for humanity, is now part of the widely sprawled Soweto landscape, literally and figuratively. It is a colourful building, and therefore very present among the houses and building structures which do not shy at all to express the social contradictions of the community of this place; it cannot just be a Black Theatre, yet also, it cannot not emerge as a metaphor of life not lived, building, a colourfully life.

The history which Sithole tells on the tour, when he was acting as a guide unravels a tapestry of the lives of this place called Soweto. It is a history full of dramatic episodes of tragedy, comedy, bravery, great human optimism, resilience, unrelenting hope and the unbreakable human spirit. To think of it and divert a bit; maybe "Kid" must consider opening a culture tours company. He is extremely good as a tour guide! He taught me many things I didn't know, even as a Sowetan, about the history of the township in which there is a great past; as so too there is the great present to that and there will be a great future which, in dramatic fashion, the past will stare into its #Yes or #No. In other words, to say history and the present are related must be interlinked and related.

The African Story must be told by the legends of African Arts

History has from a long time past made it clear that the drama of the young; in their being reckless, in their being deaf, and blind at times, in their being restless – but more importantly, in their sense of rage about the present and the past too which they find difficult to live with and in – signify a necessary future which must rupture what must be discarded so that a present to live in and a future to be lived in will stare us in the eye and ask: what must be done now?

History has never forgotten to demand knowledge about the past from us; nor has it ever forgotten to remind us to anticipate the future as the present will either be both interesting and/or dangerous to live in. In short – it is a dangerous drama when a people, any people forget their own history. That is why I will ask "Kid" Sithole whether he remembers the voice of the poets as a dramatist himself who were produced by Soweto and those together with them took the National stage by the scruff, during the struggle, giving the poor and the down trodden their spirituality, their thoughts, their being, and their voice.

I am really saying four things here, which I am also putting on the national agenda:

Firstly, I would like to pay tribute to the legends of the arts in Soweto, especially in the context of the liberation struggle in South Africa. These are the people who lived the arts when there was no government to pay anything for them, to put a play together, to put together a band, to do this or that in the arts. Sheer blood and sweat, including the fact that all of us understood at the time that what we were doing could put us in jail. I am not being romantic or sentimental when I say that, I am merely stating facts. I am saying this to say: young people who are in the frontline of the arts and culture now, must not neglect to understand the history of arts and heritage in this country. But we should also say it can be identified through people. Let me dare a dangerous thing and name them, knowing that I can never name all of them: Motsumi Makhene. Lebogang Nawa. Bobby Rodwell. Ngila Michael Muendane. "Kid" Sithole, Ishmael Mkhabela, Maishe Maponya – all of whom participated at the Soweto Theatre events as contributors and participants. To young people: if you don't know your parents' stories, and if your parents do not know their parents'

parents' stories and if mothers and fathers hide their stories from their children, those stories will express themselves through the children's madness. A history of a people is forever the identity of the future generations.

Secondly, it is extremely important that the African story must be told on the African continent. That must not mean that we must not also commit to tell other stories too – but the African voice must be emancipated, liberated and be loud clear from the African mouths in the world. The records of that history are the feel of the lives lived as expressed by the arts. What we are inside and outside of us must say about us that we come from that time, from that place and history!

The third thing I want to say is that it is very true, it is a harmonious condition of life, in the world that arts, culture and heritage have a role to play in the lives of the people and in the being of other forms of life and the universe. Arts, culture, and living, tangible and intangible heritage, are there as a collective in intricate, sensitive systems and relations, which forever demand to be known, lived, understood and forever discovered for the sake of life-arts and culture do not only build a nation, but can also sustain that nation against the greatest odds so that that nation/ nations not only discover meanings but also find the profound expression between science and spirituality, both of which attest to the fact that plans exist not coincidences.

Of course spirituality is elusive; that is if you do not understand joy, sadness, knowing, and feelings and you live without knowing how you know or do not know – these are eternal experiments and tests which happen every second, even at times when we are not aware that they are happening. What this must mean is that expression and reality forever relate and are related forever in infinite manners and measure...

The last thing which I want to say is that the arts do forever ask us: do you remember that feelings are important and that feeling is part of love? And lastly which the arts forever ask is that we must not forget to still search for that chip, the chip in our brain which says: you must remember that men and women are human.

Bibliography

Brecht, Bertolt: 20 of Bertolt Brecht's Most Famous Quotes. Available: http://artsheep.com/20-of-bertolt-brechts-most-famous-quotes/, Last Access: 25/6/2018.

Brecht, Bertolt (1992, 1965): The Jewish wife and other short plays. New York: Grove Press.

Cabral, Amílcar (1974, c1973): National Liberation Struggle and Culture. In: Amílcar Cabral (ed.): Return to the source. Selected speeches. New York, NY: Monthly Review Press, p. 39-56.

Pinholes against apartheid

A Brief History of Political Theatre in South Africa

Joachim Fiebach

The history of political theatre in South Africa is a turbulent one: The Township Theatre of Athol Fugard, that won fame in the 1970s and 1980s, just like the travelling theatre of Gibson Kente or the launch of Barney Simons famous Market Theatre, are the fruits of a theatre movement that had been growing throughout an almost hundred year period. The influence of this movement resonates right through to contemporary South African theatre – even Paul Grootboom's work would be unthinkable without Fugard or Simon.

A theatre retrospective

South African theatre first caught the attention of the European theatre scene and achieved world-wide recognition with a series of socially critical and particularly anti-apartheid productions: the beginnings of which were Athol Fugard's dramatic works in the 1970s, particularly the plays *Sizwe Bansi is Dead* and *The Island*. These were the result of Fugard's work with his Black African colleagues, the actors John Kani and Winston Ntshona. Soon following were works demonstratively developed through workshops such as *Survival* (1976) and *Woza Albert!* (1981/82).

This international success was continued well into the 1990s with the Handspring Puppet Company performances of William Kentridge's adaptations of European "classics" that were transposed into a South African context, such as *Woyzeck on the Highveld* and *Faustus in Africa*, which are still very much alive in people's memories today. These productions were financed by South African, Belgian and German funding and through international invitations and festival performances.

The montage of forms

With the montage of different theatrical forms and technical effects such as light, video and the use of puppetry, these performances point to a particular trait of South African theatre: the combination and integration of different theatrical forms and methods of expression. On the one hand this involves the utilisation and modification of Western theatre and musical conventions. On the other hand it is a continuation of the "traditional" African dramatic arts, essentially based on dance and music, and a reshaping of the storytelling theatre.

Elements of these kinds of specific artistic structures that characterise South African theatre can be traced back to the theatre practices of Black migrant workers from 1860 onwards. These workers came from the many different ethnicities of South Africa and Mozambique and streamed into the rapidly growing urban centres around the diamond mines in Kimberley, and from the 1880s onwards also flowed into the goldmine industry in Johannesburg. Besides the frequent traditional dance competitions, conditions in the mine settlements were reflected through comical and satirical sketches often performed through one-man-shows. The subject matter of these performances also came from their own established and familiar cultures. From the 1920s onwards, many professional travelling theatre groups combined both African performance techniques with musical performance practices borrowed from the Varieté shows that were imported from Western metropolises. Born of this was the specifically urban and often melodramatic syncretistic theatre form of Black South Africans.

From *No-Good Friday to Born in the RSA*

The different major dramaturgical and performance methods in South African theatre developed in parallel and then in a unified manner from the 1950s onwards from two initially quite different artistic movements: the emphatically political anti-apartheid theatre stood in contrast to the popular and musically oriented melodramatic travelling theatre. The former was initially modelled on western socially critical theatre conventions of bringing dramatic literature or written texts to the stage. The origins of which might be Athol Fugard's play *No-Good Friday*. This could be seen as the first significant beginnings of the socially critical anti-apartheid theatre from both Black and White opponents of apartheid. This play was developed in 1958 in collaboration with his Black colleagues after Fugard left Port Elizabeth and moved to the legendary Sophiatown in Johannesburg, which at that time was the highly creative focal point of South African culture. The piece revolved around "Tsotsies": young Blacks who organised themselves in gangs and attempted to extract themselves from the pressure of everyday living conditions under apartheid through anarchic violent behaviour, copied from the American gangster milieu.

Seen historically, the perhaps most important process was that of creating the play. Just as Fugard was both a creator and performer in his own piece, the other rehearsal participants collaborated in both the creation and the performance of the piece. They contributed new suggestions in experimenting with the approach and arrangement of the piece as well as to modifications in the text. From these origins begins a line that spans from *Sizwe Bansi is Dead* and *The Island* that Fugard collectively developed with John Kani and Winston Ntshona in the early 1970s, to the epochal productions of the Market Theatre's *Woza Albert!* by Percy Mtwa Mbongeni Ngema and Barney Simon, and the collective work *Born in the RSA* (1985) (for which the following creators were acknowledged in the 1986 American book publication: Barney Simon and the Cast of the Market Theatre – Vanessa Cook, Melanie Dobbs, Timmy Kwebulana, Neil McCarthy, Gcina Mhlophe, Fiona Ramsay, Thoko Ntshinga, Terry Norton). Through invitations in Europe and the USA amongst others, these pieces strengthened the front against the apartheid regime and brought an exciting variation of modern creative dramaturgy and performance methodology to world theatre.

The theatre of Gibson Kente

The other relevant movement, the popular musically oriented travelling theatre, was based on the inextricably entwined use of text, music, dance and all other historically available methods of expression with a musical and rhythmic focal point to the structural foundation of the performance. The first high point of this movement was the jazz musical *King Kong* about a Black South African heavyweight boxer that was performed in 1959 by leading Black artists in *Sophiatown*. The performance might have been the very impulse for the evolvement of a specifically South African commercial, popular and urban travelling theatre, much like the Concert Parties and the Yoruba travelling theatre in West Africa since the 1930s and 1940s.

In the 1960s and 1970s, the greatest mass impact in the townships was achieved by Gibson Kente's professional Black melodramatic productions. Following on from the musical *King Kong*, which was performed in English, he began using elements of other South African languages and integrated "traditional" African music and elements of dance with jazz in his pieces. The music and theatre historian David B. Coplan described his work as follows:

"Kente accomplished the first requirement by developing the synthesis of narrative, mime, movement, vocal dramatics, music and dance found in traditional oral literary performance into a township melodrama using urban experience and cultural resources."

At the end of the 1960s Kente took his troupe from its Soweto home base on tour in an old bus throughout the whole of South Africa. With minimal props and sets they performed in the few suitable halls available in the townships. His group functioned on a strictly commercial basis, surviving solely from the proceeds of the box office. Kente's theatre can be called melodramatic in the sense that in the stories depicted, the only way out of the crises and social dilemmas faced by the Black townships as a result of the system – which he represented in a realistic manner – were solutions that were heavily influenced by Christian morality. In the 1970s, as the apartheid regime tightened its control, he increasingly integrated political criticism of the conditions in South Africa in his moralistic evaluation of societal phenomena. His production of *Too Late* (1975) openly opposed the political system of apartheid. Afterwards, the regime threw him in prison for months.

Political anti-apartheid theatre

In connection with the spread of active opposition to the regime and the formation of the Black Consciousness movement as its most obvious sign, the specific dramaturgy of South Africa's political theatre evolved. Along with the collective productions of Fugard, Kani and Ntshona, Workshop 71 was set in motion from 1971 onwards. In 1976, the Market Theatre under Barney Simon began producing work which led to the open attack of apartheid politics in the 1980s with *Woza Albert! Bopha* and *Asinamali*. The name Workshop 71 referred to the rudiments of a working foundation – namely the collective development of texts in the production and rehearsal process. This did not eliminate the possibility of an author writing the dramatic framework for a working text. One such example was the production of *Survival*, which was commissioned by the Space Theatre in Cape Town in 1976 and produced by Workshop 71. There was no author named, nor was a collective authorship noted. The four actors and the director, who created the whole piece, credited themselves under the name of Workshop 71 Company for the production.

Playing a particular role in informing the specific dramaturgy and performance methods used in political and socially critical theatre in South Africa since the 1970s was the fundamental approach or grundgestus of (mostly traditional) storytelling theatre. In the wider socio-political sense, the representational epic storytelling appears to fulfil the function of bearing witness. In this way the political anti-apartheid theatre is described by Lauren Kruger as "testimonial theatre", and is directly concerned with protest and opposition. The combining of traditionally established forms of African storytelling with scenes involving dialogue or – to look at it the other way – the development of dialogue scenes from the grundgestus of storytelling by one or more participants, is distinguishable in the dramaturgy of *Sizwe Bansi is Dead*. Stemming from this production and similarly in *Survival* and *Woza Albert!* as with *Born in the RSA*, this manner of representation is a specifically South African contribution to those theatre forms of international significance.

The change in direction of the early 1990s

With the collapse of the apartheid regime, beginning with Nelson Mandela being released from prison in 1990 and his election as president of a new, democratic South Africa, the surrounding social framework of theatre changed. Just as opposition to the apartheid regime united the forces of socially critical and engaged theatre, they were then confronted with other urgent problems – from social instability in a rapidly expanding capitalistic urbanisation, the grinding poverty of the majority of Black South Africans, the repression of women and ethnic minorities, to the political and criminal violence threatening the stability of democratic society and infringing on everyday life in the cities.

The Market Theatre and the National Arts Festival in Grahamstown reacted quickly to these new circumstances. One such example was the adaptation of Brecht's *The Good Person of Szechwan*: In 1996 the Market Theatre utilised, under the title of *The Good Woman of Sharkville*, themes of the deep social rifts and the consequential rise in criminality in the new South Africa. William Kentridge chose similar issues for his productions with the Handspring Puppet Company at the Market Theatre. In 1992, *Woyzeck on the Highveld* (which had a big revival tour in South Africa and Australia in 2008 and is planned for a return season in 2010) was about the desperate circumstance of the socially disadvantaged in South Africa, and in 1994 *Faustus in Africa* referred to the devastating effects of capitalism, colonialism and sexism in Africa.

Translated into English by Carrie Hampel.

The text was first published in the magazine "Dawn in a land of cages. New Theatre in South Africa" as part of "Theater der Zeit" ("Theatre of the time"), Berlin 2009.

Theatre of Resistance

The Funda Community College in South Africa from the 1980s to the 1990s

Motsumi Makhene

Funda Community College, hereinafter referred to simply as the Funda Centre or Funda, and its involvement in theatre can be best understood within the history of education and the arts over a period of sixty years since the 1950s.

Funda was established in 1984 as a youth and adult education centre, by the Urban Foundation of South Africa (UFSA). UFSA was a private sector agency created as a catalyst to arrest the collapse of 1976 Youth Revolt and its economic and social meltdown. It investigated about seven policy interventions by way of commissions from 1977. The pertinent policy areas with direct impact social relations, mobility and cultural expression through theatre included education and the Group Areas Act (the Right/Privilege/Refusal to reside, recreate and work in prescribed areas). The policy decision adopted out the investigation was the promotion of adult education to mitigate growing political dissatisfaction.

In the Johannesburg city alone, there were already high levels of inter-racial engagement, several arts centres such as the African Music and Drama Association (AMDA) that was based at the Dorkay House in the City Centre. The Dorkay House also provided space and facilities for professional artists that created the internationally acclaimed musical, *King Kong*, under the Union of South African Arts. It produced generations of artists and activists in the 1950s, '60s through to the '80s.

As a Non-Governmental-Organisation (NGO), AMDA worked closely with the other city council and NGO arts centres such as the Bantu Mans Social Centre (recreational centre with dance, music and other performing arts), Polly Street Arts Centre that specialised in visual arts, the Donaldson Centre in Soweto (YMCA) which housed music, theatre and gymnasium, the FUBA Academy for the Arts, based next to the Market Theatre in the city and Alexandra Arts Centre from the late '80s. Two outstanding theatre contributions of the '70s include Gibson Kente's Production *Enterprise* that produced entertainment related genres with social messaging and *Mihloti* – The Black Theatre, a radical activist movement with a direct political messaging mission focusing on arts in schools, youth development and community mobilisation for social resistance against the apartheid social experiment.

The foundations of the activism of the sixties and seventies can be traced to the first wave of education policy resistance in the early 1950s following the *Esselen Report on Education (1954)*, a trigger for progressive resistance that saw the expulsion of four radical and prominent teachers from the education system – a move that stimulated alternative education and cultural activism movements. This resulted in Prof. Khabi Mngoma, a teacher and musician; Zephaniah Mothopeng, a teacher, musician and politician; Prof. E'skia Mphahlele, a teacher and writer; and Mr. Isaac Mahlare, a teacher, establishing alternative adult education programs that were quickly shut by the Education Department in the '50s. This further drove the four activists into various areas of survival and other professional pursuits, still agitating for alternative forms of education and culture, including going into exile. But as they say, you can leave the country of struggle but you can't leave the struggle. When Funda was established, already Soweto was abuzz, not because it was in any manner different as a township, but since the 60s it has been a theatre itself.

Curriculum of Community Development and Arts Education

As a response to the 1976 Youth Uprising, the Urban Foundation South Africa, built Funda as one of the tactics to stem the second wave of civil unrest and disobedience. Science Education, Adult Education, statement-of-the-arts library, Teacher Development and Arts Education became core to its curriculum. Between 18 to 25 different community based and Non-Governmental-Organisations established under the four education services, with the Arts Centre producing a cluster of seven (7) community based organisation in theatre, music, visual arts, photography, youth arts, arts teacher development and university distance education in visual arts.

The arts at Funda, established and directed by the 26 years old Matsemela Manaka – the poet, writer, producer, teacher, painter and insatiable cultural activist – tended to brand itself as agitating for alternative arts education, always pushing to the cutting edge of alternative arts curricula and exploring innovative ways to engage the community and main stream arts institutions, particularly the Market Theatre in Johannesburg. In the first three years of its establishment, it managed to profile itself as an alternative theatre venue, positioning itself to become a neutral multicultural space with a progressive syncretic political orientation.

Despite the inadequate multi-purpose spatial architecture of the Arts Centre, the space was adapted and converted to house a legendary small theatre that was leveraged to produce about 10 theatre productions and several exhibitions, writers workshops and rural exchange programs, particularly involving warring township and hostel migrant worker populations. Out of these, indigenous music and dance festivals, youth concerts and festivals as well as school outreach programs emerged.

Already, at the time of its establishment, Funda built on a long history of social movements from the first and second wave of cultural activism, including across the cultural and racial divide of South Africa's apartheid society. Soweto was abuzz, not because it was in any manner a unique township, but Soweto has since the 1930s and '40s it has been a theatre itself – a township theatre of many dramatic moments, from the creation of a self-ruling township (Orlando) by the founder of Soweto, 'Sofasonke' Mpanza, the launch of the Freedom Charter in 1955, the pass protests and arrests of PAC leadership in 1960, to the 1976 Youth Revolt.

When Funda was established in 1984, it brought on board people who were produced by Soweto's long history of its 'personality' and the many Johannesburg based arts centres that evolved. To name but a few: Dorkay House, Polly Street City, Orlando DOCC, Uncle Tom's Hall and many community based arts formations and theatre groups that produced Workshop '71 including Credo Mtwa's *uNosilimela*, Gibson Kente Productions, Bahumutsi led by Maishe Maponya and Malo-Poets led by Matsemela Manaka from Diepkloof where Funda Centre is located.

The Funda Centre was built as an alternative education space to apartheid education system, focusing on youth and adults. Its important kernel became the Funda Arts Centre – from a creative and cultural point of view. To the extent that, if one spoke about the Funda Centre, it was as if the entire Funda Centre was an arts centre. But it had other disciplines and dedicated units such as Science Education Centre, the Teacher's Centre and the Adult Education Centre.

Theatre as a paradigm

The idea of theatre and the role of Funda in theatre was informed by community theatre, township cinema, school literature, alternative literature – such as the *Drum* magazine, *Zonk* magazine and the *Staffrider* literary periodical. As a poet and writer, Matsemela Manaka, a comrade and friend, fashioned and established the Soyikwa Institute of African Theatre as a vehicle for research, production and youth education, contributing to and gleaning from his involvement in the *Staffrider*. Critical of the world of theatre and always looking for unique ways to express his world of the Malo-Poets (poets of Malopo/Malombo, theatre of therapy); he was active in local and global debates, exhibitions and collaborations. This experience and exposure through conferences such as "Culture and Resistance" held in Botswana in 1982, the Zimbabwe Book-fair where he built pan-African networks through his friend Dambudzo Marechera and "Culture in Another South Africa" (CASA) in Holland, resolved a number of debates in his mind and consolidated his search for a unique creative theatre practice that would define and deepen his quest of political activism, youth development passion and creative fervour through African theatre. After one of his many travels, Matsemela Manaka, in a frustrated personal conversation with me, reflects on hindsight:

"You know, I now believe that theatre is the integration of all arts and as such, African theatre is the same as that. We need to build or rebuild the type of theatre that is more integrated and not separated, where music is not just music, visual arts is not visual arts, and drama is not drama. But everything is everything. It must speak through the same medium of expression." (Manaka 1997)

In as much as Funda Centre became an alternative of Bantu Education, it was also an alternative space for three cultural pursuits. At some stage it was an alternative to the Market Theatre in town. The Funda Arts Centre had lots of robust interactions, there are many stories to go, but ultimately the two theatres were symbiotic in the world of alternative and progressive theatre. At the same time living with the creative tension between city based modes of theatre and township oriented experience of new forms of eclectic expressions and modes of rural-urban migrant culture. So, it was community-based and focusing on three ideological imperatives. One of them was about 'theatre for conscious-ness'. The second was about 'theatre for political protest' and third, which was very unique and compelling – 'theatre for identity and development'.

The notion of theatre as a integration of all arts and the mission to centre African theatre as a representative language for alternative arts in SA, raised a vexing question of how African identity could be projected among youth, during a period of advanced migrant labour social formations of multi-ethnic township communities under a colonial political economy that was disintegrating, after the 1960 Sharpeville Massacre, the 1976 Youth Uprising and the 1985 precipita-tion of 'Black on Black violence' fanned by South African State Security Forces (Bureau of State Security, BOSS). The dilemma of 'projecting youth identity' reflected more the question of how African theatre could be used to further engage youth in community social reconstruction and economic development. This was more pertinent in the '80s, given the state of fomented political and ethnic tensions and disunity among communities, particularly between hostel migrant workers and township based workers.

Identity and Development made by Soyikwa Theatre

Under the auspices of the Soyikwa Institute of African Theatre, Matsemela Manaka created two milestone productions; one is called *Domba, the Last Dance* and *Goreé*. The latter was instigated and painfully inspired by his experience as part of a political South African delegation that went to Zambia to start negotiations between the ANC and the apartheid South African government. And that delegation ended up in the Goreé Island Port of Senegal, where his spirit as an artist was literally shredded to pieces. Upon his return, he was conflicted to the extent that when he secluded and confined himself to work on memories of *Goreé*, writing poetry, painting multiple images of Goreé Island, focusing on nothing else but 'the door of no return'. Out of this personal experience, the theatre production of *Goreé* was born.

As if it was a continuation of exorcising the dark shadow of the experience as a delegate, he directed and produced the two hander musical as an intricately involved production team member, working with two fellow Funda staff members: the legendary multi-proficient singer Sibongile Khumalo and versatile dancer Nomsa Manaka (to whom he was married). Matsemela created the set, the script, and the lyrics of some songs. He was also the music producer, the lighting designer and the executive producer responsible for funding and contracting with the Market Theatre.

The *Goreé* musical was as a tribute to youth, the story about a young woman from Soweto (Nomsa Manaka) whose life, identity and consciousness would be turned around following an encounter on the shores of the Goree Island, after she missed the last ship that left for America. The musical play actually opens with a song titled 'Toro ya moAfriKa' (the African's dream), setting the scene by declaring that "toroyamoAfriKa, toro e šoro kudu. Hoo, tokologo, sellosamoAfriKa." Translated, it is a wailing cry for freedom: "the African's dream, a dreaded dream indeed, oh freedom, the bitter cry of an African." At that night, she encountered the spirit of the Oba (Sibongile Khumalo) which roamed the coast and the two, under a Baobab tree, began to converse about where she was going. She said: "I am going to America to learn to become a dancer." But at the end of that night, after she was adorned and taught to dance the 'ostrich dance' and the significance of its spirit of elegant endurance, she decided to return home to South Africa, because she realised for the first time that she was an African and her purpose was 'at home' and not in search of what she already has – the intuitive African language of dance.

Having had a successful run with full house audiences at the Market Theatre, the production raised much public interest in the Black communities and controversy around questions of Afrocentric theatre and the entry of Black-led productions in an industry dominated by White executive producers, artistic directors, lighting designers and technicians, stage managers and marketers. The most interesting media article review about it had the headline of "the paradox of painted nails" – a subtle critic from some journalists on the dancer who represented a character that projected the fervour of self-discovery and a new development mission but kept her red painted toe nails for a cosmopolitan audience, as a mark of chic.

The remark also reflected a sense of discomfort about how urban Black youth should express their identity in a complex of cultural resistance against strong media driven images of celebrity culture, whilst asserting the value of indigenous identities that most shied away from to boost their cool youth currency.

In many ways *Goreé* the musical became a seminal work that would open a new genre of living theatre and exhibitions using inter-disciplinary approaches and borderless theatre for development. At the same time, asserting an approach in protest and resistance theatre where township theatre was urged to break into established theatres and playhouses and insist on taking charge of executive production and technical staging to promote a new language of staging that was unfamiliar to the establishment. Beyond artistic messaging, the stage could a platform for anything. Sets could be a gallery of township expression as a collage of mobile images of another musical; *The Children of Asazi* (The Marginalised Children). A script could be in collaborative paintings reflecting a story on paintings, each marked by train, bus and air tickets pinned and merged into the expression of each canvas or as in the days of Matsemela Manaka's work, the conversion of his home into a neighbourhood museum where exhibitions of local visual artists and personalities would be supported by music and poetry, as part of community arts education, encouraging economic self-reliance among artists. The neighbourhood museum was also twinned with a theatre production called *Ekhaya Museum over Soweto*, a play that anticipated the marginalisation of community theatre and promoted the self-reliance of artists through a witty, anti-colonial and alcoholic character called Paki (name translates into 'the witness').

Promoting consciousness and cultural expression

Domba the Last Dance was a student production and an interdisciplinary learning method. It was developed as a collaborative musical using combined students of the Funda Arts Centre's drama, music, visual arts, photo and videography and dance. Inspired by a documentary on cultural migration and urbanisation called *Two Rivers* that interrogates the possible outcome of cultural confluence between rural Africa and western urban settlements. The documentary film triggered research on the indigenisation of Funda arts curriculum to counter Western based notions of arts education. This included curriculum research into the impact of the rural indigenous girls education on youth development and consciousness, to understand the nature and extent of limitations in the public education system on urban youth in the '80s.

Based on working with youth in the township, focus was on how Western education impacted on the forming of youth identity, knowledge and youth expression. The methodology challenged even the level of awareness, knowledge and creative capabilities of Funda arts staff, to produce authentic African genres for contemporary theatrical contexts, working with students to use eclectic language, song, imagery and dance techniques to produce convincing and commercially viable theatre ritual and ceremony.

The imitation of the dance of *Domba* by urban youth, being a sacred ceremonial graduation dance before leaving the school of seclusion to join the community as a full adult member, proved to be a complex maze of artistic techniques, style, behaviour and symbolism. This required even the teachers to be initiated in, to raise their awareness about nuances and subtleties that urban upbringing deprives us, as an imperative to achieve relative authenticity and proficiency in their teaching and creative leadership in preparation for the first performance, three days before the opening of the production.

The intervention was made through the support of Rashaka Rashitanga; an elder cultural activist and rural intellectual who organised masters of *Domba* initiation school, women drummers, dancers and singers of the ancient graduation dance for maidens. By learning about the value of rural indigenous education, cultural behavioural sensitivities, initiation into adulthood and the nature of rural communities as institutions, staff became aware of the enormity of the curriculum transformation challenge. This was the imperative to facilitate the equitable 'confluence' of rural-urban cultural expression through Afro-centric curriculum and suitable urban based methodologies.

Three frantic days before the opening of the tempered *Domba the Last Dance*, a new era of learning and teaching was born, resulting in annual festivals of indigenous music and dance, and the shaping of African dance as a language of contemporary theatre. The images and subject matter in the Funda visual arts arena, gave confidence to students to find creative expression and meaning in symbols and cultural representation that brought new techniques and aesthetics to the fore.

Consolidating the spirit resistance

Although Funda Arts Centre was part of the broader political resistance that was characterised by the spirit of political resistance, as manifested in Protest Theatre, revolts and uprisings, its creative and youth education core was different. Its environment of alternative education enabled possibilities beyond the culture of resistance struggles and therefore its theatre could not be defined in the main as resistance theatre. Even though it positioned its messages to the audiences as resistance to colonial education (*Domba the Last Dance*), inhuman industrial labour conditions (*Egoli*), *Americanisation of youth culture* (*Goreé* and *The Calabash*), oppressive Black leadership tendencies arising from colonial conditions (*Pula* and *Five Million Souls*), Funda was spurred more by alternative theatre.

Informed by its social environment, it embraced the totality of theatre that reflected other forms of social commentary theatre, such as Sam Mahangwane and the prolific Gibson Kente's cameos that explored social characters, personal relationships and socio-political tensions arising out of township contradictions and survival. These were glazed with entertainment styles that would guarantee commercial success – and successful they became. In the case of Gibson Kente, the father of Soweto musical theatre, his creative depth extended to film and television productions. In a way, Matsemela Manaka's Soyikwa Institute of African Theatre sought to continue the tradition of Black-owned theatre enterprises that constituted the building blocks for current, though brittle, commercial multimedia theatre ventures. Examples include the *Unfaithful Woman* (Sam Mhangwane) and Gibson Kente's several milestone musicals, particularly the ones that crossed the 'political censorship line' such as *Sikhalo* (the wailing cry), *Too Late*, *How Long* and *I believe*.

Funda's theatre of consciousness, resistance and identity became the culmination of a long history of urban migrant labour culture and social expression, the essential confluence of rural African and urban Western education systems. It can be argued that Funda's approach to theatre and arts education focused on both political activism and economic viability of the township arts to respond to forces of cultural marginality. The historical unequal distribution of theatre infrastructure and related resources, the lack of arts education – particularly for youth talent development – in the schooling system, the growing dominance of over-resourced state colonial outreach activities to influence community arts and the anti-arts-and-sports-in-schools campaigns of 'liberation before education' by the South African Democratic Teachers Union (SADTU) in the 1980's raised an urgent need for Funda to become a hub and strategic partnerships working with a cluster of independent production houses with strong local industry and international links. A hub to support the resistance against the dilution of township theatre, to source selected global theatre partners and stimulate local critical theatre as an alternative space that would give visibility to marginal theatre of the township and a critic of voice of social injustice through theatre.

This broader approach to the theatre of resistance meant a concerted effort by the education leadership of the Funda Arts Centre at building competencies in performance research to apply lessons towards new forms of artistic representation inspired by indigenous knowledge practitioners; it meant the exploration of innovative curriculum development approaches that centres theory on indigenous performance practice and the design of commensurate methodology to fit contemporary youth cultural interest to emerging eclectic urban culture, and the pursuit of redefining spatial conceptions, community relations and business ventures to create a new cultural ecosystem for the post 1994 political economy.

Bibliography

Manaka, Matsemela (24/7/1997): Personal conversation with the author.

The Unequal Brothers

The controversial history of the two leading South African theatres

Adrienne Sichel

Geographically The Market Theatre of Johannesburg and the South African State Theatre of Pretoria may only be some 60 kilometres apart but during apartheid they represented different countries in terms of ideologies, audiences and programming. Today they form the artistically leading couple among the South African theatres.

The Market, founded by an idealistic group of artists in 1976 (preparing to open the very moment the 1976 uprisings against the apartheid regime were happening in Soweto on June 16) embodied the dream of a socio-political utopia, of a democratic, multi-racial society. Johannesburg's old fruit and vegetable market, became the hub trading and implementing artistic visions, political beliefs and developing a singular genre of workshopped theatre. The co-founders theatre director and playwright Barney Simon and theatre administrator and manager Mannie Manim (a former company manager of the state funded PACT English Drama Company), with a group of like-minded South Africans, were determined to ingeniously break the shackles of the oppressive apartheid policy laws. In its new home the Company (which started out performing in shop windows, hotels and little theatres) created theatre which not only conscientised audiences but enriched them with art which not only took South African voices and stories to the world but brought international plays and committed artists into the wasteland of the cultural boycott and draconian media censorship.

The fruit and vegetable market theatres

Over in the Nationalist Party government capitol of Pretoria in 1981 a monolithic opera – and theatre building rose from the ashes of the city's old fruit and vegetable marketplace – which is known today as the South African State Theatre. It had been in development since 1964.

Funded and assisted by the then Province of the Transvaal this complex of five theatres, workshops, rehearsal rooms and administration offices, housed the Performing Arts Council of the Transvaal (PACT) with its opera, ballet and drama companies (which had always been split into English and Afrikaans entities.) The racially mixed Pact Contemporary Dance Company was founded in 1989.

The Performing Arts Councils (PACs') came into being in 1963 (two years after the declaration of the Republic of South Africa) when the National Theatre Organisation (which championed Afrikaans theatre) was replaced by four government funded institutions serving White audiences and artists. The cultural boycott prevented these companies in the main from staging imported contemporary works. The repertory tended to be in the European tradition.

The erosion of racial divisions

However, when the State Theatre in Pretoria opened it did endeavour to reach out to other races in terms of the desegregation of theatres, which were opened to all races in 1977. The first Black professionally produced show in the Drama Theatre was a staging of Cape Town playwright Adam Smal's classic Afrikaans play *Kanna hy Ko Hystoe* performed by the semi-professional actors from the local community of Eersterust. The writer and the performers were in accordance with apartheid policy classified as Coloured.

The racial divisions within the PACT companies began eroding somewhat. By the late 1980s a number of Black actors, contemporary dancers and singers were employed to perform at the State and Pact satellite theatres at The Windybrow Arts Centre in Hillbrow and the Alexander Theatre in Braamfontein. By 1994, the sound of the death knell was faint but a reality.

When Nelson Mandela was released from Prison in February 1990, activist artists and Non Governmental Organisations who boycotted performing with, or working for the PACs', began lobbying for a new dispensation in which all artists got a slice of the funding pie. After the first democratic elections in 1994, the pressure was on for the dissolution of the arts councils and these performing arts companies in Pretoria, Cape Town, Bloemfontein and Durban. Transformation became a buzz word which still dominates arts and culture politics today – even though institutions like the State Theatre have changed profile and transformed in terms of their management and financial compliance. All four opera house complexes are State funded cultural institutions in addition to The Windybrow Theatre, in Hillbrow, Johannesburg and The Market which acquired this status on April 1, 2005. These theatres now all fall under the Cultural Institutions Act of 1998. This funding is for infrastructure and management but not for productions. They switched from being production houses to receiving houses which have to find sponsorship and funding for in-house productions.

From production to receiving houses

Post-1994, both The Market and the State were snarled up in scandals involving mismanagement. The most high profile public drama happened in Pretoria. In June 2000 the minister of Arts Culture Science and Technology "moth balled" the theatre complex after revelations about corruption and financial shortfalls. The remaining resident performing arts companies were closed. The complex re-opened two years later. Yet, despite these upheavals and threat of closure both institutions survived to celebrate their milestone birthdays in 2006. The Market made it to 30 the State to 25.

Where did all this disruption and conflict, which only mirrored what was going on in the transforming society itself as the euphoria of democracy and the Rainbow Nation began fading and reality set in, leave the artists and art making? Mainly in distress as the promised first-time funding for dramatists and theatre companies either trickled in or didn't materialise. The National Arts Council, established in 1997, the arm's length body of the Department of Arts and Culture (which activist artists fought to be established), became the main dispersing body. The National Lotteries Distribution Fund has become a lifeline for keeping dance and theatre companies and festivals alive. That too has hit snags in terms of allocating funds with often disastrous effects on sustainability and or survival.

Revival in creativity

This hasn't prevented a distinct revival in creativity in the past three years in the calibre, quality and invention specifically in theatre predominantly in Cape Town (led by Mannie Manim at The Baxter Theatre), Johannesburg and Pretoria. Post-1994 many writers were floundering for new material. Then definite themes began to emerge. Identity being one of them. The issue-based plays of the Protest Theatre era became more sophisticated.

For her first play internationally well-established director and resident director at The Market Theatre from 1998 – 2000 Lara Foot Newton (who was Barney Simon's last protégée before he died in 1995) researched the high incidence of infant rape in South Africa in her celebrated *Tshepang – The Third Testament* (2003). In her second authored play *Karoo Moose* (2007), which again deals with poverty and child abuse, she continues to forge a theatrical language based on her evolving magical realism style. Both productions were staged at The Market. Similarly, Mpumelelo Paul Grootboom (the State Theatre's resident director since 2006), has been crafting a bold signature in plays which don't shy away from topics such as serial killers, rape, racism and xenophobia in a township setting.

Strong development work

Development is another post-1994 buzzword. A prime example of how organically proactive this can be is The Market Theatre Laboratory which celebrates its 20th anniversary this year. Co-founded by Barney Simon and John Kani in 1989 (who became The Market's Managing Trustee until 2003 and is now the theatre's international ambassador) this groundbreaking drama school unearthed new talent among disadvantaged young South Africans who wouldn't have had access to universities or tertiary education.

Among them are leading actors, theatre makers, writers, filmmakers and technicians the calibre of actor Mncedisi Shabangu who continues to tour the world in *Tshepang – The Third Testament*. Since his student days, this artist who has never lost his connections in his home community in Limpopo has proved to be an imaginative writer and director creating works with a singular physicality. His most recent productions *Ten Bush* – co-written with Craig Higginson – and *Thirteen*, all staged at The Market, illustrate his ability to engage African ritual and storytelling in a formal stage context.

The Lab's annual Community Theatre Festivals and field worker outreach programme have contributed invaluably to not only transforming lives (especially when the Lab was directed by Vanessa Cooke) but redefining what theatre is in South Africa. When Cooke – a major actress in her own right and a co-founder of The Market Theatre – retired last year her legacy continues in Matjamela Motloung who now directs the Lab into its third decade.

The era of Malcolm Purkey and Aubrey Sekhabi

Since 2002, when playwright and director Aubrey Sekhabi (Wits drama graduate and the former artistic director of the Northwest Drama Company in Mafikeng in the North West Province) became the State Theatre's artistic director audience and artist development has been a priority. His 52 Seasons Theatre Development Project, funded by the National Lottery, laid the ground work for nurturing actors, writers, directors, designers and community groups in production and networking skills through a workshop series leading to full production. The main objective was "to narrow the gap between communities based groups and mainstream companies". Erratic delivery by the Lottery has disrupted this valuable initiative which has already sown valuable seeds.

When pioneering playwright and Head of the Dramatic Art at the University of the Witwatersrand (Wits) Malcolm Purkey became artistic director of the Market Theatre, in January 2005, the standoff which historically existed between The Market and the State was about to change. The two artistic directors decided in the words of Purkey "that we were far enough apart to be colleagues, firstly, literally, then in terms of existing and emergent audiences, to be colleagues and not competitors".

Within months Paul Grootboom's *Cards* controversially graphic portrait of a Hillbrow brothel, was on the Market main stage, in Newtown, bringing in new audiences. The first Market import to Pretoria was Purkey's revival production of *Sophiatown* (created by the Junction Avenue Theatre Company of which Purkey was a co-founder). In 2008 James Ngcobo (resident director at The Market 2008 – 2009) directed Wole Soyinka's *The Lion and the Jewel* for the State Theatre. This notable production then had a season at The Market.

For the past few years, Purkey has had to weather onslaughts of accusations of being racist in his programming from small companies, or community groups, who feel they have been marginalised. Some of that criticism has ebbed way in the past two years as the fare has improved to be inclusive yet based on the criteria of excellence. Purkey's contract has been extended for a second term from 2010 to 2014.

Even if both these theatre centres continue to produce groundbreaking art and build audiences central to their operations are good corporate governance and functional, pro-active boards. After all the political and administrative dramas of this decade the institutions are on track to live up to their demands and responsibilities. There are still many battles being fought about what is professional theatre which has in the past tended to ignore or look down on community/developmental/township/grass roots theatre. The Market Lab and Aubrey Sekhabi and Paul Grootboom's work in Pretoria have held change that perspective to an extent. What was on the margins a decade ago is now partly mainstream. Post-apartheid South Africa still does not have one single subsidised drama company. Graduate actors can't learn their craft but go straight into soap opera on television and do well paying corporate or industrial theatre work. Commissioning from festivals has been a lifeline for writers and directors for actors who take the stage seriously. Given this scenario it is a miracle that South African theatre can keep its head up high.

The text was first published in the magazine "Dawn in a land of cages. New Theatre in South Africa" as part of "Theater der Zeit" ("Theatre of the time"), Berlin 2009.

Transformation in Theatre. The discourse

The performing arts as a social force

South Africa's post-apartheid theatre in the process of transformation

Wolfgang Schneider

Shots are fired in the State Theatre in Pretoria, voices are raised in the Baxter in Cape Town, demonstrations are held in the Soweto Theatre in Johannesburg. And yet people still say the performing arts are not political. In post-apartheid South Africa, theatre acts as a mirror of society, is part of the transformation process and is viewed as a real social force. And yet Blacks and Whites, old and young are arguing about the way forward, about content and aesthetics. A multi-day conference in the South African capital brought together theatre makers and cultural experts, instigated discussions and debates and met on 'the boards that mean the world' – in the exposed concrete of the State Theatre, in the 'Rostrum' on the cultural campus of Tshwane University of Technology and in the futuristic new Soweto Theatre building in the heart of this notorious township in Johannesburg.

Marikana-The Musical is the name of a musical adapted by Aubrey Sekhabi for the South African State Theatre. It tells the story of the 2012 massacre of striking mineworkers when violent attacks by the police resulted in 44 deaths. The book has now been brought to the stage with two dozen songs and a clear message, which Sekhabi, the play's director and the theatre's artistic director, succinctly sums up as "to teach tolerance".

Sekhabi represents an established theatre culture that does not shy away from popular entertainment. Indeed, it puts entertainment front and centre, but at the same time understands that artistic works also need to have social relevance. His State Theatre was one of the first public institutions to allow access to people of all races. Even as far back as the 1980s there were Black actors, dancers and singers working in the theatre. However, it was closed down by the Department of Arts and Culture shortly after the first democratic elections due to evidence of corruption and mismanagement. Together with co-director Mpumeleleo Paul, Sekhabi has transformed the institution over the last ten years into the country's premier production centre for the performing arts. It keeps its finger on the pulse and is politically engaged, with five different stages and an important role as a laboratory for cultural participation. The former artists' dressing rooms are now home to a music school, a jazz network and a dance company; the actors take part in Q&A sessions after performances and a whole department is now dedicated to community theatre.

Theatre: A political instrument or a place for art?

Grootboom is the spin doctor for form and content. He "loves his Shakespeare just as passionately as he loves a cheeky sitcom", according to the press release for the 2016 Jürgen Bansemer & Ute Nyssen Dramatists' Prize. He knows the harsh reality of the townships with their domestic violence and social upheavals. His *Township Stories* still have the ability to shock with their tales of sex and crime. Give him a podium and he is quick to condemn what he sees as the undesirable direction his country is heading in, with artistic freedom still not guaranteed and politicians banging on about 'nation building' at a time when the effects of successive economic crises are still hitting the Black majority the hardest.

Malcolm Purkey, who ran Johannesburg's Market Theatre from 2004 onwards, questioned the role of the theatre and its impact on society. In the quest for a voice in society, for a political aesthetic, theatre is an imagined space for thinking about change. But arguments rage over whether the theatre should be a political instrument or simply a place for art. Yes, theatre can hold up a mirror to society; no, theatre should stir things up, be disorientating and ambiguous.

The former artistic director of the National Arts Festival and since 2017 CEO of the Market Theatre Johannesburg, Ismail Mahomed, has first-hand experience of what theatre can be. He was not allowed to attend performances or even study, but he became a clandestine spectator whenever he could and to this day he still loves the performing arts as an educational institution in the broadest sense. He likes to think of language as a means of starting a discussion, of images as a way of exploring new horizons, and of performance as a live experience. This is why he tends to be critical of what he sees as the commercialisation of today's productions, the self-censorship that exists within many projects, and the loss of identity caused by using actors who to date have only been trained according to European standards. "Theatre is a crystal ball that allows us to constantly reimagine our society and present it anew". This is why he is pinning his hopes on the new generation of young people born after 1994.

Before this date, theatrical interventions in South Africa were predominantly protests against the apartheid state. Afterwards they revolved around stories of celebration, an era of euphoria and of honouring Nelson Mandela.

After 1999, artists once again started to write political stories – about aids, gender, and the environment. "Some of these pieces worked", says Mahomed, "but others were hopeless failures. The stories that really worked were those by artists who wrote with real conviction and who were activists in this particular area". He also made a plea for more tolerance as an artistic value, saying that fears and hopes should be taken seriously. He stated that theatre provides a way of challenging prejudices and that at times artists have a right to respond with hate and anger. It falls to the artistic directors of theatres and festival programmes to initiate critical dialogue using artistic means. And he is convinced that a curator must be a cultural mediator who "has the power to help shape society's values".

History: Is it Possible to forgive the past in order to survive the future?

Shaping is a word that is also important to Yvette Hardie. She is National Director of ASSITEJ South Africa, the international theatrical platform for children and young people, and as a theatre producer she is familiar with practical aspects of the theatre scene in her home country. She believes that theatre is confrontation, and that this provides the starting point for many works by Grootboom, Mike van Graan and others. They have a sense of political awareness and write "with a certain urgency" about emerging social issues. Another successful recent initiative has been collectively gathering and working on materials that draw on a wide range of expertise. This is how the project *Truth in Translation* was born at the Collonnades Theatre Lab. It asks the question: "Is it possible to forgive the past in order to survive the future?" The audience participates in workshops in order to explore this issue more deeply. Hardie views cultural pedagogy and artistic education as a key to the future of theatre, in accordance with the African saying: "If you plant a tree today, you can be proud of the forest of tomorrow". This is why all theatre makers are particularly focused on children's and youth theatre.

Hardie curates a festival in Cape Town that provides performances for school classes in the mornings. Performers can experiment, while the audience can make requests, get involved in the production process or have a go at being creative themselves. It all takes place in a Methodist church in the city's Observatory district. In fact, the artistic work becomes a kind of observatory: How's it going? What's it doing? What's the aim? Special contracts were awarded for this festival – for a 'School of Seeing', a project to develop the art of vision and tackle youth-related topics. *Ukwakha* deals with the complexity of relationships. Two dozen young people from the Khayelitsha township – the Xhosa word for "new home" – dance, stomp and gyrate, black bodies in white underwear and wellington boots. The audience's close proximity to the action makes the whole theatrical experience very intense, as the performers' physical movements communicate with the minds of their audience. Sbonakaliso Ndabe choreographed this hour-long piece and kept the audience enthralled with questions such as: Who with whom? When and when not? What and how? Conventions are preserved and contradicted; thoughts and feelings are laid bare. But it is not just about the authenticity of collective action. It is about the vibrancy of the work, the desire to break out of the day-to-day routine, to reflect and develop insights, to live as an individual in society. In May 2017 the ASSITEJ World Congress was hold in Cape Town, the first time in the global network's 15-year history that it was held in Africa.

Policy: too little, too late, too slow?

The third location for the conference was also new: the Soweto Theatre in South Africa's largest township, where the country's apartheid policies separated Black workers and their families. But from the very beginning, this town close to the city was also a place of cultural self-reflection – including social protest and political upheaval. Immediately behind the theatre complex there is a memorial to the 1976 high school student uprising in which hundreds of demonstrators were shot. To this day, many of the protagonists in the African National Congress (ANC), the political representatives of the country's Black majority, are still influenced by this event. During his exile in London and Amsterdam, Mongane Wally Serote used to dream of having a theatre. The former activist and ANC's Head of the Arts and Culture Department under Mandela now oversees three auditoriums and a diverse programme of productions and presentations. Of course it's still the same old story of too little, too late, too slow! As a member of South Africa's parliament, Serote was involved in writing the Rainbow Nation's White Paper on Arts and Culture that aimed to open up culture for everyone, but in practice this goal is still far from being achieved.

But young people are still flocking to the Soweto Theatre. Around 100 young, independent artists are ready to help reshape the performing arts in South Africa. They are still sitting in the audience, but are itching to be up on the stage. They are calling for the talking to stop and the action to begin. They are expressing themselves through hip-hop and funding their weekend workshops through temporary jobs. They are the digital natives whose lives are networked and who are less inclined to romanticise the revolution. They are finally in a position to help shape a future in which they can play an active role – in life as well as in the theatre. Meanwhile, an old Ibsen play is being restaged at Johannesburg's Baxter Theatre. In 2013 *Nora* finally gets to break out from the White middle classes. In the Fugard Theatre in Cape Town *District Six* uses song and dance to take a nostalgic look back at the multicultural lives of freed slaves and immigrants, traders and workers in the 19th century, and at the inhumane policies of the 20th century. But now the new 21st-century generation is breaking new ground in South Africa's theatres. They are socially aware, artistically ambitious and looking to the future – this is also a process of transformation.

Unless otherwise referenced, quotes are taken from panel discussions at the *Theatre in Transformation* conference held in Pretoria form 11 – 13 March 2016.

"Taking meat to the knives"

Report of the panel discussion "Political Power of Theatre – Cultural Policy for Theatre in South Africa"

Lebogang L. Nawa

> "We bleed
> They bleed our patient to smithereens
> as we carry their cross to the poll
> never intend on crossing swords for our patience
> when they falter,
> Had they not pleaded that democracy was young?
> Meantime, they milk the cow till it bleeds.
> They besieged the cross-carrier to tell a good story
> while patiently we watch in horror
> how the papers of the Constitution are ripped apart.
> These rulers without shame." (Maishe Maponya)

"Political Power of Theatre – Cultural Policy for Theatre in South Africa," was the title of a panel discussion in the Rostrum Theatre on the Arts Campus of Tshwane University of Technology (TUT) on 12 March 2016 in Pretoria. It probed the role of theatre in the current political juncture where it seems art has become a casualty of on-going student unrests against the slow pace, if at all, of transformation at tertiary institutions, and society at large, through movements like #RhodesMustFall and #FeesMustFall. It answered the question: is the incident of burning of paintings, including that of a Black artist, Keresemose Richard Baholo, at the University of Cape Town (UCT) on 16 February 2016 an isolated and misguided incident or does it imply that art has lost political meaning or muscle it once flexed during the struggle against colonialism and apartheid in South Africa? Similarly, in September 2015, the *Saturday Star* columnist, Tat Wolfen, also stirred a hornet's nest when he questioned in the article "Quo Vadis, Theatre" whether South African theatre is dying. On 17 February 2016, the book, *Methuen Drama Guide to Contemporary South African*

Theatre was launched at the Market Theatre amid controversy surrounding the racial composition of its contributors.

On the contrary, the demographic composition of this panel sought to give Black voices in South African theatre the deserved space and amplification. The team was also deliberately selected to give South African cultural activists an opportunity to, unlike before, air their views face-to-face on pertinent national issues. Months prior to this, some members of the panels were embroiled in public spats, through the media, on topics like the formation of the Creative and Cultural Industries Federation of South Africa (CCIFSA) to serve as an umbrella body of individual and organised cultural practitioners in the country.

The panel consisted of the playwright and theatre producer Walter Kefuoe Chakela, Wits University theatre director and teacher in performance Gita Pather, independent playwright and theatre director Maishe Maponya and the actor and director Tony Kgoroge in his capacity as CCIFSA president. The abstract read:

"Theatre created during the Apartheid years was volatile and edgy. Artists spoke truth to power. Theatre opened up windows for discussion about South African society. Theatre healed wounds. It provoked discussion. It agitated for social and political change. For the most part, the majority of artists in post-Apartheid South Africa have failed to grasp the freedoms which they have won. These freedoms are enshrined in the new consti-tution...The theatre of the new South Africa has deliberately steered far away from any kind of protest." (Mahomed 2014)

Walter Kefuoe Chakela: "Our theatre was not all about protest against apartheid. It was also about self-determination"

"I have never really experienced in our theatre any movement towards the end of the old Protest Theatre to a new Democratic Theatre. I've been looking for the demarcation for a long time. I am so far unable to see the issues of protest which inform the theatre of the years which are regarded as apartheid years. Our theatre was not all about protest against apartheid. It was also about self-de-termination. So when you look at our theatre, you mustn't be fooled and think that we spend most of our lives merely protesting against apartheid. Apartheid in fact did not define us.

I have had the honour and the privilege to grow up with Maishe Maponya, Matsemela Manaka, Ingoapele Madingoane and others. We used to dream about our theatre; how we can position our theatre in a way that it can be respected internationally? And we created theatre then which was – typical of our country – was called 'Black Theatre' and other theatre was called 'Theatre'. Ismail Mahomed used to say 'when you put up a play as a Black person, it is said a young anger Black person from the township has put up a play at the Market or the Windybrow. But when you are a young White man, the level of protest and anger is completely ignored. You are an enterprising young man putting a work of theatre.'

We worked in our respective townships. I was in Vryburg and Mahikeng. Maishe and Matsemela were privileged to be working in Soweto which, in relation to Vryburg, is considerably more privileged. But we created work that made international impact and headlines despite the fact that it came from people who had no resources to put up a production of any kind. *Gangsters and Dirty Work*, and *Egoli* by Matsemela Manaka, were all put up on shoe-string budgets. I don't know how the work I produced in the 80s it was possible out of that kind of budget. Actually, I don't even remember what that budget was. But we produced work that had a gesture of a people in struggle simply capable of celebrating themselves; a kind of work that celebrated human dignity.

We used to yearn for a time when we would all strive to achieve works which could be said to be works of human genius. Given that background, I was very curious to fight impulses within myself which say that 'now you are entering a new era, now your narrative have to be different.' I wrote a play called *Sweat/ Isithukuthu* in the 90s. It was about the labour movement, the social classes; though at the core of it, it was celebrating the life of Ingoapele Madingoane. The reason why I choose that narrative in particular was because in the early 90s apartheid was in the throes of death. So we thought we could make poetry in Funda Centre celebrating the poetry of Zimbabwean writers. But a State of Emergency was by then declared in the country. So our naivety was clearly exposed when we approached the media with the view to market the event. It was obvious that going to the media in South Africa during that period to seek permission to read Zimbabwean poetry was an open invitation for trouble.

On the day we got to Funda, there was a reception party of security police in full force armed to the teeth. We approached them and asked if we could be of assistance to them. They said 'no we have come to enjoy poetry.' We knew that it was a very cynical statement, and knowing how dangerous the situation was, we were concerned about the audience.

Ingoapele was the chairperson, Matsemela, Maishe and myself were for once just in the audience. We asked Ingoapele: 'Are you going to chair this session with the presence of the security?' Not to be outdone, Ingoapele of *Africa my beginning, Africa my ending* said 'of course!' So, we sat there in Funda Centre symbolically because we used to pretend that we were brave and not scared. But we were shaking in our boots until the end of the proceedings. That is the incident that later on informed the plays with which I toured Europe and America. But it was all about the soul of the South African, the soul of struggle, and the soul of resistance."

Gita Pather: "One size fits all cultural policy promotes imbalance among artistic genres"

"I met Walter and Lance in 1992 at the Windybrow Theatre. Walter is one of the people who opened the space for us. This was at a time when the cultural boycott had ended and we could then participate in state institutions. On Monday it will be exactly thirty years since I am being in the industry as a professional, though one has to qualify the word. When I graduated, I had nowhere to go. There was no institution to work for. I could not work for the SABC[1] or the performing councils. We all had roles which were very clear and life was simple. Some of us as activists ran, and others gave chase. Twenty two years into our democracy, we are all looking at what is the role of policy of policy the arts?

All of us wanted to make arts, and history thrusted roles upon us. We couldn't make art. We made Protest Theatre, Black Theatre, and Poor Theatre. We performed as activists on factory floors to educate people around issues about sanitation, workers, that is where we occupied the space. We began to define and interrogate who we were as an oppressed nation. From 1992 to 2016, is a long time and I am back at the same space. I worked at the Windybrow, and I went to the playhouse where I met another wonderful man who is now with the IEC[2]. He literally opened the doors and I became part of the development department. We talked about policy.

The 1996 policy said we will allow access, we need to redress pass inequalities, we need to level the playing field, and give platform to marginalised voices. I was part of the ACTAG[3] research process that went into the White Paper of which I am proud. But we were little naïve. There was a tiny little money and our visioning was that bad. And of course I would like to think we have achieved 60% or 70% of what we said out to do with the White Paper. But key things were not achieved due to legislation which was not devolved to provinces.

In 2013, the DAC[4] with all its wisdom behind, closed doors, and hired consultants for R18 millions to draw up the new version of the White Paper, which was a radical departure from the 1996 one. Now what is policy supposed to do? It merely provides a framework and then is implemented through agencies. The 1996 policy encapsulated the values of our Constitution beautifully about arm's

---

1 | SABC – South African Broadcasting Corporation.

2 | IEC – Independent Electoral Commission.

3 | ACTAG is acronym for Arts and Culture Task Group that was appointed in the mid-1990s by the first post-apartheid South Africa Arts Minister Ben Ngubane to consult with the public towards the drafting of the country's national cultural policy named the White Paper on Arts, Culture and Heritage.

4 | DAC – Department of Arts and Culture.

length funding, freedom of expression, freedom of association and self-determination. The 2013 policy is all about centralised control by the DAC. It speaks about dirty words like social cohesion, moral regeneration, job creation, and industries. It's as if DAC realised 'Oh Gosh, the White Paper of 1996 has no moral generation, and no job creation. So let's put in those terms.' When people create policy, they should at least get their terminology correct. We need to decide what an industry is, and what culture is. In this way, we will discover that one size fits all cultural policy promotes imbalance among artistic genres.

The Minister gave himself amazing powers as probably more than the president in this case. He had a final say about what could get funding. The Paper said if proposals elevated social cohesion and moral regeneration, they will go up in the pecking order. In this way, you see a swift from policy to the creation of templates of what is acceptable and not acceptable based on the National Development Plan. But thankfully, as the fraternity we kicked it out. We said no, Minister! We have the National Arts Council of 1997 which you have promulgated; we have the PFMA[5] and lots of rules which you have to abide by. And this Paper is a radical departure and more than that it is a severe compromise of the constitutional principles that artists who are people too, have those freedoms. Of course, the 1996 does need tweaking. But at least the fight was about to ensure that the White Paper of 2013 comes out – which brings me to my darling Tony here. Why has nothing changed?

We have five major state funded theatres: the Playhouse, PACOFS[6], Market Theatre, Artscape, and the State Theatre. In the bad old days we couldn't work there. Today still, artists complain about access there. Twenty two years ago, these institutions were run by Whites. Now they are run by Black people. So what we learn is that changing faces doesn't necessarily change the mind-sets. And why hasn't anything changed? It's because the institutional culture hasn't changed. And that is true for the rest of South Africa; the fact that we know people are starving, they are dying because of lack of health, and yet but we have a health department which has to roll over billions because they haven't used it. So, why do artists complain? It is largely because of like the gatekeepers of the past – and there were major gatekeepers whereby everyone's mother was a Black Sash worker. Now we kind of reflect on apartheid. These institutions seem to be designed to kick you out. Even when change happened, people like me did not find it easy going. It was literally running against a wall with your head and many bloodied foreheads happened. So what is different now yet the policy is that we will fund this flagship institutions? There is a great deal of money running into billions now. So why is it that we are still having a situation of the haves and the have-nots?

---

5 | PMFA – Public Finance Management Act.

6 | PACOFS – Performing Arts Council of the Free State.

There are two things. The DAC has forgotten its role. It is double-dipping by playing outside the policy arena. The evidence is the half-baked White Paper. Its officials have become active players in the industry. They are competing with artists. They are producing work. They are creating organisations like CCIFSA to the tune of R13million of tax payers' money. Yet to date, we have not received at least one statement about what happen to that money. I have personally lodged a formal complaint with the Office of the Public Protector because the creation of CCIFSA broke every rule within the PFMA.

The NAC[7], as the highest body established by DAC that gives money to the arts, did not follow procedure in setting up its Board. Minister Mthethwa appointed the board without the due public consultation process. And when challenged, they have just published the names now. For me nothing has changed because while we change people, what motivates us, how we understand our mandate, what is necessary for us, because the same thing of cronyism and jobs for friends still prevails. It is just who the people are that is different.

Policy has to encompass the big brush strokes of what we all want to see. It is not meant to be the mouthpiece of government messaging around social cohesion, moral regeneration or any other nice terms we can find. Those are the end-products of a democratic just society. As I said at the Woodmead Indaba in 2016: get things right, stop the polarisation our country and address issues of continued economic marginalisation of Black people and we can start to talk about a healthy society in which arts can be able to make about *arts for art's sake*. Meanwhile, there is still a huge place for artists to protest, and to challenge their own roles. Struggle is not about pre-1994, it is a continuum. The plays may have changed, but the situation remains the same."

Maishe Maponya: "For me, the struggle has not ended"

"I am going to loosely cite a few quotations and you decide where they come from and what they mean to you with regard to theatre. Somewhere in Durban, a Minister who was on a door-to-door campaign made this statement: 'We should all refrain from finding negatively and sow suspicions among one another.' Another one was said by someone we all know against this background. A few months back, as things started to come out about where the political dynamics of the country were actually headed, the man came out guns blazing and said: 'To those people who have been saying things are going wrong in this country. Some of them were general secretaries but today they are criticising the party. They kept quiet while they were still in the party. They only got wisdom after they had left. If they say the party is weak, they must have weakened it.' Yesterday, Mpho Molepo said that 'we have inherited a wrong status quo.'

---

7 | NAC – National Arts Council of South Africa.

Paul Grootboom, who was on the same panel, indicated very clearly that I am very pessimistic about the state of theatre in this country today and whether theatre can actually effect change. These are very strong statements. You take these statements and put them together with what has already been said then you begin to understand where we come from. And then you also take the statement about people refraining from fighting negativity, and basically what it does is to shut off any debate related to the status quo. And that's where the problem is. That if anyone stands up say anything about the wrongs that this state and the ruling elite, then people begin to make these statements.

In 1985, I was given the Standard Bank Young Artists Award as the first Black person. When that nomination was made, I didn't accept it immediately. I took it back to the township to consult my colleagues and friends like Ingoapele Madingoane, Matsemela Manaka and Makhubu. We engaged very thoroughly about whether to accept it or not. They said it is your choice to accept it. We have given you our views. It was called then called the 1820 Settlers Foundation.

In 1986, I gave another production that deliberately dealt with the realities of the time. For those who have an idea of poetry, it would be something like what Mothobi Mutloatse called *Proemdra*, a fusion of prose, poetry and drama. If you read the reviews that came from that, there was just fear expressed by journalists because we spoke in different local languages and said things we wanted to say. An example is a poem called *Ugly Brown Canvass Uniform* about the army trucks in the streets. And because of that, the term *angry young Black man* was also attached to me.

I now want to talk about theatre today and policy. For me, the struggle has not ended. On hindsight, we probably did not inherit a wrong status quo contrary to what was said earlier. The 1996 White Paper created a kind of status quo as a basis upon which we should now be going forward. We are supposed to have inherited that White Paper as the law for the arts and culture in this country. Today, when politicians, for very simple reasons of convenience, decide that they don't like that White Paper and yet have not really made an effort to ensure that some of the good things are kept within the Paper, they make sure that those things don't exist. For example, the national, provincial and local government spheres don't talk with each other in terms of arts and culture. The provincial arts council are supposed to be set up but the national department sits back and say those things will happen by themselves. The provincial government have not been put as a programme by the national government."

Tony Kgoroge: "The sectors of policy are often developed in sectarian silos"

"I would like to use this opportunity to clear misconceptions about certain developments in the cultural sector in the country and set the record straight to make people understand where we come from, what we are about, and what we do. I am sitting here as the President of CCIFSA which represents the voice and the vision of cultural and creative industries in this country. CCIFSA was officially registered in May 2014. It operated through an Interim Committee until 23 March 2015 when we were elected into office as the new leadership by conference. CCIFSA's primary objectives include the following: to encourage the development and promotion of cultural and creative industries in the Republic South Africa; encourage the establishment of sector-specific industry councils; guide and encourage transformation, including acting against any form of bad practices in the cultural and creative industries; act as a body in the delivery of cultural and creative awards in recognition of excellence and achievements; address the skills requirements in the cultural and creative industries; improving access to finance for sectors in the cultural and creative industries and create cross-cultural sector fertilisation.

In our industry, we have lots of organisations that are dynamic in their approaches. However, we have also realised that we are very fragmented. For instance, there are no structures that link music, film and fashion design. And for that, the sectors of policy are often developed in sectarian silos; limiting the scope for synergies and the emergence of new solutions. All these challenges have had a negative impact on how the industries function. In order to address the challenges, the DAC assisted the cultural and creative to establish CCIFSA so that it can create the necessary linkages in a comprehensive manner. The ultimate objective for the cultural and creative industries is to achieve maximum contribution in the economy, nation building and social cohesion. Therefore, the establishment of CCIFSA is meant to ensure that strategies in the cultural and creative industries are aligned and more importantly are underpinned by sound research to ensure effectiveness, efficiency and sustainability of the sectors. Of each relevant issue, from skills develop to access to finance or the world market, these strategies will identify what can be tackled by generic policies and instruments, and what requires tailored approach in respect of each sector. As we speak, we are currently going to every province, organising sectors from local municipalities to district to come up with provincial sector councils, as well as to lobby support for sector-based policy in addition to the umbrella national cultural policy.

I don't think the DAC is doing away with the White Paper. It is basically looking into what policies aspects are possible. They have recognised that in light of the problems the country is facing, the policy is not really rooting out or bringing in more people to benefit out of whatever the sector they operate from. Now they are saying: can we look at this Paper? If whatever works we can carry on with it, if it doesn't work, we do away with it. There would be consultations, going through provinces in making sure that people can affect. So, nobody is doing away with anything. All of these things bother me these days as we are going through these provinces.

We are having a problem within our sector; we have White artists and Black artists. Indeed the notions of 'Black Theatre' and the 'White Theatre' still exist. People from townships complain about these things. They say that they are suffering from White monopoly. Is that a fact or not a fact? It is for us to see that the policy addresses this. What is sad is that we only find Black people in those gatherings. We sent letters to White organisations, but they never come. I don't think that is a South Africa we are trying to build. We need to change the mind-set to make sure that we get people to get to these gatherings. We must stop this obsession with postings on Facebook and become part of what is been undertaken. These things roll into other things.

If you look into the film industry, you will find that you have Lokshin[8] bioscope and film; same pattern that Bra Walter was speaking about. Lokshin bioscope is meant for Black filmmakers about funny stories of low budget of R300 0000. You come into the proper film, they are given better budget. And who are doing these proper films? The White folks are making films. You also go into what our broadcasters are doing. MNET[9] has three channels dedicated to Afrikaans. I am not saying that is bad, but can we look at other languages and learn from our Afrikaans colleagues to make sure that we uplift other languages? The SABC has exclusive Nguni, Sotho, Afrikaans and English channels. What does that say about us? We are still building the 'Us' and 'Them' mentality. Until we get to the point and sum up all these things together and come with a solid voice that is South African, these things will go on. As CCIFSA, we will fight these kinds of things and carry on with other things. With unity, we can reach out to far worlds.

Just to correct, Gita. My sweet heart, I don't know where you get the information about the misuse of money by CCIFSA? CCIFSA's interim committee was given R5 million and carried on until the conference. From then on, the new leadership that came into office after the elections. At the conference, we were given R3.7 million. It was hard to operate from this R3.7 because it came in tranches. So I don't know where the R13 million comes from. Whoever came with that figure for you fabricated facts."

---

8 | Lokshin is a colloquial and euphemistic reference to the word Location, mostly referring to Black residential township dwelling.

9 | MNET – Private television channel.

Deliberations by the panel and members of the audience

Gita Pather: "The figures you and I have euphemistically quoted come out of 172 pages of the DAC, attempting to hide information. I went through it. It is called creative industry. I don't hold Tony personally responsible. However, I also want to guide against political speak. When you are reading CCIFSA, it is the voice of the artists. Who is the artist, what is the voice, what is happening, and whether is R13 millions or R3 millions? It is important for us to ask questions. If you use the EFF[10] line, it's an irony coming out of Julius Malema's mouth 'payment back the money' because politicians in this country; the way they speak and the words they use speak are polarising. This is not a Black and White issue. If I was in that community, this is what I would tell you; go to KwaZulu-Natal and see Linda Bukassine. She gets the lion share from both from KwaZulu Arts and Council, municipal council, provincial and national governments. Ask her who is keeping the doors closed? You may want to ask the same question in Gauteng. Go and ask Aubrey Sekhabi, Annabel and James. In the Free State, ask the same questions.
There is a simple question that must be asked: what is CCIFSA, what does it do, where is the monthly report? If you are the voice of artists; which artists are you talking about? If you sent a letter, please show me the letter. It's about asking the uncomfortable questions. If I was marginalised pre-1994, I feel marginalised now because government is attempting to control not just the arts, but the while country. And I as an old ANC[11] member, I know what people do when they start losing control. The tenders get in, they get people in there and they close the space. And when they do that they think they are in control. For your benefit, Tony, this is not a Black and White thing of who got the monopoly. We have to stop and interrogate the situation and say, actually, there are no Black people holding the purse string and stop in platitudes, using old tired the language. I mean there is Ismail Mahomed who runs the National Arts Festival. So, let's talk the facts. The only White person who runs a White Theatre is Lara Foot at the Baxter. Athol Fugard. There is Katrina Theatre that is underfunded on the bend. There is Pop-out in Maboneng run by Hailey. And you know whom she makes space for? Lots of young radical talents. So, let's ask questions. Of course some are asked louder than others."

Mandla Maseko: "I am in the music industry. I want ask how we transform music industry to actually benefit the theatre sector? The first point I want to make is that it hurts how we interact with information and distort and still continue that's how it is because it is written down. I was one of the people who were part of the CCIFSA Interim Committee appointed by the Minster to make sure that transformation and access in arts happens. Please don't look at it from an angle of privileges, urbanised community. For me, it is the resistance that we see when we talk transformation. So, I want to check with the panel. Is this panel saying when government talk transformation and access it is now taking

---

10 | EFF – Economic Freedom Fighters.

11 | ANC – African National Congress.

control? Every single Minister of Arts and Culture has met with the majority of artists in various communities, sectors for as long as I remember. All of them are telling the Ministers the same thing; i.e. the problem is access and transformation.

It is time for this industry to slightly move the narrative that understands that the majority of people who make theatre, music are still feeling marginalised and they die in the brunt of poverty. I am turning the rail because I can see I am ageing and I am one of the artists who started one of the spaces I see today. There should be a generational dialogue about how do we see theatre and the music industry going forward. In the music industry today, the majority of our people have been marginalised into the physical business of music like live performing and selling of CDs. And when they are no longer selling, you are pushed out of the system. And they are no telling you that the copy right laws accord to you 50 years of royalties. 74% of the money collected from music played in South Africa leaves the country. So, whatever affects you in the theatre affects other sectors. All we are asking the panellists and the learned colleagues who are teaching the arts: please, ensure the narrative of access and transformation does not end in books."

Mpho Molepo: "Maishe, I want to confirm what I said yesterday. We have been made to accept a fake status quo starting as far back as the Sunset Clause and the Rainbow Nation idiom that emerged from the CODESA[12] negotiations. But we can see now that something did not go right. How long should the transition have taken? In the arts, the transition has taken 20 years to review the White Paper. I look at it as a document that was helping us to transit from apartheid to the now which is dangerous. Even though I am made to believe that arts go beyond colour, the non-racialism in the arts is fake. We continue to administer the racialised intuitional model today. Changing faces has not changed anything. The other problem with South Africa's cultural industry is we are constantly beginning all the time. We do not make reference of what existed before like previous conferences in the country and overseas before 1994. Furthermore, nobody writes about our narratives as Black practitioners. There seems to be concerted efforts by White commentators to ignore what we do as Black artists and position the White practitioners as the faces of the country. Please, let's correct that."

Gita Pather: "Indeed, there is so much appropriation in this country, including in the arts. Look at the recently launched book, *Methuen Drama Guide to Contemporary South African Theatre*. Out of the 22 writers in that book, only one (1) is Black; a Nigerian wrote about Zakes Mda and Sekhabi. Is this reflective of us? If as Black artists we don't sit down and put theory to what we do, then other people will appropriate our stories. It is really our responsibility to start writing down the history. And until we have done that, we cannot throw any stone."

---

12 | CODESA – Convention for a Democratic South Africa.

Tony Kgoroge: "I wish I could take everyone to the provinces, especially the rural parts, and make them to hear what the people are saying about what is happening in the country. Look at the #RhodesMustFall and others. It is a Black and White thing, whether you like it or not. For others, the statue of Cecil John Rhodes is a heritage that shouldn't be taken away; and for others it is a symbol of oppression that has to go. And this controversy comes to us as policy makers as a challenge to think about what do we do with spaces like these. It is a problem about which we have to think strongly."

Walter Chakela: "Mine is just a rhetorical question: can anyone really read the 1996 White Paper thoroughly and still feel there is need to create structures like CCIFSA?"

Maishe Maponya: "Yesterday I went to see *Bohemian Rhapsody*. There were only four Blacks in the theatre. Before that, I've gone to see *Singing in the rain,* and there Blacks constituted less than 3%. I am using this as an example to put a spot light on Pieter Toerin; the biggest cultural boycott breaker who now runs a theatre that was established by government. The government granted licenses to the casinos like Emperor's Palace to establish their social responsibility programmes. Now the very government is not demanding accountability from these institutions. Four years ago when I checked, they had about R100 million of social responsibilities in other coffers that was not used. We need to investigate this scenario."

Facilitator's remarks: A postscript

Of all the conference sessions, this is the one that graphically dramatised the tipping point at which the country is poised in terms of racial disharmony and disillusionment in the current political dispensation. The heated exchanges laid bare suspicions, mistrust, and resentments that have come to characterise social relations within shared spaces. The arts space in South Africa is the actual barometer of national disillusionment. It is a space where signs of bubbling discontentment are first witnessed before they explode onto the surface. In 2013, I cautioned:

"No society will ever be at peace with itself if it does not come to terms with the cultural tenets that define it [...] The consequences of leaving cultural intercession to fate are too ghastly to contemplate. South Africa's history has illustrated the repercussions of allowing cultural misunderstandings, suspicions, and tensions to simmer. Certain cultural explosions in South Africa have actually come to punctuate historic moments, and have thus influenced the charting of new political trajectories..." (Nawa 2013)

Twenty two years after the supposed attainment of liberation against colonialism and apartheid, the country is back to where it was in 1976 when the issue of language domination literally set the country on fire. The nation is now at war against itself because it has, through its state organs, failed to match political freedom with economic emancipation and cultural leverage. It is against this backdrop, that panel members spoke about appropriations and misrepresentations of Black experiences, racial scaling of theatrical productions and ambivalent policy trajectory. They have demonstrated that the notion of transformation has not only failed to lived up to its meaning, but that it is essentially used as a buzz word to ironically negate change to the nature of the society that is inherently favourable to the minority at the expense of the majority. Essentially, South Africans still exhibit, much against claims to the contrary, social behaviour originally programmed along racial and economic scaling. This is unsurprising because human-made systems are not known for relinquishing characters to appease those against them. According to Biko,

"the system concedes nothing without demand, for it formulates its very method of operation on the basis that the ignorant will learn to know, the child will grow into an adult and therefore demands will begin to be made. It gears itself to resist demand in whatever way it sees fit." (Biko 2004: 100)

Thus the vicious cycle continues. And it appears it will not stop anytime soon as long as the socio-economic structures remain intact under the watch of a government suffering from political apostasy or inertia. How do they manifest in the arts arena? The crux of the country's erstwhile bifurcated education system was to produce, from the Black populace, sewers or wood and drawers of water, and masters or owners of the economy from their counterparts. Literally, this means that the latter were exposed to tutelage that inculcated skills relevant to framing, packaging and marketing concepts that set them ahead of competitors. As such, they continue to wallow in superiority complex of doing good for the unskilled fellow citizens who are in turn expected to reciprocate with infinite gratitude and never with queries about the misrepresentation of their aspirations for the deserved transformation of the status quo. Two decades after the 1994 democratic dispensation, the change in the education system is in such a snail pace, if at all, that it is just as good at perpetuating the colonial and apartheid legacy with 'gatekeepers' among the drivers of the process(es).

Gate keeping in the cultural policy domain in South Africa deserves exposure and condemnation in strongest possible terms. Cultural policy is not a subject of academic expertise in South Africa, at least with regard to curricula at all levels of education. At tertiary level, there is no single university in the country that offers undergraduate degrees in the field. The University of Witwatersrand offers the subject at Masters Level for dissertation purposes. PhD qualifications are yet to be produced by the institution this regard. Incidentally, I happened to be the first and thus far only PhD qualification recipient in cultural policy in South Africa from the University of South Africa (UNISA), but neither receives recognition nor commission or procurement for services by government and tertiary institutions alike. Meanwhile, there are several self-proclaimed experts who are feted with accolades and honours by cultural agencies nationally and overseas. Some of these culprits are mere economists turned culturists whose best competence is to throw statistics at South Africa's cultural face. Back in the country, these self-styled gurus have endeared themselves to the high echelons of government and its agencies where they occupy positions from which they veto allocations of opportunities, as well as approval for policy considerations. By the same token, government establishes own agencies like the South African Cultural Observatory (SACO). But almost immediately afterwards, calls are made for its transformation on the basis that it is already too White, especially at the higher echelons. This being the case, why is it that government doesn't do things right from the onset when opportunities arise rather than try to rectify later?

True to the racially-charged and divided South African populace, it was shocking yet unsurprising to hear Mpho Molepo, in one of the inaugural panels the day before, publicly accusing South African cultural practitioners of Jewish descend for allegedly monopolising the cultural industry and framing it ways that, at the very least, frustrate authentic aspirations of their Black counterparts. Notwithstanding perceived subjectivity or political inconvenience of the charge, the stark reality is that indeed there is a critical mass of opinion bubbling beneath the cultural landscape in Black townships to the effect that White cultural practitioners by and large occupy crucial spaces from which they set anti-Black cultural agenda with deceptive chic as was the case historically with the dilution of African ideals within the mass democratic movement.

I submit respectfully, and without reservation, that South Africa will never experience genuine racial harmony until all sources, layers, configurations, dimensions and complexions of social stratification are categorically addressed. This includes the manifestations of all forms of discrimination according to South Africa's race schema, in this hierarchical order: White, Indian, Coloured, and Black. Sugar-coating of any part of the matrix is treasonous. The sporadic upheavals that the country is currently witnessing evidence the rejection of artificial rainbow-nationalism based on racial reconciliation without restorative justice. Genuine nationhood exists only when people within a shared space cultivate and embody common identity and patriotism in an inclusive cultural ideate. "South Africa's cultural diversity requires some elements of local relativity to prevent history from repeating itself." (Nawa 2013) Stated differently, the practice or tendency of adjudicating African culture(s) through universality must cease for restorative justice to South Africa and the entire African continent as well.

My first-hand experience of gate keeping within the arts in South Africa is worth sharing. In one of the several sessions I have attended on the review of the White Paper [Woodmead Indaba, 2016], I happen to have been part of a commission that strongly called for the review of a section of the Constitution of the country that was perceived as disfavouring the role of local government in culture. This call resonated with a series of serious academic studies that have been conducted on the subject beforehand. The facilitator of this commission was one of the top officials from the DAC who tried in vain to dilute or mollify the bid for the Constitutional amendment; arguing that what was required was clarity in respect of concurrent functions of the spheres of government on culture in the doctrine, as opposed to the actual alteration. But the commission stood its ground on its position.

The mischievous manoeuvre by the official could perhaps best explain how some pertinent recommendations of the ACTAG Report that gave birth to the national policy were ignored in that despite public consultations final decisions rest with the high echelons of government. Hence the country now finds itself having to revisit the document to close glaring gaps that could have been avoided initially had public sentiments been taken seriously. As history has a knack of repeating itself, it would come as no surprise if this current review process is once again equivalent to *manipulative charge*, or to put it idiomatically in SeSotho languages: "Go isanamakodithipeng (taking meat to the knives [butchers])." Only vigilance as displayed throughout the conference will guarantee the acceptance into the new cultural policy recommendations on sector-based aspirations as well as seamless sharing of competencies or functions on culture by all spheres of government. Otherwise, the likelihood of the convening of a series of similar public charades in future on the same topic cannot be discounted while the status quo remains.

Unless otherwise referenced, quotes are taken from panel discussions at the *Theatre in Transformation* conference held in Pretoria form 11 – 13 March 2016.

Bibliography

Biko, Steve (2004): I write what I like. Johannesburg: Central Books.

Mahomed, Ismail (2014): Reflections: Two decades of SA Theatre. Available: http://www.artlink.co.za/news_article.htm?contentID=35329, Last Access: 31/10/2016.

Nawa, Lebogang L. (2006): We must recognise all cultures. In: *City Press*, 1/2006, Last Access: 31/10/2016.

Same old apartheid drama or new democratic play?

Report of the panel discussion "The State of Theatre in Soweto"

Lebogang L. Nawa

On Sunday 13 March 2016, about hundred people gathered at the Soweto Theatre to listen to a panel discussion on the topic: "The State of Theatre in Soweto: Same Old Apartheid Drama or New Democratic Play?" The panellists were: journalist and writer, cultural activist and arts manager, former Member of the Parliament, Mongane Wally Serote; poet and producer, composer and musicologist, arts and cultural policy analyst Motsumi Makhene; entertainer and comedian, theatre producer and film actor, president of the Creative Worker Union of South Africa Mabutho Sithole; and theatre maker and film producer, master in social sciences and drama for life, community theatre movement activist Bobby Rodwell. Lebogang Lance Nawa, the convenor of the event, facilitated the discussion. The abstract of the debate read:

"When Soweto sneezes, the rest of South Africa catches cold! So went the saying during the height of the liberation struggle in South Africa. As the biggest Black township in South Africa, initially Apartheid planners saw Soweto as little more than a dormitory for Johannesburg's black domestic workers and gardeners, mine and factory workers. But it has long been a cosmopolitan centre of political and artistic life for black South Africans." (Bryson 2010)

The event programme, from which the abstract is drawn, serves as an outline of this report. The report presents a blow-by-blow account of the proceedings as they unfolded in chronological order. However, due to space constraints, not all items on the programme are contained herein. Only covered in the report are: the history of Soweto Theatre, profiles of panellists and respective presentations, deliberation between the panellists and the audience, panel moderator's remarks, reviews of the panel, and post-scripts by some panellists.

The Soweto Theatre is one of the three entities that form the Jo'burg Theatres umbrella. There are two are the Johannesburg Civic Theatre, and the Roodepoort Theatre. They are all owned by the City of Johannesburg Metropolitan Municipality and are overseen by a single Board of Directors. The Soweto Theatre was established and inaugurated in 2012, as part of the 2010 FIFA World Cup as part of its Soccer Legacy projects, to serve biggest Black township in South Africa with a population of about 4 million. Worth R150 million, the construction of this facility commenced in June 2009 and it was fully operational and officially opened on 25 May 2012. The venue is the first of its kind in the township and perhaps South Africa in that it a futuristic architectural spectacle that has become an eye-catching landmark which serves as a multi-levels multipurpose venue with a theatre of a sitting capacity of 420 in its main attraction, two smaller venues for 180 and 90 patrons respectively, an indoor foyer, dressing and storage rooms. Easily accessible from main roads and a nearby Rea Vaya bus rapid transit station, and located next to the busy Jabulani Mall on the corner of Bolani and Koma Roads. It is central to the development of the Jabulani business node, which will eventually house a R320-million shopping mall, a 300-bed Jabulani Provincial Hospital, and a residential area (cf. City of Johannesburg 2011).

This section deals with the actual main focus of the event. It first profiles each panellist and respective individual input, then broadcasts a conversation between the panellists and the audience, and then with remarks by the facilitator. Each of these three components is treated separately and sequentially. The panellists' submissions and audience participation are presented verbatim with just minor editorial for grammatical and space considerations. The names of participants from the audience are matched to corresponding comments to attach actual real people with their names to the discourse.

Mongane Wally Serote: "Arts and culture can build a nation"

"Firstly, I would like to pay tribute to the legends of the arts in Soweto, especially in the context of the liberation struggle in South Africa. These are the people who lived the arts when there was no government to pay anything for them, to put a play for them together, to put a band together, to do this or that in the arts. Sheer blood and sweat, including the fact that all of us understood at that time that what we were doing could put us in jail. I am not being romantic or sentimental. I am conveying a message to young people who are in the front of arts and culture not to neglect to understand the history of arts and heritage comes from in this country. One way of doing this is through the identification of people who have made indelible marks in the cultural arena for Black people. You need to study and accept from what they did and go forward. Their list is long. Others have already been mentioned today. Those not yet mentioned are

Mothobi Mutloatse who used to run a publishing house called *Skotaville*. For the context of this debate, Mothobi coined a phrase *Proemdra*; short for prose, poetry and drama. This shows how artistic genres in our era were integrated into one.

We were also in the front with the likes of those present here. I have worked very close with Lebogang Nawa for many years in many key fronts of the arts; and also this one who calls herself a White woman, Bobby, with one focus: to build a South African nation. I am saying this to remember that the arts, culture, and heritage build a nation. We are where we are today at a point where some people say they are disgruntled and others say the country has lost direction. There is another stalwart here; Ngila Muendane, to whom I have listened many times on radio. He is active in many ways and fortunately he has also been able to record the history of this country from many angles which otherwise if they were not recorded, we would not have known about them as they would have been lost. With these few words, I am really trying to put four things on today's agenda.

The first is an advice for young people: if you don't know your father's story, and if your father did not know his father's story, you are a lost person. So let's be very careful about that. Let us not be misled by people. It is an African finding which is the foundation of our existence. The second thing I want to say is that it is very true the world over that arts and culture and heritage have a role to play in two ways; arts and culture can build a nation and make sure that that nation does not starve by contributing significantly into the economy. Those who are doing PhDs must study this. This must find a way to look into it and ask: is it true arts and culture can build a nation, that it make sure that it contributed significantly to their livelihoods, quality of life and create liveable spaces?

In this country, theatre played a very significant role; starting with bo Gibson Kente and Sam Mahangwane. You know, Mhangwane play, *Unfaithful woman*, played to full houses wherever it was staged: What can we do now to reclaim these stalwarts of theatre? History of theatre in South Africa, especially Black townships, is long and it must be studied.

The last point I am making is that as cultural workers, we must express deep disappointment to our government for having put arts and culture in the backseat. I was once with some of the key officials of the DAC and I said to them: the department cannot afford to be so disliked by the people of South Africa. What is the mistake that you did? You must identify it for yourself. Another person I have worked with very strongly when it was not fashionable to be in arts is Maishe Maponya (in the audience). Maishe, we have to find a way to reconnect; all of us and say somebody has lost a path. But we must never forget that revolution did make gains and those gains cannot be reversed. We must find a way to acquire more gains now than in the past."

Motsumi Makhene: "Theatre for consciousness, theatre for protest, and theatre for identify and development"

"I want to make certain connections because this feels like a holy space all of a sudden. I'll just share a bit of information about Funda Centre; the role of Funda Centre in theatre. Bra Wally spoke about Donaldson Orlando Community Centre and YMCA in Orlando. There was Dockay in the City of Johannesburg, and many other Centres that have produced the generations from the 50s through to the 80s. Funda Centre merely took the cream of the crop from 1984 onwards. It has a long history that starts in 1954 with the Esselen Commission which produced a report about education of a Black person called Bantu Education. It was created as an Adult Education Centre. Some of the four radicals or rebels produced by that report include Prof. E'skia Mphahlele, Prof. Khabi Mngoma, Mr. Zephaniah Mothopeng and Mr. Isaac Mahlare; all of whom have since passed on. The four of them were all teachers who were involved in that period of the 50s of the 80s. Some of the like Mphahlele and Mahlare left the country for exile at some point. And you can leave the country but you can't leave the struggle.

When Funda was established, already Soweto was abuzz not because it was in any manner a typical township, but that Soweto has since the 60s has been a theatre itself; a township theatre of many things. So when Funda was established, it brought on board people who were produced by Dockay House: the *Bahumutsi* (I mention *Bahumutsi* because *Tlou* [Elephant as totem clan name] is here [in the audience]: Maishe Maponya); and Malo-poets from Diepkloof where Funda Centre is located.

One important canon of that is if you spoke about Funda, it was as if the entire Funda Centre was an arts centre, yet it had other disciplines. At that time, Soyikwa Institute of African Theatre was established by my friend and comrade, Matsemela Manaka. He had lots of experience, debates and international encounters. He came back at some stage from his travels and said: 'You know, I now believe that theatre is the integration of all the arts and as such African theatre is part of that. We need to build or rebuild the type of theatre that is more integrated and not separate; where music is not just music, visual arts is not visual arts, and drama is not drama. But everything is everything. It must be within the same expression.'

In as much as Funda Centre became an alternative of Bantu Education, it also became an alternative space for Market Theatre in town. We did have lots of interactions with the Market Theatre for which there are many stories to tell, but ultimately the two theatres came together. Essentially Funda was about three things in respect to theatre, namely: theatre for consciousness, theatre for protest, and theatre for identity and development. With regard to the last, Matsemela created two milestone productions; one is called *Domba (The last dance*) and *Goreé* because he happened to have part of a delegation that went to Zambia when negotiations started to happen between the ANC and the then South African government. And that story ended up in Goreé[1] where his spirit as an artist was literally shredded to pieces. And when he came back, he was conflicted to the extent that when he was working on *Goreé*, he was the artist who created the set, the script writer, and the artist that painted a series of portraits of the location; focusing on nothing else but the door on no return. The play paid tribute of a young lady from Soweto whose life, identity and consciousness would be turned around because she had lost a ship that had left the shores of *Goreé*. At that night, she encountered the Spirit of the Oba which roamed the coast. And the two began to converse about where she was going. She said: "I am going to America to learn to become a dancer." But at the end of that night, she came back to South Africa because she had realised for the first time from the dialogue with the Spirit that she was an African.

Mabutho "Kid" Sithole: "My wish is for the young to become change agents"

"I am particularly inspired by the presence of many young people. I want to challenge them to think very deeply about becoming change agents in this industry because they still have the energy, the technological advancement and other tools they need to become impactful change agents. What inspires me to speak to them is where I come from; a time when it was not fashionable to be in these types of gatherings. And I am glad the facilitator started by referring to us as cultural workers – and for heaven's sake not celebrities because I can't be seen to be celebrating poverty.

I want to talk about labour matters in the arts because we tend to take for granted that we are not working. Often when I hear brothers strumming their guitars and I go to them to ask where they would be performing that night, a common response would be: "SidlalaeMarket Theatre. Si-a-dla-la (We-are-PLAYING)." My wish for theatre is that all of us who are practitioners must understand that when you strum your guitar, when you pound your drum, when you take to your flute or saxophone, when you take to the script and run your lines, you are on duty. There is no difference from a person who is a teacher in classroom or a policeman in a police station and so on. My wish is for young who are here to become change agents. How?

The people who are next to me will tell you that we used to have a structure that was called TMSA (Theatre Management of South Africa). That is the structure that pulled together all the theatre managements. I don't know whether it

---

1 | *Goreé* is an island on the coast of Senegal which served as the largest slave-trade post in West Africa. It is declared a UNESCO World Heritage Monument.

is still available, but I doubt. The change agency will have to look at bringing back those kinds of structures. The Creative Workers Union, of which are I am President, recently formed CIFSSA (Creative Industries of South Africa Association) and the Independent Producers Organisation (IPO) of this world. Why am I mentioning this? Because most of them have been in charged with particular groupings: IPO in charge of putting together the productions; and many such organisations. Why do I propose that they come together? They come together to make sure once you want to be a cultural worker, there is therefore a body that could possibly assist that there must be a theatre or creative arts bargaining council so that they must be an employer-employee relationship that comes out of it. So that all the other things that are needed to make the life of this theatre practitioners comfortable are done there. So that this seasonal type of scenario that we find ourselves in is addressed. So that the IPO issues are addressed, so that the local contents issues are addressed. All those can happen if you can begin to understand that *aodlale, oyasebenza* (You are not playing; you are working). When do you begin to understand that you are not a celebrity, but that you are a worker? I am calling for change agents so that this scenario changes for the better."

Bobby Rodwell: "The past is in the present and no one seems be responsible for putting it there"

"The focus of what I want to say today is based on this question: are we suffering from the past nostalgia in South African theatre? A few years ago, about two years ago in this very theatre, I was presenting in a *Drama for Life* Conference on unfinished business of the Truth and Reconciliation Commission (TRC). And I was speaking about a play that we had done fifteen years earlier called *The story I am about to tell*; which dealt with personal testimonies told to the TRC. And perhaps the issue is the way I presented; speaking about the story as if it were yesterday. Or perhaps it is because we were investigating theatre around the TRC that prompted post-doctoral researcher, Gibson Seman, to ask me whether we were experiencing the past nostalgia in the South African theatre. That got me thinking: why we are we staging plays so many plays from the early 1980s and early 1990s?

One year after that conference, we brought the play to the Soweto Theatre; thanks to the then artistic director, Warona Seane, a great visionary in theatre. Thank you to Warona we brought the play and we re-envisioned it somewhat with a new young director, Monageng Motshabi, and previously been directed by Robert Coleman; and a great new casted headed by Sello Sebotsane. Together the new team took the story forward without losing the integrity of the original production, though in the original production people told their own stories. It wasn't the actors telling the stories. They then gave the story to the actors to tell the story. The play was seven year old. Did it work?

Performances were completely sold out. The theatre was filled beyond capacity every performance. And this was in a climate when filling houses in theatre is difficult. Sadly, for the last three performances we had to turn away lots of people. So why was it so full? It is not as if it was an amazingly superior production compared to other productions that were been staged in the theatre at the same time. What we did as we have done before is that we performed for one hour and we engaged in a discussion with the audience for another hour as part of the performance around the TRC. And this gave me an opportunity perhaps to get an insight to why the play was so successful.

The lens had shifted from 1997 when it was first done to 2015 when it was first redone. The lens had shifted from people telling their own stories, and the emotional healing power of storytelling and also debates around the TRC process. And the debate now in 2015 was very much around race and disparities. The script hadn't changed, but the context and the names had changed. And in the discussion afterwards, questions ranged from "we should just have killed all the White people at the time" to "the ANC has totally failed this country", to "what was the point of the point of the TRC?" One of the saddest points for me was made by a student from Naledi High school – and if we remember, Naledi was one of the forerunners of the Soweto uprisings of the 1970s. The students said we are angry as young people and yet we do not fully know our history. We are not even taught our history at schools. So the question then was to what degree did the 1980s discourse really challenged issues of colonisation and coloniality?

This is the question that ran though the debate after the play and I am sure that something that the universities students are asking our generation. So thus the seven year old paly, examining the past, was successful and perhaps one of my favourite lines in the play, which perhaps speaks to that, is that "the past is in the present and no one seems be responsible for putting it there." For me the role of the 1980s and 90s plays that are surfacing, I think, allows us to debate to ask how far we have come, or as the late Gibson Kente would say How Long? And I think Matsemela Manaka's Egoli at the Market Theatre recently, written in the 1980s about the mining industry and migrate labour in South Africa. The play, written thirteen years ago, asks the question: what has changed? The ghost of Marikina was in the theatre, the ghost of Lily Mine was in the theatre. The director had brought Marikana with a single green blanket that one of the players wore. The question wasn't about thirteen ago. It was about that was about thirty years ago and this is today.

I mentioned only two plays of the past, but of course there is a long list. There have been a lot of plays from the 1980s and 1990s being redone but at the same time there have been an incredible blossoming of new plays by new young playwrights. Again, I mention a play that Warona Seane produced in this theatre; Philip Lekgotla's *Ke a lla* which deals with the racial massacre that happened post-1994. Warona also produced Kgafela Monageng's Rainbow Nation, dealing with the not-too-futuristic capitalist constructed elitist government, or the intellectually challenging *Poet of all time* by Jeff Tshabalala. All presented in this theatre. Or Thabiso Ramano's ... dealing with the issue of circumcision which has not yet been staged at this theatre but I am sure it will. I am asking questions of whether that play would have been done in the 1980s or not? This is all brave new theatre and it is breaking news ground. I mentioned again only three of the plays that came to mind.

The other day I was speaking to Philip Lekgotla about the issue of the past nostalgia and how it is important it is to be doing plays of the 80s and 90s. He is in his 20s. He blasted me out of the water, saying that he is having a different point of view, and the old plays are taking the plays what the new playwrights are trying to create. There are a lot of young people today who may agree with that position. He said that the old plays are getting good audiences, but the new young playwrights are struggling for audiences, and how do we breach that gap?

Of course, the old plays are better known but perhaps it is because our society is being made to re-examine where we came from and where we are now. And our theatre is reflecting that as it always does reflect the times. There is a process of re-examining, with a nostalgic memory, not the harsh realities of the political and racist society of the 1980s, but rather the ideological paradigm of the vision of the new society. This is healthy and necessary for our theatre while at the same time there is a wonderful growth of new ideas, new plays and new playwrights germinating right next to these plays. And it needs to be respected and space preserved for both. South African theatre is in great space to be in today."

Discussion among panellists and audience
Can we firm up intergenerational and international connections?

Smangaliso Mnisi: "I want to ask Bra "Kid" what is actually the point of the Creative Workers Union? Why are we positioning creative as workers instead of a force to be reckoned with? Shouldn't we put ourselves as employers because you will find in production houses? Let's take the SABC TV soapy *Generations* for example. The actors said we were not paid enough, and the producer Mfundi Vundla then fired everyone and hired everyone else. That's what happens when we regard ourselves as workers. Shouldn't we position ourselves as employers of a section that at least we can put our foot down if we feel that we are not getting what we deserve?"

Simphiwe Twala: "How can you guys connect us with people who have been there because there is a huge gap between cultural workers before us and now?"

Dikeledi Molatoli: "My observation has been that young people today, young cultural workers or artists for that matter, find themselves struggling a lot when they go knocking on the doors as individuals. I would like the panel to comment on the importance of young people to work as collectives because that is what we are trying to do in MollowaDitshomo. To say there is power in numbers. Secondly can we really firm up these inter-generational and international connections?"

Mabutho Sithole: "Let me start with our friend Smangaliso there on the question of positioning ourselves as what? The reality of this industry whether is theatre, television or film and music is that you find that as a practitioner, you are sometimes called to be two-in-one. You are a Ringo Mandligonzi and you are hired by a City of Jo'burg to do a particular show on romantic Ballads. At that stage the musician is an employer because he has been commissioned to sing romantic ballads. At another stage, in the same project, he is going to be an employer because is going to hire a backing band.
Let me bring it closer to theatre, you have a Motsumi Makhene who is a producer of a particular *Goreé* theatre production. First, he will have to negotiate with the management about this space here. In that play he is also a lead actor. So you can't deprive him his dual roles. Yes, the important part is to belong to a collective so that with the numbers you are able to bargain, to make sure that all times the interest of you as arts practitioners are covered. So working as a collective is critical.
The other sad part of our history is that seemingly we are going backwards. After we got our freedom, and it is now easy for a child from Orlando to be a student at Mondeo High School, which was previously not allowed. Maishe and I we were in the same school, Orlando High; we couldn't go to the neighbouring Noordgesig High School – it was not allowed. Since our liberation our children are taken to the schools which seem to be academically advanced than our township schools. But what happens in the process? They are going there to amass quality education and academic levels that are supposedly higher than that of townships. Simultaneously, another sad thing is happening: cultural erosion chips. We used to sit as the family, *umndeni*. It doesn't matter whether with your mother, father, uncle, aunt or so forth. We used together and share things. Today the youth say: "he is not my friends, he is not my peer. I am going to sit with my peers." That did not happened with us. This is what one can safely call the unintended consequences of amassing the so-called quality western education at the expense of African culture. And then all of the sudden there is this generational consciousness."

Should an artist be a worker or employer?

Motsumi Makhene: "On the question of whether an artist should be a worker or employer? We are citizens first. And what Bra "Kid" had said is that we have a missing link in the transformation of South Africa. This link has to be filled by an active consciousness. And only artists can lead because before they are employers, before they are workers, they must do something about our community's level of consciousness so that institutions like this one, the one in Roodeport and the one in the City centre, should be institutions where artists are most active in trying to communicate to the community through all integrated arts about what the community should become because there are many lies, and deceptions and deflections. Our multimedia is a powerful medium that makes you not to think, to unbecome. Multimedia is preparing a new nation of tomorrow that does not know itself, that consumes what is given. Artists must begin here to create that consciousness. And theatre is one of the instruments. South Africa has grown into a nation that it always looking forward for something to be delivered to it. We need to shift from receiving delivery to creating the future."

Maishe Maponya: "I want to say we are where we are today disgruntled. Cultural workers must express big disappointment to our government for putting arts and culture at the back. Arts and culture is actually in the front but it is manipulated by cronyism. A new debate of the review of the arts and culture has been emerging from 2013 and 2014, but I can bet my last penny that Bra Wally has not been, or is not, part of that process due to cronyism and political manipulation."

Warona Seane[2]: "I want to speak to the notion of the *State of Theatre in Soweto* from two angles. What artists need to do essentially is to look at if you are your collective, what is the value-chain and that collective? We can't be doing the same job. How do you work together to help each other to ensure that the collective stay strong? An easy example is that of the *Word N Sound* collective. All of them realised that we have different skills, degrees, and diplomas. They put together their skills and now they have a company that is pushing boundaries around poetry. They are now doing tours all over the world raising funds by themselves. They are running a business; not a Non-Profit-Organisation. Their intention is to ultimately get *Word N Sound* listed on the Johannesburg Stock Exchange. They have taken all the skills that all the poets have and they are putting them together to brand a company. That how you need to start thinking as well because there are lots of structural gates that would stand in the way if you are not compliant; which means your company is not properly registered, it doesn't have tax certificate and all other kind of all things the government can use to get tax from you. You need to have these things ready so that your company can really be fully functionally and so nobody can

---

2 | Warona Seane is the former artistic manager of the Soweto Theatre from 2013 to December 2015.

use the fact that you are not compliant as an a way to not give you space and access to resources that belong to you.

I finished working at November last year [2015]. This is March now, and there is still no replacement for the Artistic Manager and General Manager. That worries me about this space because it needs to continue to run. Before I left, I had created a programme that would run until May this year with money left for the incumbent to actually dream about what people would do in June as part of the 40th celebration or commemoration of the (Soweto) Uprising. If that programme had been followed, we would still have theatre here. We would not been sitting here right now. Perhaps we would be sitting in another venue while the cast Have you seen Zandile?, directed by Khutso Bakunzi-Green, is setting up a performance for the afternoon.

The programming has not been implemented and still there is no replacement for the artistic manager. The space needs an artistic manager as urgent as yesterday otherwise the State of Theatre in Soweto will continue to be a problem and people will knock on doors and find nobody to talk to because nobody is there to look towards furthering perhaps the first three years of the institutional history memory until such a point it shifts when someone new – who has a different vision – is appointed. I am saying this with the board here so that they can rush the process of finding a new artistic manager and general manager, otherwise the State of Theatre in Soweto is not improving and my last three years would amount to nothing."

Have the arts become over-corporatized?

Carl Johnson[3]: "One of the big problems in the country at the moment is that the arts have become over-corporatized. There are these interchangeable positions of Chief Financial Officers (CFOs), Chief executives Officers (CEOs) and Chief Operating Officers (COOs). We find these professionals jumping from sector to sector, but it doesn't neces-sarily mean they know anything about theatre. One of the main reasons that made me to leave the Jo'burg theatres is that of the technocracy of the executive management team; the COO in particular doesn't understand theatre. We are perfectly safe in this building at the moment, but you need to know that the smoke detection and ventilation system in the building does not work because this man would not allow a normal piece of business in the municipal management system. He would like to have a specialist service provider to carry on doing the job it was doing when it was paid to do the building. I must put it out to the market which does not have the special skills relevant to theatre. I have tried for three months after that I just gave up.

I must speak with respect to the chairperson of the Board and other board members present here. You have a serious problem when the industry is been dictated to by bureaucrats as opposed to them learning how to run the industry from the so-called industry experts and then applying that into the various government acts they have

---

3 | Carl Johnson is the former general manager of Soweto from 2012 to February 2016.

to apply: e.g. the MMFMA and BFMA the Cultural Institutions Act. They must take the knowledge they learned from the specialists, apply to the specialist BComm or whatever degree they got and apply it back into the industry. That would save the country millions of rands, grow the industry more. And this is not applicable only within the Jo'burg theatres. It is across the board."

What do we hope this theatre will be for the people of Soweto?

Yvette Hardie: This theatre has been a dream for a very long time. I remember people asking: "when are we going to have a theatre in Soweto?" And finally, the theatre is here for the last four years. Warona had an extraordinary vision for this theatre and tremendous energy to implement that. Where is that dream now? What do we hope this theatre will be for the people of Soweto and how is it going to nurture the next generation of theatre makers and the audience?"

Ishmael Mkhabela[4]: "What we have just heard about the Soweto Theatre touches me because I was the Chairperson when it was launched. I remember vividly once saying that this facility is not going to make artists on its own, but artists would make themselves artists. We need the energy of everybody here, but we need to draw a line: that there is a board and there are artists; there is management and there are artists; management knows it all and artists know it all and we draw the line. Mutual recognition would be helpful. As Board members, we cannot work this way on our own, and neither should we allow the you-and-us-approach to dictate our relationship."

Linda Mash: "I am feeling very encouraged that we are here, young and old. We are concerned about the state of the arts and theatre because I feel like that's where solutions are going to come for us. I also feel so good to see the presence of our elders here. There is a lot of disgruntlement because art is no longer a profession that you grow into and you survive. When we tell our parents that we want to be artists they discourage us. They ask us: "how are we going to eat, raise your children, and buy a house?" This forces us to go to places of work that we don't want to be in just because we want to survive. If we are artists, it's like we are condemning ourselves to die hungry. Our parents even give us examples of other struggling artists by saying: "do you want to be like that one?" to a point where it feels like abandoning the arts. It is a very painful thing to abandon the arts to survive. So, while it is encouraging to see people from all over the world here to discuss something with us, but at the same time – and I am sure many peers will agree with me – we have been in many meetings like these with adults. It's nice to see you here. You are important somewhere and you have your labels and titles. But are you really going to make a difference to us, actually be part of our lives, or are you just here

---

4 | Ishmael Mkhabela is the Board Member of Jo'burg Theatres under which the Soweto Theatre falls.

to say "in 2016 we were in Soweto?" Ten years from now, would I be able to say this event has changed my life? You can see we are ready. We can even break into song right now. But you guys are the ones with the money, connections and power. We need you. So please let's just not be here; formal and important. Let us make a difference. We want to see action more that talk. We are tired of talk."

Who do I identify with, who am I going to help, who I can collaborate with?

Ngila Muendane: "This is a historic meeting because it sets the stage for the future of the arts post-1994 dispensation. It is how we approach that subject, our occupations, our vision and missions, and what we got to do in this life so that you don't pass through this life without a sound. And you cannot make a sound when you are focusing on problems, when you are using your energy to complain. Because the energy that you have can either for complains or for creativity. You can't use it for both. The youth has played a very important role in the history of this country. It was a 26 years old who formed the ANC. It was a 24 years old who formed the Youth League of the ANC. It was a 28 year who formed the PAC (Pan Africanist Congress). It was Steve Biko later on who formed the BCM (Black Consciousness Movement). And in each time there was change in this country, it was the youth. So the ball is in your court. I want to challenge you. I want you to remove yourself from expecting old people like me to create your future because I am not going to live in that future. My one leg is already in the grave. The elderly don't know how to create the future they are not going to be part of. Only those people who are going to live in that future can create it because it is theirs. It would be interference on the part of an old like me to dictate how the youth must prepare for their future.
Another point is that when you build, you build brick by brick, and who are the bricks of this society? The bricks of this society are individuals who must be brought together? How do you that? You use mortar. The arts are that mortar in this nation. This is what brings us together. If we want to live for a very long time in this country, we must have an approach that we are as artists the combiners of individuals in this nation. The social cohesion that we are talking about, as an antithesis of disgruntlement, can only be achieved through the arts. It is all very well that the government is not doing anything. But it is the pressure you put. And you don't have to fight, you can protest. What is it therefore as the mortar that is going to solve the problem? It is identity. Identity simply means: who do I identify with; which means who is going to help me, who am I going to help, who I can collaborate with? But it also has many levels. It is not just simply to say I am an African."

Lebogang Mnisi: "The problem about the arts in our country is that our industry is used as a dumping ground or detoxing place. It is not respected. People go and work as accountants and when they are bored they come to this industry. We have lost the identity of our talent within the process. That is why we are losing the meaning of the arts. Not all of us go to school to be grounded in the arts; some of us are born with and into the arts. But we are now at the point in this country that we are being scaled through certificates. Why do we need piece of papers to validate us as artists? When you take people from varsity and you put them on stage, they are dead!"

The demographic inclusitivity of the cultural space. Facilitator's remarks

My comments are based on observations from the actual proceedings of the event as well as the aftermaths. To avoid rehashing the event proceedings, the commentary is limited to selected themes that emerged from the conversation. The composition of the panel was deliberately designed in such a manner that it reflected an eclectic mixture of the social fabric of Soweto. To this effect, the panellists were drawn from different facets of theatre experiences in the township, from the 1970s to the present. It is against this backdrop that Bobby Rodwell mischievously introduced herself to the audience as a "White Woman in Soweto." There is no gainsaying that she intended to debunk the stereotype of Soweto as an exclusive Black enclave as decreed by apartheid laws. Indeed, while the infamous political doctrine had officially designated Soweto as a restricted Black settlement, cultural activists across the racial divide crossed the artificial boundaries and made the place their preferred trading site as well as home. Driven by Heinrich Boell's philosophy of 'meddling' as captured in her biography, Bobby was one such activist who frequented cultural sites in Soweto, and elsewhere, when it was socially unfashionable or curios as well as politically risky in terms of apartheid laws. In light of this, I disclosed to the audience that on 10 April 1993, the day the militant ANC stalwart Chris Hani was assassinated; Bobby had been spending a weekend with my family at the village. The significance of this point is that this bastardly act could have plunged South Africa into a racial war. It is for this reason that when the news broke out on radio, my mother, been the first to have heard the news and of course fearing for Bobby's safety, rushed out of the yard to searched for us in the streets to convey the message. Fortunately, no harm happened to Bobby. Reverting to Soweto; judging from people who associate with the current theatre, the demographic inclusivity of the cultural space is being con-solidated. This inclusivity mirrors the integrated theatre production approach in the Black townships; from the artists, artistic genres, logistics and so forth. The first point still requires some improvement, though.

Several concerns were raised in the panel about an apparent generational gap. In line with Muendane submission that the young are their own liberators, it must be disclosed that the local organising team was requested to identify young cultural practitioners to be on the panel. By their own admission, they felt intimidated and not confident enough to share the platform with house-hold names, yet they turn around today and get vocal about generation gap between cultural practitioners. Nevertheless, the symbolic presence of a 16 months old toddler in the audience augurs well for the closing of the genera-tion gap as well as the development of future practitioners and audiences from an early age. This is the matter cultural practitioners and government should take up earnestly through arts education curricula and campaigns at schools, varsities and communities.

Theatre as a business and not as a non-profit-making ventures

The panel affirmed the continuation of Mothobi Mutloatse's legacy of *Proemdra*. According to Makhene: "We need to build or rebuild the type of theatre that is more integrated and not separated; where music is not just music, visual arts is not visual arts, and drama is not drama. But everything is everything."

The point of departure in this regard, according to Dr. Serote through the analogy of *Know your father's house*, is for young artists to know their history from which to tap knowledge, inspiration, and benchmarks for the future. To support this point, I referred the audience to Kwame Anthony Appiah's book, *In My Father's House: Africa in the Philosophy of Culture;* quoting very loosely a line that said something to the effect that 'it is only a bastard who does not know his father's house.' The statement was moulded philosophically or exis-tentially rather biologically; and was accordingly received as such. To reinforce this point, I further cautioned South African cultural practitioners against fig-uratively chasing western butter-flies instead of adoring African totems.

From the cultural policy domain, dissatisfactions were raised about the current trajectory adopted by government as well as the exclusion from the dis-course of cultural policy pioneers like Dr. Serote who had charted a culture-ori-entated policy path from which government has clearly deviated. During the water-shed 1993 Culture and Development Conference, convened by the ANC in Johannesburg, Dr. Serote, in his capacity as Head of the ANC's Department of Arts and Culture, presented a post-apartheid cultural policy in these categor-ical terms:

"Legislation will have to be put in place that ensures that all South Africans have access to cultural expression and activity. This principle must permeate the implementation of the RDP: when housing is planned, cultural recreation facilities must be included in those plans; when health schemes are devised, art must be included as legitimate forms of counselling and therapy; when the departments of defence and safety and security develop their programmes, they must embrace arts and culture as bridge-building exercise...If we refuse to recognise the importance of culture, we will be removing the potential for development." (Mayibuye, 1995: 5)

The sensitive issue of labour exploitation in the arts in South Africa cannot be overemphasised. Generations of artists have traversed the globe drawing and wooing millions of fans and supporter, yet they die poor in the country of their birth. To counter this from one angle, Seane encouraged young artists to ply their trade as business and not as non-profit-making ventures. This call is informed by the fact that government and private funding agencies in South Africa view the arts as non-money-making ventures or hobbies instead of careers. Funding schemes like the National Lottery Commission require artists to apply as collectives rather than individuals under the umbrellas of Non-Profit-Organisations (NPOs) or Non-Governmental-Organisations (NGOs). Consequently, artists end up setting bogus entities to access funds and then in turn get accused of dishonesty.

Theatre needs cultural policy and management

The tension between theatres ran by non-artistic professionals as opposed to by theatre practitioners, as raised during the event, is not necessarily antagonistic. Artists are not outrightly rejecting the infusion of professional management in the sector, they are merely advocating for a culture-sensitive professional administration and policy. The issue of arts management and policy is currently plaguing government and the academia alike. I am privy to attempts by government agencies to commission academics, including myself, to assist them with improving their systems and structures after realising that the majority of officials in their employ have no clue about how to manage the arts. Yet the academics, from which salvation is sought, are few. The source of this drought is the absence of tertiary institutions in South Africa offering undergraduate degrees in cultural policy and management. Similarly, short-term or bridging certificates and diplomas for artists and government officials in this field are few and far in between.

Another instance of cultural exploitation as raised by the symposium's local organising team during the preparations of this event is worth matched with a plea: the principles of *nothing for mahala* (nothing for free) *equal payment for equal work* ought to be upheld. International academic institutions are obliged to reserve sufficient funds for payment of knowledge they intend to extract from South Africa and the continent. Otherwise it is regrettable for scholars or academics, in general, to condemn human exploitation as well as depletion of resources – especially in Africa – in their theories, yet perpetuate the very injustices in practice, knowingly or otherwise.

Furthermore, allocation of sufficient time for events of this nature is also crucial because the abundance of data available at any given site cannot be extracted or generated from a short period as was the case with the conference.

In conclusion, some positive spin-offs have since surfaced over-time after the conference. The call for research or studies to be conducted on theatre in Soweto seems to have fallen on fertile ground. Days after the conference, Andile Xaba, who had attended the session, approached me with a request to connect him with Makhene for his PhD research. In May 2016, the Jo'burg Theatres appointed Nomsa Mazwai as the General Manager for the Soweto Theatre and Salvataris Koloti as the Marketing Executive, respectively. Similarly, processes are currently underway to reclaim and revive Funda Community College to its glorious past.

Unless otherwise referenced, quotes are taken from panel discussions at the *Theatre in Transformation* conference held in Pretoria form 11 – 13 March 2016.

Bibliography

Appiah, Kwame A. (1992): In My Father's House: Africa in the Philosophy of Culture. Oxford: Oxford University Press.

Bryson, Donna (2010): "The Soweto Theatre making theatre again," article from 24 May 2010, Mail & Guardian newspaper, http://mg.co.za/article/2012-05-23-the-soweto-theatre-making-theatre-matter-again 21/10/2016.

City of Johannesburg Metropolitan Municipality (2011): "Soweto Theatre brings arts to the people",http://www.joburg.org.za/index.php?option=com_content&view=article&id=6407:soweto-theatre-brings-arts-to-the-people&catid=110:arts-and-culture&Itemid=193 21/10/2016.

Mayibuye (1995): Looking forwards looking backwards: Culture & Development Conference. Bellville: Mayibuye.

Soul food

South Africa's theatre shows how the country is seeking its future role

Henning Fülle

It was a coincidence, but a fitting one. South African Mpumelelo Paul Groot-boom, one of the protagonists of the *Theatre in Transformation* conference, was awarded the Jürgen Bansemer & Ute Nyssen Dramatists' Prize in Germany in May this year, while the German delegate to the eponymous conference held in South Africa in March was overcome by a kind of tragic yearning that went well beyond the romanticism of enlightenment or even revolution as he listened to the profound and very serious discussions on the future of theatre. Such intensive and respectful discussions between theatrical stakeholders and pro-tagonists would have been welcome in the wake of German reunification or the Second World War: times when we needed to make decisions about the future of theatre as we emerged from difficult entanglements.

It is already 22 years since the end of apartheid, marked by the first free elections in 1994 and the accession to power of the African National Congress headed by the newly released Nelson Mandela. Nevertheless, the discussions showed all too clearly that there is still a great deal of controversy and vague-ness about what the role of theatre could and should be in today's society and in building South Africa's Rainbow Nation.

This was the focus of the workshop initiated and organised as part of the international cooperation between the UNESCO Chair for the Arts in Devel-opment at the University of Hildesheim and the Tshwane University of Tech-nology (TUT) in Pretoria. The conference that ran from 11 to 13 March at the State Theatre Pretoria, the TUT and the Soweto Theatre brought together the key stakeholders and protagonists of South African theatre to take part in a number of panel discussions.

"We don't know how to mirror what we live"

The self-critical and poignant words from Paul Grootboom summed up the mood of the first day of the conference, when the floor was given to theatre directors and artists who had taken part in the struggle for apartheid and actively contributed to its downfall. They told how the old structures had of course been overthrown and a White Paper produced in 1996 that set out the guidelines for a cultural policy that would help to create a Rainbow Nation. This stated that existing theatres should be receiving houses and production houses rather than repertory theatres, but despite this, theatres are still a long way from finding their role in society. The abolition of repertory theatres took the powerful theatrical institutions – which were already open to all races in the 1970s – out of the hands of the White minority. But their new managers have generally been weak, rushing to obey the funding decisions of the Arts Council and chasing supposedly populist tastes, hugely influenced by the TV "soapies", as they are affectionately known here. It is about entertainment rather than building an emancipatory social consciousness With all due respect and sympathy for the "old fighters" against apartheid and colonialism who are still voicing their strong criticism of the current bad government under Jacob Zuma and his followers, it cannot be denied that at the end of the first day there was a general sense of blight and melancholy that reminded the German observers of the discussions about the decline of East Germany's rebel theatre culture after the fall of the GDR.

Therefore it was no coincidence that it Paul Grootboom was on the panel on both the first and second days of the conference. He initially responded to the old fighters and their visions as a sceptic with his honest self-doubt, then on the second day he joined representatives of the next generation for whom the quest to determine the future role of theatre can neither be based on pragmatic survival strategies nor on calls for resistance and struggle. These representatives were director Kayelihle Dom Gumede, who last year created a furore at the Market Theatre in Johannesburg with *Crepuscule*, and Omphile Molusi from the community theatre, the free theatre in the townships that goes beyond the major theatres and institutions to address people's existential issues and in this way does not talk *about* them but *with* them. Both in their late twenties, they have lived most of their lives in the post-apartheid era and have no melancholy memories to affect their view of the present. They see there is a lot to be done and that the ideas of the old fighters are of very limited use in battling the violence and injustice, nepotism and corruption, arrogance and authoritarianism of South African society. But everyone at the workshop agreed that theatre is an important, even essential, medium for waging this fight in society.

PS: At the end of the workshop, film and TV star Mabutho "Kid" Sithole led a guided tour to some of the key places in the struggle against apartheid. This triggered a revolutionary, romantic thought: perhaps the descendants of Frantz Fanon's "Les damnés de la terre", who could not bear another moment of oppression and discrimination, now possess the means and tools to continue the fight for their goals and utopias in today's globalised world via the arts and theatre.

Translated into English by Gill McKay.

The text was first published in the magazine "Theater der Zeit" ("Theatre of the time"), Berlin 2016.

Theatre for Protest.
The political dimension

The State of the Nation's redress re-dressed

The new forms of protest in South African Theatre and the

Theatre of *Excess*

Nondumiso Lwazi Msimanga

"We are not passive victims to this oppression. *Siyazabalaza*. We are revolting. We are re-imagining the kind of society that we want to belong to." Simam-kele Dlakavu's (2017) translation of *siyazabalaza* into *we are revolting* is a useful phrase for imagining the characteristics of theatre in post-apartheid South Africa. *Siyazabalaza* means *we are struggling*. Struggle is understood as going through difficulties but, in the sense that Dlakavu says, "We are not passive victims to this oppression", it means that *we are struggling* against repression. A #FeesMustFall activist[1], as well as an anti-rape activist in South Africa, Dlakavu sees herself as one of the beautiful ones that have been born for change. The phrase 'The beautiful ones have not been born' comes from a novel of the same title by the Ghanaian author Ayi Kwei Armah. It tells the story of disillusion-ment with the post-colonial dispensation in Ghana in the last years of Kwame Nkrumah's presidency. Nkrumah was Ghana's first president after indepen-dence from the British colony. The plot of the novel revolves around a man who resists temptation of corruption to the scorn of those close to him.

The #FeesMustFall protesters have modified the phrase to 'the beautiful ones have been born', but they are *ugly* – in revolt! They mount their struggles in the face of derision – even from their families. They do not shy away from revulsion and have mobilised a language of impoliteness as part of their revolt against what they see as issues not properly dealt with – if at all – since the new democracy in South Africa with its language of reconciliation and not of redress as it was supposed to be. "We are re-imagining the kind of society that we want to belong to," Dlakavu (2017) says. This re-imagination is not, in my

---

1 | #FeesMustFall is a mainly university-based movement and/or campaign of students in South Africa calling for free and decolonised education system in the country.

opinion, merely theorised in the philosophies of decolonisation; it is being put into protest action.

This chapter focuses on protest and its fresh expression in new South African performance. It is understood as informing the history and current state of the country in its continual struggles for freedom(s). Located within the existential and phenomenological insights of German Philosopher Martin Heidegger (1927), protest characterises South Africa's democracy as a site of *excess*. *Excess* as a concept is applied for its ability to allow for meaning to be understood as permeating in different directions rather than mere binary identifications. The *being* of South Africa and its contemporary performances is seen as a form of rupture from its past and politics with the view to create its new self as truly free. The struggles identified here speaks to a need for *being* to become more than mere survival in a free nation.

Against this backdrop, the chapter weaves different performances in the frame of protest from an assertion that the current live experiences of the South African nation can be philosophically described as *excessive*. The manuscript is divided into two sections. The first deals with discourse around the meaning of the concept, *excess*. The second part provides the geopolitical context within with *excess* manifests in political action and theatrical innovation.

Life itself and theoretical context of its *excess*

"We need to live first of all; to believe in what *makes* us live and that something makes us live-to believe that whatever is produced from the mysterious depths of ourselves need not forever haunt us as an exclusively digestive concern. I mean that if it is important for us to eat first of all, it is even more important for us not to waste in the sole concern for eating our simple power of being hungry." (Artaud 1958: 1)

Artaud's theory of theatre as a protest is an event in rupturing theatre's focus on form towards the vision of theatre as *excess*. *Excess* is necessary for his sense of theatre as life itself and not mere representation. It is a vital protest and hunger for freedom. In democracy, this theatre is a reminder of hunger not be wasted by simple consumption (the postcolonial politics of the stomach) but as a force for creation. His protest stands in opposition to the concept of culture as separate from life. Artaud's theatre and postcolonial theatre 'assembles the true spectacle of life' and in an evental process of the spectacle invigorating life such that it is then in retrospect 'renewed by the theatre'. Thus, if revolutionary theatre is life itself – a culture expressed through the language of struggle – it is a theatre of *excess*.

The language of protest or revolt is seen as the language of new protest performance that attempts to free itself from current conventions. *Excess* is a language of struggle to attain greater freedom. In South Africa, *excess* is decolonial in the country's attempts to understand its being anew. It is also queer in its overflow of past traditional theatre parameters. It emerges from different angles and levels to create new means of expression in an Artaudian fashion of rupturing the current bourgeois norm. In theatre, *excess* is protest against form.

"Excessiveness is meaning out of control, meaning that exceeds the norms of ideological control or the requirements of any specific text. Excess is overflowing semiosis, the excessive sign performs the work of the dominant ideology, but then exceeds and overspills it, leaving excess meaning that escapes ideological control and is free to be used to resist or evade it." (Fiske 1989: 114)

In defining *excess*, Fiske discusses social norms and what they deem as extraordinary. He examines how social order is maintained by disciplining bodies as well as any action that is deemed out of control morally, legally, and aesthetically. For Fiske, *excess* becomes meaningful by producing the sensation of freedom, even fleetingly. This freedom is seen as confined by laws and regulations that deem freedom disruptive (cf. ibid.). Saddik defines the theatre of *excess* as one seeking liberation by using laughter, the grotesque, ambiguity, and chaos to celebrate the irrational (cf. Saddik cf. 2015: 5).Whilst both authors discuss *excess* by calling on the grotesque, carnivalesque, and parody, Saddik goes a little further through an Artaudian analysis of Tennessee Williams later plays as political due their use of *excess*. Her exploration of *excess* in these plays reveals the world as ambiguous, chaotic, and irrational. The madness of the world is portrayed through morbid humour. Laughter, *excess* laughter, shifts the centre of meaning-making and splinters it across space in varying directions. It cannot be contained. It is liberated from social mores and theatrical conventions by being "too much".

In the Heideggerean sense, *being*, with its meaning overflowing any ideological system, text, or law is applicable only in an event which works in both the direction of meaninglessness and meaningfulness but always *exceeds* meaning in the process of its rhetoric. These can be historical events and others like the state of emotion; pleasure or pain. The event is not one that appears and disappears like a flash mob at a grocery shop, but more like the protests that arise at different sites with different or the same people.

Making visible what is invisible

Skelly notices that "the strategy of attributing immoral [ity to] *excess* has also been used to stigmatise certain groups and individuals, often within the contexts of racial, ethnic, gender, and sexual differences" (Skelly 2014: 3). To her, *excess* is linked to desire and consumption. In early post-apartheid, *excess* was a badge of democracy, but it is now connected to a gluttonous government. Critics of the apartheid Protest Theatre like Zakes Mda and Njabulo Ndebele point to the need for multiplicity in the performances and literature of protest, respectively. At the heart of the important criticism of *excess* by the South African thinkers is the question of the action performed by apartheid protest art relating to the meaning of *being*.

Both Mda and Ndebele do not deny the potency of *excess* but advocate for deeper philosophical engagement with the *being* that protests against and the *beings* protested for. Mda argues that Protest Theatre placates its White audience and marks a shift to what he calls theatre of resistance in the vein of Black Consciousness's self-awareness. It speaks directly to Black people to liberate their minds in order to fight for freedom (cf. Mda 1994). Ndebele argues that protest literature was *excessive* but only in a reactionary mode because of the *excess* of the times. He cites the famous Rolande Barthes (1972) essay 'On Wrestling' and calls protest literature a spectacle at the loss of engagement with the ordinary loves and laughter and ambiguous lives of South Africans (cf.Ndebele 1984).

Discourse on *excess* is not new in the racial history of South Africa, yet it is a rare but growing academic inquiry. Skelly mounts the probe from feminist and queer perspectives devoid of racial context (cf. Skelly 2014). Abbott posits the concept as an approach for dealing with social issues anew thus:

"Many great problems of our era are problems of excess: massive pollution, sprawling suburbs, glut of information. [...] Confronted with excess, we nevertheless make scarcity the center of our attention. [...] I want to sketch the foundations of a social theory based on the premise that the central problematic of human affairs is not dealing with scarcity, but dealing with excess. [...] By rethinking in terms of excess those problems that we usually conceive as problems of scarcity – poverty, domination and so on – we might find completely new approaches to old questions." (Abbott 2014: 1-2)

The proper name of *being* is 'The Void', writes Badiou (2005). Thomas Sheehan's and Richard Polt's Heideggerean conceptualisation of *being* is labelled *excess*. All three acknowledge the contradiction at the essence of *being* as self-concealing; an *excess* that is a void beyond discernment. Sheehan states:

"Beingness in all its historical forms conceals a certain relation to [the hu]man. The beingness of beings is fundamentally not something 'out there' in beings but rather the meaningful relatedness, the intelligible presentness of things to and for [the hu]man." (Sheehan 1979: 4)

The presence, not just of the performers but also of the spectators, becomes the means to access the *excess* of *being* in relation to silence. On the other hand, the absence of activity, intermittent in play *DE-APART-HATE*, creates the access to *excess* – void that is *being*. The discourse is not merely of making visible what is invisible (which is significant in the politics of subjectivity), but it is also an event that manifests *excess*. By playing with frequency, celebrating and parodying the church, *being* still and listening, many possibilities of meaning shift with every new moment of the event. This, according to Žižek is a discourse that is not only evental, but an event in Heidegger's sense of the moments or states that exposes the *beingness* of *being*. It is an improvised play that is pleasurable and paradoxically painful (cf. Žižek 2014).

South Africa as a protest nation

Duncan observes that "Past and present-day South Africa has truly become a country defined by its protests: a protest nation." (Duncan 2016) News of protests are reported on the news almost, if not in fact, daily along with morning traffic report to alert the public where protests could be happening and causing traffic through blockades or mass gatherings. These events constitute day-by-day trauma in the protest nation. The event of Simamkele Dlakavu's popularisation as an activist was actually a solidarity rape protest by female students against a spade of rape of on the Rhodes University campus where she was interviewed, bare-breasted; thanking fellow protesters. Disturbing events like the Rhodes protest against rape link the micro to the macro in a continuous feedback loop that creates something new, albeit unconventional.

The idea of an event is not mere incidence, but it is theoretically conceived. Protests are events because they take place suddenly and they disrupt, not just the flow of traffic at any given time, but they are also geared towards hinder regular business functioning. They also seem to appear out of nowhere because abruptly, people amass and gather together. Slavoj Žižek identifies a crucial feature of an event as "the surprising emergence of something new which undermines every stable scheme" (Žižek 2014: 6). Badiou concurs: "Events happen in certain times and places which, unlike the minor contingencies of everyday life, rupture with the established order of things." (Badiou 2005: 27) These events can transform a situation as they open up the space for a new praxis that destabilises the previous orthodox. In South Africa, freedom as an essential aspect of *being* is seen as new.

In *Moving the Centre: the Struggle for Cultural Freedoms*, Ngũgĩ Wa Thiong'o addresses the notion of event as a necessary deconstruction for the creation of decolonial freedom in the continent. In his other book, *Decolonising the Mind*, the Kenyan philosopher discusses this new praxis in terms of language. He states: "Communication creates culture is a means of communication." (Wa Thiong'o 1986: 15-16) Dlakavu's responds to Wa Thiong'o uses the language of struggle as one of *excess* in that young activists are revolting against perceived indoctrination by the current government to render them passive spectators of their democracy. Dlakavu proposes a decolonisation that is intersectional to include women and queer people in its reimagining of culture as life itself. Along this thinking of the theatre of *excess* as a fresh intersectional space whose mode of action is queer, Gindt opines: "The open mesh of possibilities, gaps, overlaps, dissonances and resonances, lapses and excesses of meaning when the constituent elements of anyone's gender, of anyone's sexuality aren't made (or can't be made) to signify monolithically." (Gindt 2014: 254)

Changes inherent in world, and the gaps and overlaps of its borders, are crucial to revolutionary performance. Wa Thiong'o shares Artaud's the idea that culture, like theatre, is a vital force of communication for protest – for change. In concluding *Decolonising the Mind*, he cites Bertolt Brecht's poem 'Speech to Danish Working Class Actors on the Art of Observation':

"We now ask you, the actors
Of our time – a time of overthrow and of boundless mastery
Of all nature, even men's own – at last
To change yourselves and show us mankind's world
As it really is: made by men and open to alteration." (Wa Thiong'o 1993: 108)

In this citation, Wa Thiong'o recognises writing the book as a protest action. A call to decolonise internally as well as externally. He concludes:

"A call for the rediscovery of the real language of humankind: the language of struggle. It is the universal language underlying all speech and words of our history. Struggle makes history. Struggle makes us. In struggle is our history, our language and our being." (Wa Thiong'o 1993: 108)

If struggle characterises South Africa as a protest nation now, then it has moved beyond its Brechtian Protest Theatre and has involved the real-time world outside of the theatre's separation of performer and audience, creating a vigorous interaction with lived reality. Therefore, struggle bursts the seams of theatre as a building such that "[n]ow the oppressed are liberated themselves and, once more, are making theatre their own. The walls must be torn down" (Boal 1979: 95).

Theatre manifestation of protest

Siyazabalaza is not just about fleeting protests that are reactionary, but a constant struggle as a mode of *being excessive* by challenging the status quo through direct action. Protest actions are not necessarily anti-democratic. On the contrary, "Protests are an essential form of democratic expression" (Duncan 2016: vii) in that they are "expressive acts that communicate grievances through disruption of existing societal arrangements, bring[ing] problems in society to public attention in direct, at times dramatic, ways" (ibid.: vii). The communication is direct in that it circumvents bureaucratic protocols of societal order to raise awareness about social problems to both the public and governing bodies. Duncan regards the right to protest as a distinguishing feature of *being* in South Africa in that protest occurs anytime and anywhere in the streets, shops, conference rooms and/or lecture halls (cf. ibid: 1). Similarly, democracies around the world are currently experiencing their fair share of protest actions as global calls to redefine society and governance. There too, protests are also intersectional in their politics. Protests in South Africa are increasingly self-aware of this significant discourse. Protest trolleys overflow with issues around race, gender, sexuality, corruption, economic freedom, service delivery, and environmental awareness, etc. The very intersectionality of the disruptions to social conventions reveals a significant space of questioning boundaries as a way of *being*.

In *Reading the Palms of the Time*, a collection of post-apartheid plays, Seane writes a piercing dissent against democracy. She begins her foreword to the collection by citing Plato's critique of democracy as a means of maintaining ignorance amongst the masses. She critiques the media's representation of South Africa's reconciliatory transition to democracy as a peaceful one (cf. Seane 2016: 5). Seane's appraisal centres on the supposed White-washing of some stories for the narrative of a less complex political rhetoric. She highlights "the politics of the stomach" (ibid.: 8) that are at play for South African citizens yearning for tangible and economic change but instead fall prey to *excess* exploitation by bogus people, often politicians, who thrive on systemic corruption now infamously termed 'state capture' (the alleged pilfering of money and usurping of political power from government entities). Seane connects the political with the personal by observing how political propaganda is manifested in the personal interactions of discontentment.

The paradox in the different ideas of democracy between Seane and Duncan is a paradox at the heart of South Africa in the post-apartheid space. Where Duncan sees protests as communicative and necessary expressive acts against the state, Seane's sense of the 'politics of the stomach' speaks to the state of its people as having a yearning that is in *excess* because democracy itself is false, as exposed by the concluding play of the collection by Monageng 'Vice' Motshabi and Kgafela Oa Magogodi. Titled *Book of Rebellations,* the play portrays a state similar to that described by Badiou in *Being and Event*: "The situation was actually quite paradoxical. On the one hand, dominating public opinion, one had 'democracy' – in its entirely corrupt representative and electoral form – and freedom reduced to 'freedom' to trade and consume." (Badiou 2005: 13) Similarly, in *Book of Rebellations,* when faced with a state of 'the politics of the stomach', it is only the character Gogoa (meaning to scream), like Artaud's iconic scream, who is capable of rupturing reality with *excess* shriek; indicative of the space where words fail (cf. Grant et al 2015: 54).

At the ICA Live Art festival in Cape Town (24 February 2017), Dean Hutton, a White non-gender-conforming performance artist, discussed their work *FuckWhitePeople* as an attempt to deconstruct Whiteness in South Africa such that, by so doing, they expose the *excess* of their own Whiteness as privileges component of the South African nation. The actors created a three-piece suit with the words *FuckWhitePeople* printed closely together all over each piece of the white clothing worn in daily performances in actual reality in public spaces. For instance, by sitting in a taxi full of Black people and walking through the city of Cape Town in the suit displaying the slogan, Hutton company is a walking event of *excess* where the audience is both those who laugh along at the absurdity of *being* and those who refute the rupture. Hutton's suit is like mad-laughter at the irony of those fighting for Whiteness in a postcolony, post-apartheid; where self-awareness is critical. A protest against an exhibition of *FuckWhitePeople* paraphernalia occurred when members of the Cape Party assaulted the gallery's two Black staff members and stuck a poster saying, 'Love thy neighbour' over a print of *FuckWhitePeople*. Hutton retorts: "How do you preface a message of love with a violent, criminal act which has no respect for the bodies of people who have been oppressed for centuries and who still experience daily aggression and trauma?" (Hutton 2017)

Hutton's reality theatrical stunt spilled over into other theatrical production like *Interracial* by actor-director, Nompumelelo Paul Grootboom. Staged on 25 April 2017 at the launch of an anthology of plays *Reading the Palms of the Time*, Grootboom's play ends with a monologue in which he tells the audience that he experienced difficulties in recruiting White actors to help him put together the piece to tell his new South African story. Those approached refused to be auditioned, he complains. So he resorted to casting Black actors to play White roles. In the monologue, the actor rages on about how new stories cannot be told if White people don't want to be involved in works written by their Black counterparts:

"Fuck White people! How long must we keep on proving ourselves to them!?
Fuck them! Fuck White people!
(The song goes up and down again)
Fuck this shit man! Fuck White people! Fuck them! Why the fuck did God have to make us 'different' from each other? Look, sorry guys, let's go home... I don't wanna have to make such a story, such a play... Fuck White people, man!" (Grootboom 2017: 190)

The post-mortem of the play through question and answer session between the playwright and the audience reverberated with the phrase 'Fuck White people' such as when one audience member merely repeated the phrase when he was handed a microphone to comment on the play. Incidentally, the audience in the 100-seater theatre was predominantly Black. There were only 4 White people present; 3 of whom associated with the production of the play as either sponsors or part of management. It is also notable that this play has never been fully staged since its debut then when one of its rape scenes was graphically performed to the applause of the audience. The act brings to the fore this question by Skelly: "Is excess akin to freedom?" (Skelly 2014: 7) The query seeks to indicate that it is critical to be aware of how protests can be problematic in the use of *excess*. Nevertheless, what meta-theatrical play offers is critical self-reflexivity in creating new performances.

Recalling Hutton's invocation of the historical and daily trauma endured by Black people in South Africa, conceptual whiteness is as a sign of infection at the site of trauma in that the very construct of Whiteness is an event that created the trauma that constructed its privileged identity. The concept of Whiteness is an *excess* and Whiteness is evental. Evental "is a manifestation of a circular structure in which the evental effect retroactively determines its causes or reasons" (Žižek 2014: 2). Whiteness emerges in the circular structure of having the effect of determining the reasons for its own existence. It performs excessively to maintain its privileged position and so Hutton's performance of *excess* in the refrain *FuckWhitePeople* is a challenge from within the *being* of Whiteness to invoke the possibilities of this *being* outside of the status quo. The work is not an effect but an event; a disruption, a questioning of what makes Whites retain their privileged status quo after apartheid's traumas.

The traumas of freedom

Trauma stands in opposition to understanding. It refutes logical meaning-making strategies but it does, paradoxically, throw a person into the too-much-task of trying to make sense of something they can never entirely understand (cf. Caruth 1991: 182). This is the *excess* of the site of democracy as a space of daily trauma. It eludes understanding in so many aspects of its political *excesses*. Trauma is the site but when it reveals its *excesses* (the infection-pus on the wound [Artaud 1958]), it means the event of the injury has already occurred; and so, South Africa becomes a country struggling daily to cleanse itself of its traumas, past and present.

On 12 April 2010 – a year in which South Africa was in celebratory mood as a post-apartheid construct due to its hosting of the FIFA World Cup – Achille Mbembe used the phrase "the trauma of freedom" (Mbembe 2010) to analyse the popular politics of the time. The paradox is useful because whilst freedom was the clear goal of the struggles against apartheid, the pain of living in a free country, and yet still having to fight racism, poverty, homophobia, rape, and femicide, amongst other struggles, is a pain with no discernable end. Hence, the joys of festivities such as football tournament are experienced in relative *excess*. Mbembe discusses this as a dichotomy of '*Excess* and the Creativity of Abuse'. The image he paints is of the postcolony as a game of power-grabbing and power-grubbing. Like in the postcolonial Ghana depicted in *The Beautyful Ones are not Yet Born*, where a dug-out toilet becomes a passage of escape, Mbembe states:

"The emphasis on orifices and protuberances has to be understood in relation to two factors especially. The first derives from the fact that the *commandement* in the postcolony has a marked taste for lecherous living. Festivities and celebrations, in this regard, are two key vehicles for indulging the taste. But the idiom of its organisation and its symbolism focus, above all, on the mouth, the belly and the phallus." (Ibid.)

Mbembe argues that citizens show their awareness of own government's performances of power by performing mockeries of the *excess* festivities and celebrations as ways to quell their daily dissatisfactions. Such performances, grotesque as they may seem, are a necessary parody, he asserts as he calls these parody performatives the revenue of "auto-interpretation, and of negotiating that interpretation and the forces which may shape it" (Mbembe 1992: 7). Stated differently, these communicative acts are performances of protest that occur in real time and they simulate the performative *excesses* against – which they protest – to not only reshape their world, but to also actively take part in the cleansing and interpretation of their democracy. This point is demonstrated graphically in the performance *Take In, Take Out* by Albert Ibhokwe Khoza. In this play, the actor performs a cleansing ritual, in real time, to literally wash away the traumas that exceed the past and spill over into the present. Khoza drinks and regurgitates, performs colon hydrotherapy, and slaughters a chicken in front of the spectators. The actual cleansing is done after having called upon the ancestors a part of the ritual that is traditionally secret. The invocation of the different ancestors is done humorously through telephones after the requisite burning of *impepho* (incense). This cleansing ritual theatrical performance opens up access to the space of the sacred to both those previously exposed to or familiar with, and asks for a higher form of *being* to become possible for the people whose life has become a struggle of merely existing. Khoza performs African rituals that were rendered private and/or – at worst – immoral, barbaric or uncivilised during colonisation.

Marion's *Interpreting Excess* agrees that sacred ritual works in the realm of the extra-daily. It is a real ritual made public to different contestations regarding its *being* made public. Its protest, with its multimedia projection of colonial events, documentary clips on poverty in Africa, and then celebratory indigenous dances, is not against but for something. It is for the affirmation and celebration of African culture as a way of *being*. It creates access to the *beingness* of *being* African. Hence, the experience of this ritual with its use of telephones by Khoza to perform a conversation with the ancestors we don't see as an audience to embrace *excess* in African ways of *being*. Using telephones is not only a playful strategy but allows for the concept of communication itself to be visualised.

Wa Thiong'o recalls Karl Marx's challenge: "The philosophers have only *interpreted* the world, in various ways; the point, however, is to change it." (Wa Thiong'o 1993: 107) Wa Thiong'o describes the moment of Marx's statement as an event in itself in that its effects exceed its occurrence. He ponders: "Change it?" (Ibid.: 107) Duncan responds by indicating that an event can transform something crucial in society and the individual who partakes in it because *excess* is existence. It can be used for repression or its inverse liberation. When it is a protest it can empower by manifesting as an event in praxis. In this way, *excess* can create and not merely re-imagine. *Excess* puts us into contact with the vital forces and uses our core drives and struggle to transcend itself in the queer space of liminality. It is crucial in the times of revolt and in the theatre of protest not to waste the energy of this hunger in mere consumption but to access this force to "live first of all", as Artaud (cf. 1958: 1) says. Not to be passive victims of this oppression, as Dlakavu said in response to Wa Thiong'o's lecture. It is freedom that is exercised in the new theatres of *excess*. The freedoms are not easy to perform. They can be risky, but they formulate their own language. If these events can amass the emergence of a movement as a grand event, we can only know retrospectively. But while these events are happening, there is no question that they offer new forms of praxis. Their call is to participate; not just to interpret. The language of the new culture is struggle. It is: Action!

Bibliography

Abbott, Andrew (2014): The Problem of Excess. In: Sociological Theory 32 (1), p. 1-26.

Artaud, Antonin (1958): The theater and its double. London: Grove Press (Evergreen books, E-127).

Badiou, Alain (2005): Being and event. Bloomsbury revelations edition. London, New York: Bloomsbury Academic (Bloomsbury revelations).

Boal, Augusto (1979): Theatre of the Oppressed. New York: Pluto Press.

Caruth, Cathy (1991): Unclaimed Experience: Trauma and the Possibility of History. In: Yale French Studies (79), p. 181-192.

Dlakavu, Simamkele (2017): Response to Ngugi Wa Thiong'o lecture. Wits University, 2/3/2017.

Duncan, Jane (2016): Protest nation. The right to protest in South Africa. Pietermaritzburg: University Of KwaZulu-Natal Press. Available: http://

search.ebscohost.com/login.aspx?direct=true&scope=site&db=nlebk&A
N=1385575.

Fiske, John (1989): Understanding popular culture. London/ New York: Routledge.

Gindt, Dirk (2014): Your Asshole is Hanging Outside of Your Body?. Excess,
AIDS, and Shame in the Theatre of Sky Gilbert. In: Romita Ray und Julia
Skelly (eds.): The Uses of Excess in Visual and Material Culture, 1600-2010.
Burlington: Ashgate Publishing.

Grant, Stuart; McNeilly, Jodie; Veerapen, Maeva (2015): Performance and
Temporalisation. Time Happens. New York: Palgrave Macmillan (Performance Philosophy). Available: http://gbv.eblib.com/patron/FullRecord.aspx
?p=1986788.

Heidegger, Martin; Macquarrie, John; Robinson, Edward (1962): Being and
time. 35. reprint. Malden: Blackwell.

Hutton, Dean. Available: yesfuckwhitepeople@fuckwhitepeople.org, Last
Access: 11/5/2017.

Khoza, Albert Ibhokwe (2017), 11/14/2017. Personal Interview Nondumiso Lwazi
Msimanga.

Mbembe, Achille (1992): Provisional notes on the postcolony. In: Africa 6 (01),
p. 3-37.

Mbembe, Achille (2010), 12/4/2010.

Mda, Zakes (1994): The Role of Culture in the Process of Reconciliation in
South Africa. Paper presented at the Centre for the Study of Violence and
Reconciliation, Seminar. 9, 11/30/1994. Available: http://www.csvr.org.za/
publications/1751-the-role-of-culture-in-the-process-of-reconciliation-in-
south-africa, Last Access: 6/30/2018.

Motshabi, Monageng (2016): Vice. Johannesburg. In: Reading the Palms of the
Time.

Ndebele, Njabulo (1984): Rediscovery of the Ordinary: Some New Writings in
South Africa. New Writing in Africa: Continuity and Change Conference.
London.

Polt, Richard (2011): Meaning, Excess, and Event. In: Gatherings: The Heidegger Circle Annual 1, p. 26-53.

Saddik, Annette J. (2015): Tennessee Williams and the theatre of excess. The
strange, the crazed, the queer. Cambridge: Cambridge University Press.

Seane, Warona (2016): Foreword. Johannesburg. In: Reading the Palms of the
Time.

Sheehan, Thomas (1979): Heidegger's Topic: Excess, Access, Recess (4) (4), p.
615-635.

Skelly, Julia (2014): The Uses of Excess in Visual and Material Culture, 1600-
2010. Burlington: Ashgate Publishing. Available: https://ebookcentral.pro
quest.com/lib/gbv/detail.action?docID=4905479.

Thiong'o, Ngũgĩ wa (1986): Decolonising the mind. The politics of language in African literature. Portsmouth: Heinemann Educ Books (Studies in African literature).

Thiong'o, Ngũgĩ wa (1993): Moving the centre. The struggle for cultural freedoms. Portsmouth (Studies in African literature).

Žižek, Slavoj (2014): Event. A philosophical journey through a concept. London.

Political Theatre and Cultural Activism in the Free State Province, South Africa

The vacuum left by the death of Thamsanqa Duncan Moleko

Montshiwa K. Moshounyane

"Comrade Moleko was a giant among men; he knew that in order to fulfil the majority of the aspirations of our artists, he had to sacrifice his artistic career." (Roda 2013: 14) The aim of this Chapter is to profile the life and times of the late Thamsanqa Duncan Moleko as a pioneer of political theatre and cultural activism in South Africa's Free State province, with the view to highlight the void left by his untimely death in 2010. This task is by no means easy for several reasons loaded with contradictions. Firstly, the province is generally treated as if it is on the periphery of South Africa's map and life-world or experience, yet it is geographically the centre of the country's topology. Secondly, due to its vast rural character, there is no strong arts-focused media that ordinarily broadcast contributions and impact of artists in the cultural and creative industries. The focus has always been on big metropolis like Johannesburg, Cape Town, Pretoria and Durban.

Ironically, Free State has produced the pioneering Black scholar, Solomon Tshekisho Plaatje: an intellectual, journalist, linguist, politician, translator and writer. Plaatje is the first Black person to write a novel in English, *Mhudi*. He also translated four of William Shakespeare's plays into his native language, SeTswana. As a politician, Plaatje was a founder member and first General Secretary of the South African Native National Congress, later renamed the African National Congress (ANC); South Africa's current governing party. Incidentally, the ANC was officially inaugurated in the Free State in 1912. The last point leads to the third reason about the lack of literature on cultural activism in the Free State.

Moleko's contribution to the South African cultural landscape came at a time when the country was still emerging from the euphoria of the post-1994 democratic society, and as such he entered an uncharted space where his pro-Black rhetoric, carried out with bravado, was misunderstood and labelled as against the new order and its mantra of racial reconciliation; hence he was regarded as an agent provocateur worth ignoring and erasing from sight and memory.

A comprehensive overview of the personality and cultural work of Moleko will always seem miniscule when compared to that of those cultural activists who carry out their work in the cultural mainstream provinces like Gauteng, Western Cape and KwaZulu-Natal. This sometimes creates doubt in the minds and hearts of those who knew his cultural activism, felt it and were impacted by it. However, these reasons are not enough to ignore his legacy. It is through cultural activism and unheralded leadership that a paper on the vision for cultural and creative industries was officially specially presented in the Free State Provincial Legislature in 2008. Moleko's life story easily qualifies as a subject of lengthy Masters or PhD dissertations, but the brevity of this Chapter demands that it be condensed under four headings below.

A life between political activism and artistic work

Thamsanqa Duncan Moleko was born in Rocklands, Bloemfontein, on 11 April 1975. He started his basic education at Tebelelo Primary School, and matriculated at Lereko Senior Secondary School in 1991. The latter is credited for shaping both his artistic talent and political activism. It is at Lereko where he was recruited by Moses Lechuti to join his drama group, Zatja, in 1986. Simultaneously, Moleko also worked with the Siyababa Drama Group under Peter Nthwane, who died in 2016. Lechuti is one of the best theatre directors to have come out of Bloemfontein. Moleko's debut performance as an actor was in 1992 in the play, *Tears won't make it right,* written and directed by Lechuti. In 1995, he also performed in the subsequent production, *In Limbo.* In the same year, he got involved in a workshop production, *Shukumisa,* at the Market Theatre Laboratory Community Festival. *Shukumisa* was selected as the best production out of thirty-eight other renditions, and was subsequently given a run at the Laager Theatre wing of the main Market Theatre precinct in June 1995. In 1996, *Shukumisa* featured in the *Arts Alive Festival* in Johannesburg, as well as the *Calabash Arts Festival* in Taung where it was awarded the prize for the most promising new production. In 1997, together with the late actor, writer and director Bushy Shikishi, Moleko left Bloemfontein for Johannesburg for full-time training in the dramatic arts at the Market Theatre Laboratory.

Upon his return to Bloemfontein, Moleko reactivated his political activism originally cultivated whilst still a student at Lereko years ago where he was part of the Congress of South African Students (COSAS) and its Cultural Committee. He attempted to reconnect with his peers whom he had met earlier in the ANCYL (African National Congress Youth League) and ANC offices in Bloemfontein, with the intention to open an academy styled on the Solomon

Mahlangu Freedom College (SOMAFCO)[1] model. Moleko approached the Performing Arts Council of the Free State (PACOFS) and other independent institutions, with no success. Later, he decided to produce artistic works on the life of Robert Sobukwe, the Pan Africanist Congress (PAC) leader who was incarcerated in solitary confinement at the infamous Robben Island. He also trained people in his Rastafarianism religion and poetry. He continued to engage with lots of people whom he had identified as potential partners for his envisaged academy. However, he experienced challenges in securing capital for his ideas. His militant, rebellious and confrontational political approach to the arts gradually got pronounced and it soon became a threat to some people. Moleko's cultural activism should be understood in the manner described by Verson as:

"Cultural activism is campaigning and direct action that seeks to take back control of how our webs of meaning, value systems, beliefs, art and literature, everything, are created and disseminated. It is an important way to question the dominant ways of seeing things and present alternative views of the world." (Verson 2007: 171-186)

Pinder describes cultural activism as "those radical and creative practices that are critical and politicised in relation to dominant power relations and their spatial constitution" (Pinder 2008: 731). Duncombe views cultural activism as a practice of cultural resistance in that it disrupts commonly held assumptions and expectations about the world (cf. Duncombe 2002: 12).

Moleko's cultural activism articulated new imaginaries and meaning, intending to transforms spaces of cultural productions into political schools and political spaces into spaces of cultural engagement and production. His activism was about immediacy, presence and confrontation against the status quo. This he found in three resources: the currency of ideas, creativity and political will (or political participation). Ultimately, his contribution was mostly successful in the small moments of unheralded leadership exercises, creative rationality and self-sacrifice. His greatest gift was the ability to inspire, transfer ideas and ideals into discussions, and art into politics. He was popular because:

"He spoke the language of the artists, and not the capitalists and the opportunists. He did not demand a crowd of 10 000 people in the arts centres for him to address artists. His words directly touched the artists and reciprocally the masses reasoned with him without chasing the newspapers, Facebook pages and Television. This made comrade Moleko to be loved and adored by the artists." (Roda 2013: 4)

The cultural landscape that Moleko entered and wanted to change commonly held assumptions, notions and expectations on culture in the post demo-

---

1 | SOMAFCO was built by the ANC in Tanzania for its members while in exile.

cratic South Africa, particularly from the national cultural policy perspective. Whereas the 1996 White Paper on Arts, Culture and Heritage (WPACH), as the *defacto* national cultural policy, was clear on policy directives, its implementation was a set-back. Prolonged problems with policy implementation meant that the Free State, like other provinces, was confronted with issues of the transformation of the theatre sector. Two major controversies in the WPACH were the transformation and restructuring of performing arts councils[2] into receiving houses and not production houses; as well related budget cuts to be rerouted to the envisaged National Arts Council[3] (NAC) (cf. Department of Arts and Culture 1996: 26).

Community access, capacity building and art making

Although the nonexistence of viable cultural industry in the Free State has demoralised many passionate and promising artists, Moleko believed that people should continue to organise for local change. His cultural activism was based on three cornerstones: community access to creative and dedicated spaces of art-making; production and dialogue for capacity building and training; and concrete action (e.g. poetry recitations, open stage performance, and socio-political debates). The anticipated outcome was the destruction of social conditioning of complacency, despondency and apathy and lastly campaigning for artists' inclusion and consideration in strategic government related events, posts and legislative processes that affect their wellbeing; i.e. the practice of art, as well as access to information for empowerment in the cultural and creative sectors. He also advocated for the deployment of artists in government institutions because he believed they would serve the sector better as they understand it unlike the current crop of government officials many of whom have no clues what the arts are (cf. Roda 2013: 14).

Of the many tools at his disposal, Moleko used political education and trade unionism in the arts to inject political consciousness into the arts. Through the self-initiated *political school*, Moleko advanced a belief that artists would not achieve anything without the ability to be politically aware and involved. For Moleko, art is nature is political as per Maritain's assertion that

---

2 | Before 1994, South Africa's arts scene had the Cape Performing Arts Council (CAPAB), Performing Arts Council of the Orange Free State (PACOFS), Performing Arts Council of the Transvaal (PACT), and the Natal Performing Arts Council (NPAC).

3 | The National Arts Council (NAC) a statutory body tasked with addressing issues of access, redress and participation to which individuals, cultural organisations should apply for funding for projects in new centralised manner.

"if one regards art as a virtue of the practical intellect and politics as the ordering of communal life with a view to moral and intellectual excellence, then it seems reasonable to speak of art as a political good, that is, a good to be achieved in political association" (Maritain's 1960: 51).

At that time, these views were extremely radical in a province or a society whereby it was convenient for artists to consider themselves non-political. But Moleko reasoned that while the arts could be not always be viewed out of a political context and making political art was not necessarily infusing political themes in the work, it is the 'art as an expression on freedom' which made it political. The political school programme entails, amongst others:

- Advocacy and lobbying of government's structures (Department of Arts and Culture [DAC], Provincial Arts and Culture Council, Free State Legislature, Premier's Office, PACOFS, Free State Youth Commission and other departments that tap into the creative economy sectors
- Total transformation of PACOFS and its relationship with the arts sector, including lobbying of artists to be part of the board
- Lobbying for funding for projects for job creation in platforms like the annual Mangaung Cultural Festival (MACUFE)
- Capacitating of artists with regard to government legislations, institutions, and programmes related to the arts.

As Chairperson of the Free State province of the Creative Workers Union of South Africa (CWUSA) between 2007 and 2009, before is deregistration in favour of the Cultural and Creative Industries Federation of South Africa (CCIFSA). Moleko used the union to improve artists' conditions of employment, as well as to lobby government and employers to protect and promote the rights of creative workers. Moleko's general vision for the cultural and creative sector in the Free State through trade unionism was to:

- Create sustainable arts industry in the Province for sustainable job creation
- Recognise all artists as workers and their craft as work like in income generating industries such as textile and mining
- Organise arts organisations, including in the labour industry, to deal with the exploitation of artist as well to improve their living conditions and standards
- Create or offer training opportunities through formal training institutions and informal platforms like workshops and other platforms
- Represent artists in legal matters, political forums, government and its agencies' programmes and activities.

The Power of Political Theatre

Moleko was a proponent of political theatre; generally defined as "drama or performing art which emphasises a political issue or issues in its theme or plot" (Patterson 2003: 34). Kirby argues that "theatre is political when it is concerned with the state or takes sides in politics in a way that distinguishes it from other forms of theatre" (Kirby 1975: 129-135). Kirby further says, "if the theatre piece is intended to be political and the intent is not perceived, there is no need to categorise that performance as political theatre, thus is the presentation does not attempt to be political it cannot be political, it is not political" (ibid.: 137). Moleko's political theatre "sought to narrate and not only record events, but to establish causal connections between events" (Lukács 1971: 107). This intentionality and the establishment of the causal links underpinned Moleko's political theatre. It is the very concept that prompted Moleko to temporarily leave Bloemfontein. Setumo summarises Moleko's preference for political theatre thus:

"He wanted to explore the use of art as a political vehicle and a developmental tool. He got tired of being aligned to institutions and wanted to explore establishment of an institution that will focus on history of art in SA, Africa and also acknowledge foot soldiers and institutions in the arts that contributed in the development of the sector. Part of it was to also focus on African literacy." (Setumo 2016)

While overt political theatre receded with the advent of democracy, there are reasons now in the post democratic South African for its resurgence. One of the prevalent discontents with the current political dispensation and a sense that the media is fail to bring meaning and context with the contemporary realities facing the society. The power of political theatre is that it communicates through symbols, gestures and signs; searching for meaning, creating meaning placing meanings in aesthetical context. Political theatre informs and heightens consciousness.

Moleko reasoned that politics are part of everyday lives regardless of whether people refuse to acknowledge that by declaring themselves non(a)-political or acknowledge that, yet choose to do nothing about it. He convinced many that politics is embedded in daily existence: how people experience life and well-being (or lack of it) in the communities in which they live in; as well as in education, safety and access to resources. His productions narrated stories that sought to establish a causal link between events and community education. He was always aware of his role in the society and wanted to use his position and his artistic talents to stimulate thinking. This was one of greatest assets; hence in most case on stage he performed with a certain boldness and purposefulness to achieve his political objectives. In this way, he was an "artist who is supposed to be the conscience of his people has no time for dreaming he wants some action, revolutionary action to be taken" (Rive 1983: 5-6).

As prolific writer, he collaborated with like-minded playwrights in political productions like *Dead Politician* (2008) and the *Grave Dream* (2012). The *Dead Politician* was staged at the Market Theatre Laboratory (2008) and at PACOFS in (2008) while *Grave Dream* (2012) has not being staged yet. It is interesting to note that Moleko preferred writing his drama scripts, poems, and speeches by hand instead of typing. Sometimes he would sit and dictate to someone else typing.

The theatricalisation of social life

The contemporary state of theatre in the Free State lacks political content and intent. When it does happen, it only offers social commentary and spectacle. Debord terms this the "spectacle of society a mode of perception, of passive consumption and by definition conceals its own construction" (Debord 1992: 20). This is where the concealing of the construction becomes important, while the theatricalisation of the social life of society has received attention. Political life needs to reveal the construction, mobilise the spectator and question the basics of the spectacle because in a society where the political has become the norm, it becomes questionable when theatre doesn't respond accordingly. The following Facebook status aptly summarises the situation:

"Free State Arts industry, especially theatre and drama is continuously getting controlled by political artists (PL) than art producers (AP). People suddenly use social networks to voice their lack of productivity in the name of the Arts. A lot of you PL's have never produced, directed, written anything for the past five years." (Pholo 2013)

While this post speaks to the 'lack of theatre making' it speaks also to the proliferation of the political norm, but more so it speaks volume about the absence of political theatre. This void is conspicuous in both professional and developmental platforms like the Homebrew Developmental Theatre Productions in 2016 during the MACUFE Festival and PACOFS' incubator developmental. While conditions for political theatre in a post-democratic South Africa are very fertile, it has become almost impossible to imagine a society fundamentally different from this one. This is not due a lack of political actions and ideas, but rather to their proliferation. Perhaps the claim that "everything has become political and therefore nothing is political" (Baudrillard 1993: 9) aptly contextualises the lack of political theatre in Bloemfontein currently. Therefore, it seems plausible that the political theatre and cultural activism in the Free State province might have been buried with Moleko. In the years after his death, it

seemspolitical theatre has been marginalised mainly by the practitioners themselves in favour of personal material benefits.

Thamsanqa Duncan Moleko died on 21 April 2010 from natural causes. Yet
even in his death, he continues to be celebrated and also recently inspired collective or united action by cultural practitioners in the Free State. In a memoriam
on his birthday, Ayanda Roda eulogies:

"On 11 April 2013, we mark the birthday of the late comrade Thami Moleko who contributed massively in the struggle of the artists in this country and in the Free State. He led
the struggle of the arts with no hope of being paid or getting funding from any department in this country and he strongly believed the arts and cultural fraternity needed
political intervention. I hope that the current future generation can know this hero of our
struggle in the arts. He would be disappointed to see the artists still struggling and the
rot that is bedevilling this industry." (Roda 2013: 14)

On 26 March 2016, his memory inspired a decisive action by artists from the
Free State during CCIFSA'selective conference at the University of Free State,
Bloemfontein. This is when the delegates witnessed and experienced the
political astuteness and cultural activism of the Free State. Many wondered
then, after the announcement of the results, how come leadership of such an
august organisation has not gone to the cultural mainstream provinces like
the Gauteng, KZN and Western Cape, but to the Free State in the person of
Tony Kgoroge as CCIFSA's inaugural President[4]. The plan was quite simple,
and at its heart was Thamsanqa Moleko's teaching and influence. This is
how it unfolded. In order to wrestle power from the mainstream provinces,
the smaller or so-called peripheral provinces, led by the Free State[5], formed a

---

4 | CCIFSA conference was highly contested between two factions: mainstream prov-
inces led by Gauteng (Gauteng, Western Cape and KZN) who campaigned for Eugene
Mthethwa and the peripherals provinces (Eastern Cape, North West, Northern Cape,
Limpopo, Mpumalanga and Free State) led by the Free State which lobbied for Tony
Kgoroge. Although the Free Stators managed to mount and execute a brilliant plan, the
Province itself was divided into two factions, namely: one for Mthethwa and the other
for Kgoroge. This standoff split into two the province's vote of 120 delegates. In the end,
Kgoroge faction emerged victorious.

5 | The Article on AFAI website 'Cultural and Creative Industries Federation of South
Africa' (CCIFSA) – 29 March 2015 exposes a certain negative disposition to the these
peripherals provinces: 'By the end of the CCIFSA conference, the less resourced provinces – Limpopo, Northern Cape, North West, Eastern Cape, Mpumalanga and the Free
State – had succeeded in nominating and electing a Board comprising mainly of delegates from these Provinces. For many, the outcome was better than expected' (www.
afai.org.za).

cohesive force against the big three and that's how symbolically power returned to the Free State[6].

Thamsanqa Duncan Moleko was a significant cultural activist and a proponent of political theatre in the Free State. He seized the chance to employ his politically consciousness and voice to heighten public attention on the association between the arts and politics. He persuaded through dialogue, theatre creation, writing opinion pieces, speeches and by listening. He cultivated a sense of optimism and personal responsibility which was felt, embraced and laudable. He was determined not to see the world happen to him, but rather believed firmly in making the world.

Bibliography

Baudrillard, Jean (2017): Symbolic exchange and death. Revised edition. Los Angeles, London, New Delhi, Singapore, Washington, DC, Melbourne: SAGE (Theory, culture and society). Available: http://lib.myilibrary.com/detail.asp?ID=980085.

Debord, Guy (2010): The society of the spectacle. Reprint. Detroit, Mich.: Black & Red.

Department of Arts and Culture (1996): White Paper on Arts, Culture and Heritage. Available: https://www.bit.ly/18fpmAM, Last Access: 25/11/2016.

Duncombe, Stephen (2002): Cultural resistance reader. London: Verso. Available: http://www.loc.gov/catdir/enhancements/fy1311/2002028053-b.html.

Kirby, Michael (1975): On Political Theatre. In: *The Drama Review: TDR* 19 (2), p. 129-135.

Lukács, Georg (1971): Realism in Our Time: Literature and Class Struggle. New York: Harper & Row.

Maritain, Jacques (1960): The Responsibility of the Artist. In: *Art Journal* 20 (2), p. 114-116.

Patterson, Michael (2003): Strategies of political theatre. Post-War British playwrights. Cambridge: Cambridge University Press (Cambridge studies in modern theatre).

Pholo, G. (2013). Available: https://www.facebook.com//posts/, Last Access: 30/11/2013.

Pinder, David (2008): Urban Interventions: Art, Politics and Pedagogy. In: *International Journal of Urban and Regional Research* 32 (3), p. 730–736.

---

6 | In the article for the Daily Maverick Marianne Thamm, 25 March 2015, writes that CCFISA elective conference: chaos, 'bullying' and 'political agendas'. Ismail Mahomed, the then Artistic Director of the National Arts Festival.makes a snide remark: 'The Free State Province was a stark example of how political lobbying and greed was engineered to undermine the conference'.

Rive, Richard (1983): Advance, r Advance, Retreat: Selected short stories. Cape Town: D. Philip.

Roda, A. (2013): A Tribute to Thami Moleko. Available: https://www.ncexpress/docs/express 27mar 2013, Last Access: 21/11/2016.

Setumo, P. (10/6/2016): Electronic Interview with author. Interview with Montshiwa K. Moshounyane.

Verson, Jennifer (2007): Why we need cultural activism. In: Do it yourself. A handbook for changing our world. London, Ann Arbor, MI: Pluto Press, p. 171-186.

Ubulution!

A re-imagining of protest and the public sphere in contemporary theatre

Janine Lewis and Katlego Chale

The political climate in South Africa post-1994 democratic settlement has been significant. The governing party is at the centre of a transition period which has been characterised by instances that persist in the minds of some South Africans when considering the country's politics. Recent prominent examples where politics has been at the fore have included the Life Esidimeni tragedy[1], the #FeesMustFall Movement[2] and the Marikana Massacre[3]. In these moments of social heightened awareness, theatre makers are often moved to create works that provide commentary on and examine the issues; thereby creating spaces where the public can engage matters of interest. The creation of such environments has the potential of providing a site where citizens can gather and exercise the tenets of democracy, leading to theatre becoming a public sphere. Balme argues that "the theatrical public sphere invariably focuses attention on theatre as an institution between the shifting borders of the private and public, reasoned debate and agonistic intervention" (Balme 2014). Harbermas opines that public sphere:

1 | The Life Esidimeni tragedy occurred where ninety-four people died after the Gauteng Health Department moved them from Life Esidimeni and other facilities, to NGOs (cf. Khosa 2018).
2 | #FeesMustFall is a student led protest movement that began in October 2015, in response to an increase in fees at South African universities (cf. BusinessTech 2016).
3 | On 16 August 2012, the South African Police Service (SAPS) opened fire on a crowd of striking mineworkers at Marikana, in the North West Province. The police killed 34 mineworkers and left 78 seriously injured. Following the open fire assault – 250 of the miners were arrested. This event culminated after an intense week-long protest in which the miners were demanding a wage increase at the Lonmin platinum mine in a wildcat strike (cf. SAHO 2012).

"[...] is made up of private people gathered together as a public and articulating the needs of society with the state. Through acts of assembly and dialogue, the public sphere generates opinions and attitudes which serve to affirm or challenge – therefore, to guide the affairs of state. In ideal terms, the public sphere is the source of public opinion needed to legitimate authority in any functioning democracy." (Habermas 1991: 176)

Ideally, this type of engagement allows citizens a shared space to express their views about things which affect them on any of several levels. Arnold informs us that "the public sphere is a constitutive element of democracy" (Arnold 2008). Theatre makers thus can consider their role in a functioning democracy by approaching selected works for carving a public sphere for audiences to engage matters which bind them to their state.

Ubulution (2016) is one such theatre production making satirical commentary about corruption and greed that tends to befall those in power. Created with the purpose of commentary on democracy and politics inherent to South African Protest Theatre history, this production further chose to instil at its heart the voice of the people in protest. As a universal human right, South Africans have always turned to protest as their voice of dissent against the perceived wrongs inflicted by the state, which has persisted well into post-apartheid democracy. However, these protests often become volatile, especially when the needs of the people are perceived not to be heard. This then leaves more devastation in its wake than originally intended, and may also be indicative of the unresolved issues that remain simmering just below the surface of the public sphere, that often boil over, erupting quickly. Without offering solutions, *Ubulution* integrated this 'need' to protest and observation of what such action may leave in its wake.

This paper looks at *Ubulution* as contemporary protest commentary within the conception of the public sphere. It considers how finding Marx in Protest Theatre may be conceived as a vehicle for marshalling public opinion as a political force in South Africa's socio-political climate. To further understand the impact of a non-linear and non-literal storytelling through utilising theatrical satire and a layered metaphorical commentary on current issues, the source work and dramaturgy of *Ubulution* is revealed to interpret the political themes intertwined in the play. These themes are then considered to determine whether they indeed may offer an expression of public opinion in relation to the South African state.

In search of a contemporary Protest Theatre

Protest Theatre is an accepted international genre for theatre in which communities can scrutinise themselves and endeavour to live according to targeted goals sought by a people who aspire to be a democracy. Where messages are relayed to docile societies urging them to embark on new ideals that would eventually remove the taxing burden of silence, to make a stand, to protest for a better life. It has been proposed then relatively all theatre is essentially theatrical protest.

Specifically, in South African Protest Theatre as a genre became a voice shouting for change from the 1970s when as repression grew and the voices of political activists were increasingly silenced. Theatre became an important means of voicing the protests that were banned from the streets and political platforms of the country. Protest Theatre in South Africa was seen for over a decade to be the voice of reason in the wilderness, the hope of many and the opportunity to make a stance for change. This style of theatre thrived right into the 1994 post-apartheid democratisation. However, the existence of Protest Theatre in the new South Africa was criticised for not transforming with the times: "Protest Theatre has struggled to come to terms with itself after 1994. The didactic agitprop forms of the 80s and 90s have clung on for dear life even though the traditional object of their scorn...is virtually extinct" (Rayneard 2004). Van Graan ponders:

"Now, we have a Constitution that guarantees us the right to freedom of creative expression, and more than ten years after the dawning of democracy, we consider it brave for a playwright to be doing a play like Green Man Flashing[4]. What does it say about our society? About our government's sensitivity to criticism? About the self-censorship that has become endemic to our society? What does it say about our democracy? What does it say about our theatre industry? About us as writers, theatre-makers?" (Van Graan 2006: 285)

Contemporary award-winning plays are being produced, and witnessed by the masses. They tell stories of struggle heroes and the past they have vanquished with promises of a better future; thereby perpetuating a "theatre of nostalgia" (van Graan, 2006: 279) that offers a spectator a walk down memory lane,

---

4 | *Green Man Flashing* is a fast-paced political thriller theatre production written in a filmic style. It explores themes of personal and political violence, as well as the lengths people will go to in the name of greater political good. All this is played out against the backdrop of a young democracy still dealing with its racist history, but where violence against women is of national crisis proportions. Written and produced by Mike van Graan; and first performed at the National Arts Festival, 2-9 July 2004.

instead of (re)presenting the reality we are currently facing. Taking a cue from German playwright Bertolt Brecht who reasons if the intention for art is as a mirror that reflects reality, or a hammer used to shape it; perhaps then theatre should be used as a tool to hammer home some powerful messages about life and society in general.

Theatre is essentially political, and despite that politics as theatre is not wholly or necessarily negative. South African political analyst Brent Meersman likens the political arena to theatre by attributing the seriousness and content as the trouble in attracting audiences, so too is the level of political debate: "Theatre is quintessential to the nature of politics therefore we should acknowledge and not lament it. We should use the analogy to better understand the nature of public discourse. For this is theatre with lives – reality theatre as it were." (Meersman 2008: 292-306)

Theatre makers are spoiled for choice in South Africa for social and redemption themes to tackle in our theatre. So much so that they often err on the side of including too many topics in one play or use the theatre as a platform for information sharing. Instead choosing the theatre platform and a style that allows them to voice their concerns for the myriad of issues that they face in their daily lives, but not tackling the root of a solution that may be faulty or the one in need of a mirror. According to van Graan:

"Theatre - like all art, education, the media and other institutions of socialisation – inhabits the realm of hegemonic conflict, the battle to provide leadership with respect to ideas, values, worldviews, and ideological assumptions to inform the development of our society and of our own individual lives. Whether we like it or not, whether we acknowledge it or not, the act of making theatre is essentially a political act. What we choose to make theatre about, and what we decide to leave out, who we decide to do theatre for, which audiences and at which theatres or buildings we do theatre, are in essence, politically strategic choices." (Van Graan 2006: 286)

Protest Theatre advocated the struggle of the lower-class individual which provided an abundant source of inspiration for writers during South Africa's apartheid era. Contemporarily, the potential for theatre to be used to bring about social, political and economic change to the lives of the oppressed is being realised more and more clearly. Marxist values are gaining traction essentially in response to the unfair social conditions being experienced by the Black majority. For a time after democracy creating theatre from a Marxist conceptual vantage point allowed for the inequality that prevailed to be brought into question. Whether this type of theatre can be termed protest should be questioned but perhaps becomes irrelevant if it speaks the truth.

Finding Marx in Protest Theatre

A Marxist vantage point requires the inclusion of the elements that compose the theory, namely the factors of social and economic production in society. Marx resolved that "if contemporary humans appear to act as self-interested individuals, then, it is as a result not of our essential nature but of the particular ways we have produced our social lives and ourselves" (Rupert 2007: 3).

Based on this view, it follows that if human beings were to critically reconsider the way they produced their own reality they could liberate themselves from any form of human imposed oppression.

There also seemed to have been a further fragmentation of the representation of society through the arts sector directly because of political management of the arts sector. As a result, Irlam notes that much of the literature, and theatre, which emerged out of post-colonial South Africa has been in a state of division where separate communities used theatre and literature to promote the histories and values of their own belief systems (cf. Irlam 2004: 698).

When writing a play for a South African audience, the playwright or theatre maker must consider the socio-political/economic/cultural contexts of their audiences. The problems encountered in the post liberation era had several economic ramifications for different sectors in the countries. Holding playwrights accountable for the current, however, would not be a complete exercise unless we acknowledged the role that the past has had in constructing our current realities.

The new dispensation of South African writers should seek to integrate the masses and find ways of reconciling for past discrepancies. When van Graan said, "It is imperative that, whatever we call it, we see the rise of theatre that boldly, unequivocally and unashamedly speaks truth to the powers that be," (van Graan 2006: 287) he captures what Marx and Engels would have liked the writer who operated in line with Marxist ideology to seek to achieve as an artist.

To this end, the *Ubulution* production was devised as part of academic research into the role of the dramaturge within a South African context. This practice-based project focussed on the collaborative processes of the scriptwriter-dramaturge, when interacting with a director, a cast of actors, an animator and a puppet maker (cf. Chale 2016a) towards developing a socially relevant commentary. Produced by the Tshwane University of Technology Department of Drama and Film, the production was performed in March 2016 in the Breytenbach Theatre, Sunnyside, Pretoria.

Ubulution. Narrative and Context

Ubulution speaks to a continuation and recurrence of the Ubu tales as started by Alfred Jarry and referenced in such pivotal pieces as *Ubu and the Truth Commission* (1998) by Jane Taylor. The narrative captures the tale of Pa Ubu; the manic man in charge who is in pursuit of an empire and its perceived reward, hoping to gain ultimate capitalistic power. The play *Ubu and the Truth Commission* is itself based on an adaptation of Alfred Jarry's *UbuRoi* (1896). "*UbuRoi* follows the political, military and criminal exploits of the grandiose and rapacious Ubu, a kind of parodic Macbeth who, together with his wife attempts to seize all power for himself" (Taylor 2007: iii, Jarry 2007). Ever since the creation of the Ubu concept in France, Ubu has spread through the world. Ubu made its debut in South Africa in 1996 with the advent of the Truth and Reconciliation Commission (TRC)[5]. In this version, Ubu represents the police agents who were responsible for carrying out the orders that secured the political interests of the creators of apartheid. As a response to the TRC, *Ubu and the Truth Commission* came to life through the hand and vision of Jane Taylor, William Kentridge and the Handspring Puppet Company.

Ubu and the Truth Commission follows the life of a policeman named Pa Ubu, from the apartheid era, preparing to testify at the TRC. According to Taylor, the story considers the perpetrator's side of the story within the context of the security police who provided the muscle for many of the atrocities visited upon the Black masses by the National Party through White minority rule (cf. Taylor 2007) The non-linear story focuses on the element of testimony within the TRC using puppetry, projections and motion graphics. The play required a transdisciplinary collaboration which brought together actors, crew, puppeteers, animators and videographers.

Through several readings of the various *Ubu* scripts, the central characters of Pa Ubu and his wife Ma Ubu are portrayed as a greedy couple who are only willing to take any action when there is something for them to gain. They act without considering how their actions will affect the people around them. They behave like children, as is evident from the Punch and Judy type actions in *UbuRoi* (cf. Piepenbring 2015) and the nappy-like costume of Pa Ubu who wears underwear throughout *Ubu and the Truth Commission* (cf. Taylor 2007).

Further, more Ubu represents an excuse for instigators of crimes against humanity. Theatrically, he uses strange language which shows that he is trapped in a different time. The intention of *Ubu and the Truth Commission*

---

5 | The Truth and Reconciliation Commission (TRC) was a series of hearings held in South Africa in 1996. The hearings were intended for agents, victims and survivors of human rights violations perpetrated during apartheid to give testimony of their experiences (cf. SAHO 2017).

was to take the Ubu character out of the burlesque context in which he was originally created by Jarry, and to place him in a realm where his actions had consequences. Taylor calls this a narrative dependent upon agency, where "the stories of those who do are more compelling than those who are done to". She adds: "Ubu's story is, at one level a singular story of individual pathology, yet it is at the same time an exemplary account of the relationships between capitalist ideologies, imperialism, racism, classism, sexism, religion and modernisation." (Ibid. 2007: vi)

Ubu and the Truth Commission provides a source text to develop a contemporary Ubu script for South Africa, titled: *Ubulution*. The aim of *Ubulution* was to develop a newly devised, indigenous production through collaboration that brought the themes of political theatre into the twenty-first century. Through the development of scenarios that required the implementation of Marxist ideologies, *Ubulution* narrates the story of the downtrodden worker who is finally fighting for freedom by any means necessary.

Ubulution. Synopsis and Themes

South African readers and audience members may attribute subversive parallels to real people and situations when considering the actions and qualities of the characters in *Ubulution*. In compiling the text, many themes and topics were referenced that included the following ideas: global economic trends; intelligence agencies and alliances through the world; monopolies within an economy; the principles of protest action; the history of pre-colonial African monarchs; and African folk tales.

As an original script, *Ubulution* was conceived in the tenets of the Ubu traditions with the principal characters of Ma and Pa Ubu representing caricatured elements of being overly ambitious, self-indulgent and unrealistic about their expectations; and with no sense of remorse for whoever suffers by their hand.

Pa Ubu is a merciless tyrant, dictator and Black Economic Empowerment (BEE) business man. According to the guidelines of the policy, formulated in 2001 and implemented in 2003, all businesses with a turnover of R5 million and more had to adhere to a BEE scorecard to enable them to achieve a BEE certification. The government decided to expand BEE to B-BBEE or Broad Based Black Economic Empowerment in 2007 and that has since been the measure ever since (cf. RSA 2007). However, there have been many aspersions cast against the policy (cf. Du Preez 2017). It was on these elicit elitist Black enrichment critiques that Pa Ubu's character's business dealings were framed.

Pa Ubu has monopolized the economy and is on a mission to colonize the world. He has monopolized the fast food industry, the mining industry, the alcohol industry and just about every industry that is economically viable. He rides the backs of his workers who slave day and night to build the Ubu Empire. Pa Ubu considers himself to be a man above the people who is a saviour unto himself, yet at the cost of others. Literally depicted as inflated in the live performances with the character on stilts, Pa Ubu shrinks throughout the play as he diminishes in size and stature. His deflation symbolizes his weakening grip on the power he believes himself to wield.

Ma Ubu is the estranged wife of Pa Ubu. She starts the play on ground level, but inflates in size and stature throughout the play. Her inflation symbolises her rise to power in the absence of Pa Ubu whilst out on his mission to execute Chief Whip Mansa Musa. When she was growing up, Ma Ubu had very big dreams. Her vision was to put the world on a string up until Pa Ubu came along and swept her off her ankles. Ma Ubu used to be a supervisor in Pa Ubu's favourite factory where he was impressed by her level of diligence and obedience. Whenever Pa Ubu was around, she would forget her bossy tendencies and become a very sweet woman. His macho bravado made her weak at the knees and she fell in love with the way he demanded the control of any situation.

Ma Ubu was attracted to Pa's power because it reminds her that she also had a dream to be the most powerful woman alive. Now she sits in their house all day populating Africa (which is symbolised by her constantly blowing up balloons and casting them adrift on the stage) whilst waiting for Pa to return. Ma Ubu is convinced that Pa Ubu is a secret polygamist, pretending to be a good Christian monogamist like her father who only cheated on his mother, but never disrespected her by marrying other women.

Ubulution includes the introduction of an original set of puppet characters which represents the working-class society in the play-land of the Ubus. The puppets resemble a spectrum of South African animals in skeletal form who are anthropomorphised. Their human traits are further personified through the actors' interpretation. These puppets represent a group of workers who make up the work force of Ubu and constitute the main ingredient in the recipe for revolution; but remain easily swayed by whomever provides them with the most entertaining or controversial argument. The puppets are 200mm in height and so they performed on stage with their puppeteers, which was further recorded and projected in a live feed – all visible to the audience. This is done intentionally to emphasise that this cross-section of a few puppets was representative of an entire workforce.

Unencumbered by wit, the workers are happy to do their duty daily without complaint, hesitation nor fair compensation. As decreed by Pa Ubu they work barefoot in the factories to ensure that no one's shoes discriminate against another's. Pa Ubu rewards diligence and long service with the sole ambition of all his workers: a pair of black gumboots – these are only ever seen worn by the union boss, which brings into question the allegiance of said union leader to the manipulations of his boss. The workers live in fear of violating the five cardinal rules of the factory. "Rule #1: Good Workers Never Strike. Rule #2: Good Workers Never Talk to the Media. Rule #3: Good Workers work from 9 to 9 to 9 to 9. Rule #4: Good Workers Enforce Nepotism and Child Labour. Rule #5: Good Workers Know, Pa Ubu is the King. All hail Pa Ubu." (Chale 2016b)

The puppets work for Ubu under the charge of Jannie, the Union leader. This leader is often seen as the instigating force behind getting the workforce to strike, yet despite him managing to sway the puppets and get them to speak, Jannie proves ineffectual in combating the economic elitism.

Ananzi, the spider trickster, is a character based on African folk tales (cf. Barker & Sinclair 2007). She is introduced as a pivotal character in bringing down the Ubu's capitalist empire. Ananzi is shown as always watching things unfold, whispering things that make the scene take a turn when you least expect. She gets people to do things as if by their own will, but it is always Ananzi's will that comes to pass. She is a trickster, who makes herself seen only when she can gain something out of it.

Ananzi is instrumental in getting Pa Ubu to face his corrupt actions at a commission where he is confronted by many witnesses who tell of their suffering under his leadership and corruption. However, Ananzi's plans are floored by the strategic Ubu's who manage to escape without consequence.

During the commission various larger witness puppets are introduced. These are manipulated by performers who may be seen by the audience, akin to the Handspring Puppet Company and Bunraku puppetry techniques. These witnesses use text taken directly from accounts after protest actions in South Africa; including Marikana, #FeesMustFall, and all service protests mentioned in the media.

When the play begins Pa Ubu comes home from a long voyage "out at sea", so he says where he was honoured with the bull for being an important man. This bull gifted to the couple increases in size every time it strategically appears throughout the play as a metaphor of the greed and power. The prevalence of the bull is a direct reference to the 2012 Lonmin board member's (the then deputy president of South Africa, Cyril Ramaphosa's) R18-million bid for a buffalo at an auction. This auction took place a mere month after the Marikana Massacre that saw 34 miners killed due to wage negotiation protest action at Lonmin mines. Although he lost the bid for the bull, Ramaphosa came under attack for such ostentations in comparison with the low wages of Lonmin workers (cf. Falanga 2014).

When Pa Ubu first appears, he is on stilts wearing a jacket filled with all sorts of top secret paperwork which he extracts and feeds to the bull, while Ma Ubu is sitting on a low chair. As the play progresses, Pa leaves on another mission which will see his status elevated beyond any other; however, this represents a trick by Ananzi the spider, who intends to fill Ma Ubu's head with doubts about her husband's activities. Ma Ubu also escalates her power and influence over her husband's henchmen (Boomba and Moloi), and ultimately the workers they in turn manipulate. She experiences a rise in her own status as can be seen through her seat which is elevated throughout her 'hot air' conversations with Ananzi. During this process, the bull ascends a pair of stilts – as a symbolic shift he is growing in stature through corruption and conniving. By the time Pa Ubu returns after finding out that he was tricked he has been reduced in stature, where he comes down to the lowest level, of being merely a man, emphasised in contrast with the oversized bull figure.

Ananzi sends Pa Ubu away on a mission to kill the spirit of Mansa Musa[6] to create the space for her to influence anarchy amongst the workers in Pa Ubu's factories. Mansa Musa is proposed to have been the most powerful man on the earth, rumoured to have died in the 14th century, and represents the level of ambition which Pa Ubu aspires to emulate. This further and echoes the spirit of *UbuRoi* appearing to Pa Ubu in *Ubu and the Truth Commission*. Ananzi tries to trick Pa to go look for him, not knowing that Mansa Musa's spirit is still alive[7]. Only Musa's amplified voice is heard in the production, the audience never see a physical representation. When Pa Ubu converses with Mansa Musa, he is warned about the anarchy brewing in his empire because of the actions of a certain spider, which Ubu considers to be ancestral intervention.

Ananzi's only detractors are Pa Ubu's ever hungry henchmen Boomba and Moloi. They throw their weight around in his absence and mistreat the union boss (Jannie) in the presence of the worker puppets. Ananzi and Jannie both plan a rebellion, but it is the acts of Boomba and Moloi that ultimately lead to the revolt and the uprising by the worker puppets. The henchmen are reminiscent of the military within an African state.

Upon Pa Ubu's return, his workers have turned against him and his empire is about to crumble as the commission of enquiry set up by Ananzi finds him guilty of gross violations of his workers and the world in general. In the fictional world of the Ubu's, there is no accountability, which leads to Ma and Pa Ubu evading prosecution as they ride off into the sunset on the back of the bull, which renders them literally untouchable.

Non-literal staging and the active spectator

Theatre makers should have opportunities for self-actualisation without discredit or condemnation. Whilst this philosophy should garner support and be advocated for the freedom for an artist to speak their minds, it needs to be

---

6 | "One of Mali's greatest leaders, the emperor Mansa Musa, awakened the world to Mali's power on his pilgrimage to Mecca in 1324 when he spent and distributed so much gold that it deflated its price in Cairo for the next twelve years." (Pulambo 2010: 5)

7 | This references the importance of ancestors in African culture.

acknowledged that theatre makers as individuals should not speak on behalf of another or a community – with or without that community's consent. Without the insight and meaning-making from an audience, the theatre maker should see their work as being incomplete. The consent comes in the form of acknowledgement and attendance of the theatre.

Therefore, this non-literal theatrical style calls for an 'active spectator'. An active spectator is one who participates in the performance event – by having to unravel, emotionally engage, or even physically participate. An active spectator controls the meaning-making. The focus should shift from individual responses to seeing a live performance to the collective's condition that make theatre, and spectator's experience of it, possible. Social-cultural-circumstance determines the interpretation of any perceived social commentary experienced through theatre. And further establishes the relevance for and personal association by the spectators, again investing them as active participants in the performance.

As with its precursors, *Ubulution* is created in a non-linear and non-literal theatrical style. This theatricality lends itself to the inclusion of satire and expressive performance narratives (cf. Lewis 2010) which requires interpretive meaning-making from all participants – the theatre makers and the spectators.

The spectator is immersed in the performance from the beginning; they are invited to sit on stage facing the backstage area where the action took place. This provides for a very intimate experience. They also each find a hard-hat on their chairs to wear during the show, symbolising their engagement with the workers. During the performance, the henchmen demote the Union leader and randomly select a member of the audience to take his place – this further entrenches the literal involvement of the audience.

It also allows for the suspension of belief in that the spectator can immerse themselves in a play-world that is familiar to reality but does not hold the ramifications of being seen to be subversive in merely attending, and to adopt a critical perspective on self-distinguished social reality. In this manner, a sense of theatricality is upheld whilst the spectator is enticed into making their own choices and conclusions through the social public sphere.

Public spheres and transference of power

Theatre makers need to remain cautious to keep from becoming biased in terms of dealing with the content whilst maintaining the truth of our sources. In *Ubulution*, a sense of protest are integral both in the depiction of action on stage (thereby influencing the narrative) but also in the development of the text in the first place. Certain influential events in the text were developed from material crafted in literal environments that were forged by ordinary citizens that were engaging with the state through protest action, environments which could be called public spheres. It is important to note that although the narrative advocates for a revolution and referenced the protest actions, it doesn't offer solutions. Instead, it merely depicts the possibility of such being ineffectual or destructive if not correctly implemented for the greater social good.

Habermas warns against undermining the public sphere; arguing that "manipulative publicity" could lead one to assumptions. This too is pertinent to a theatre maker selecting material from a public sphere. Habermas further warns against propaganda being presented as truth because of those in authority trying to enforce their power (cf. Habermas 1991, 178; 195; 206; 245).

The danger posed by creating political theatre which is steeped in propaganda is asserted by sentiments that such instances stunt the freedom of expression of participants. "Even arguments are translated into symbols to which one again cannot respond by arguing but only by identifying with them." (Habermas 1991: 206) This notion suggests that theatre makers need to steer clear of the trap of making assumptions on the parts of the views and ideologies of our audiences, but that we should create spaces for them to interpret for themselves – as active spectators.

Kellner further captures Habermas' sentiments about presupposing and the media's role in the public sphere:

"For Habermas, the function of the media have [sic.] thus been transformed from facilitating rational discourse and debate within the public sphere into shaping, constructing, and limiting public discourse to those themes validated and approved by media corporations. Hence, the interconnection between a sphere of public debate and individual participation has been fractured and transmuted into that of a realm of political information and spectacle, in which citizen-consumers ingest and absorb passively entertainment and information." (Kellner 1990: 11-33)

Theatre makers are also caught up in this fray especially when creating content that has elements of factuality and politics. According to Livingstone and Lunt:

"At one end the populace has little direct role in politics, but policies should be enacted in the public interest with the consent of the people. At the other extreme, ordinary people participate in the political process through voting, lobbying, inquiry, membership of political parties and trade unions, and so forth. The poles of this opposition can be used to understand a transformation from an elite to a participatory democracy." (Livingstone/Lunt 1994: 11)

Theatre makers must ensure that their work allows viewers to remain individuals in a democratic society. As Harbermas suggests, "Citizens act as a public when they deal with matters of general interest without being subject to coercion; thus, with the guarantee that they may assemble, and express and publicize their opinions freely." (Harbermas 1989: 231) If theatre makers can deal with material in an unbiased manner, they can free audiences to feel the necessity of adding their own voices to the unfolding, unbiased conversation taking place before them.

To this end, *Ubulution* sought to create a space where the audience could engage content sourced from and reminiscent of the literal public sphere, presented within the theatrical public sphere (cf. Balme 2014). The final show also ends with a question and comments session between the cast and the audience. Questions about text, acting and directorial decisions are duly responded to. A point of reflection during this session proves to be a moment where the collective present audience reached a consensus about the fact that there is a general feeling amongst members of the public that our country is separated into two spheres. First, the world of the constitution, where all are equal, and we are all equal beneficiaries of the policies and promises of the Constitution and the Freedom Charter; and second, the real world, where such actions as State Capture, Life Esidimeni, #FeesMustFall and Marikana happen; suggesting that we have chosen callous leaders to ensure that our ideals are fulfilled. This insightful conclusion is drawn specifically out of reflection on what the spectators had perceived from watching the production and was not the explicit objective of the playwright/theatre makers.

Without the spectator's involvement in the theatre experience, the production is impossible. It is the active spectator who completes the interpretation of the narrative into a contemporary context to a greater or lesser degree. Without the spectator to witness the transposition, the story is layered and vital to the context in which it found itself. Despite the intentions of the performers and the director, or the entire creative team, it remains the spectator who places the production within their own social-cultural circumstance.

The spectators are forced to claim their role

Marxism warns that if politics would not rise to challenge the unequal situation presented by capitalism then the lower class would come to accept their position over time – at their own peril. Rupert expands:

"To the extent that people understand existing social relations as natural, necessary and universal, they are prevented from looking for transformative possibilities, precluded from imagining the social production of alternative possible worlds. In short, they may abdicate their collective powers of social self-production. Ironically, then the unprecedented development of productive capacity under capitalism has as its historical correlate the disempowerment of collective human producers." (Rupert 2007: 6)

Ubulution represents this as a phenomenon of the working class through their desire for revolution explored through protest. It theatrically presents protest as an indicative option of the downtrodden, offering a mirror to society; but also, in so doing, assumes the subversive stance of being labelled as theatre that is protest – a hammer to shape it. *Ubulution* spans a range of topics which reflect the sentiments of different sectors of the community. Yet, the production manages to focus attention on the protest action and draws from the public sphere to allow audience members to engage with themes as opposed to prescribed ideas.

However, these questions remain: is it Protest Theatre or is it merely social commentary. Is social commentary on stage not Protest Theatre? Is not the theatre in which the communities are able to scrutinize themselves and endeavour to live according to targeted goals sought by a people who aspire to be a democracy, Protest Theatre?

Perhaps this 'contemporary' form of Protest Theatre does not share the same aggression or urgency as the older versions in this country. It may be labelled agitation or propaganda whichever so long as the resultant cause is a reaction in a spectator to participate – to actively get involved in their social reform.

In its non-literal theatrical rendering of social commentary for interpretation and meaning-making by audiences. *Ubulution* defines protest implications. The performer/creators make their contribution by daring to collude in presenting the performance to an audience without any devious or confrontational intentions. But the ownership shifts. The protest now sits squarely with the spectator. Everyone may choose to make of it what they will – to voice their disapproval, to oppose or make an objection. Or to affirm their role in making a difference to their world, affirm or declare their allegiances and assert their opinions, or question their social conditioning. In whatever form, the spectator is forced to claim their role, own their voice. Everyone is entitled to their opinions. They cannot turn their back on what they experienced; even their silence would be interrupted by their interpretations.

Bibliography

Arnold, Anne-Katrin (2008): Worldbank. Available: https://blogs.worldbank.org/publicsphere/defining-public-sphere-3-paragraphs, 7/1/2008, Last Access: 10/4/2018.

Balme, Christopher B. (2014): The theatrical public sphere. Cambridge: Cambridge University Press.

Barker, W. H.; Sinclair, Cecilia (2007): West African folk-tales. Chapel Hill, NC: Yesterday's Classics.

BusinessTech (2016): Damage to SA universities hits R600 million – and counting. BusinessTech. Available: https://businesstech.co.za/news/gover nment/138169/damage-to-sa-universities-hits-r600-million-and-counting/, Last Access: 8/1/2018.

Chale, Katlego (2016a): Identifying a South African interpretation of drama-turgy in collaborative theatre. A reflexive study. Pretoria.

Chale, Katlego (2016b): Ubulution. Pretoria. Tshwane University of Technology. Department of Drama and Film.

Du Preez, Theo (2017): the new #BEE – the real enemy of SA. myNEWS24. Available: https://www.news24.com/MyNews24/the-new-bee-the-real-ene my-of-south-africa-20170703, zuletzt aktualisiert am 1/8/2018.

Falanga, Gabi (2014): Blood on his hands? 'McCyril' testifies at Marikana inquiry. Mail and Gaurdian. Available: https://mg.co.za/article/2014-08-11-blood-on-his-hands-mccyril-testifies-at-marikana-inquiry, Last Access: 1/8/2018.

Griffiths, Martin (ed.) (2007): International relations theory for the twenty-first century. An introduction. ebrary, Inc. London: Routledge. Available: http://site.ebrary.com/lib/alltitles/docDetail.action?docID=10205731.

Habermas, Jürgen (1991): The Structural transformation of the public sphere. An inquiry into a category of bourgeois society. Cambridge, Mass.: MIT Press.

Habermas, Jürgen; Seidman, Steven (eds.) (1989): On society and politics. A reader. Boston: Beacon Press. Available: http://www.loc.gov/catdir/enhance ments/fy0736/88043321-b.html.

Irlam, S. (2004): Unraveling the Rainbow: The Remission of Nation in Post-Apartheid Literature. In: *South Atlantic Quarterly* 103 (4), p. 695-718.

Jarry, Alfred (1896): UbuRoi. Paris. Théâtre de l'Œuvre.

Jarry, Alfred (2007): UbuRoi. New York. Grove Atlantic.

Kellner, Douglas (1990): Critical Theory and the Crisis of Social Theory. In: *Sociological Perspectives* 33 (1), p. 11–33.

Khosa, Amanda (2018): I dip my head in shame – Makhura on Life Esidimeni. Eye Witness News. Available: https://www.news24.com/SouthAfrica/News/i-dip-my-head-in-shame-makhura-on-life-esidimeni-tragedy-20180226, Last Access: 1/8/2018.

Lewis, Janine (2010): Physical actions as expressive performance narratives: a self-reflexive journey. In: *South African Theatre Journal* 24 (1), p. 175-198.

Livingstone, Sonia; Lunt, Peter (1994): The mass media, democracy and the public sphere. Routledge. London. Available: http://eprints.lse.ac.uk/489 64/1/Amended%20_Livingstone_Mass_media_democaracy.pdf.

Meersman, Brent (2008): Democracy, Capitalism and Theatre in the New South Africa. In: *South African Theatre Journal* 21 (1), p. 292-315.

Piepenbring, Dan (2015): An Inglorious Slop-pail of a play. The Paris Review. Available: https://www.theparisreview.org/blog/2015/09/08/an-inglorious-slop-pail-of-a-play/, Last Access: 1/8/2018.

Pulambo, Joe (2010): Mansa Musa. African King of Gold. Los Angeles: University of California Press.

Rayneard, Max (2004): Green Man Flashing, 6/7/2004. This Day.

RSA (2/2/2007): Government Gazette 500.

Rupert, Mark (2007): Marxism. In: Martin Griffiths (ed.): International relations theory for the twenty-first century. An introduction. London: Routledge.

SAHO (2012): Marikana Massacre. South African History Online. Available: https://www.sahistory.org.za/article/marikana-massacre-16-august-2012, Last Access: 1/7/2018.

SAHO (2017): Truth and Reconciliation Commission (TRC). South African Theatre History Online. Johannesburg. Available: https://www.sahistory.org.za/topic/truth-and-reconciliation-commission-trc, Last Access: 1/7/2018.

Taylor, Jane (1998): Ubu and the Truth Commission. 1. publ. Johannesburg.

Taylor, Jane (2007): Ubu and the Truth Commission. 2 ed. Cape Town.

Van Graan, Mike (2006): From Protest Theatre to the Theatre of Conformity? In: *South African Theatre Journal* 20 (1), p. 276-288.

Artists as "Seismographs", Theatre as a "Mirror" of Society?

Conversation with Cultural Activists: Yvette Hardie, Ismail Mahomed and Omphile Molusi about Social Transformation

Isa Lange

It is said that artists could be seismographs in times of crises and changes, register in processes of transformation movements in the society. They help to give people a meaning in life and determine human purposes. How is it working, what are the experiences in post-apartheid South Africa, why does it make so important to watch the Performing Arts? The answers of the experts in Theatre for children and young people, the artistic director of the National Arts Festival and the dramatist, actor and writer are focussing of the social relevance of theatre.

Is theatre a mirror of the political condition in the whole country? Can you give an example?

Yvette Hardie: It is to some extent. There are certain plays which capture a kind of zeitgeist for a moment and reflect the political conditions. Mike van Graan is particularly good at doing this – finding a story or incident which encapsulates a particular confrontation within South African politics and dramatising it in a way that presents the complexities and questions raised from several points of view. Plays like *Green Man Flashing* (which speaks to government corruption and manipulation and whether the rights of the individual are more important than the needs of the party/collective), *Rainbow Scars* (which confronts the 'easy' notion of the Rainbow Nation and picks at the its inconsistencies and implausibilities) and *Brothers in Blood* (which demonstrates the very human dilemmas which emerge when characters from different religions and racial backgrounds come into contact in a tragic misunderstanding) come to mind in this context. There are also plays like *Protest* (Paul Grootboom) and *Marikana – the Musical* (Aubrey Sekhabi) which represent a significant moment or occurrence in contemporary society and which express – with some cynicism and also some glossiness – the times we live in.

Ismail Mahomed: Theatre often is a mirror of the society in which our theatre makers create their work. Sometimes the work is reflective; and in which case the artists are either looking back at historical moments in our society either nostalgically or critically. An example of nostalgic reflection is the production *Kanala District Six* which is produced at the Fugard Theatre in Cape Town. The production looks back at an area and a community that was destroyed by the Nationalist government's Group Areas Act. Malcolm Purkey's *Sophiatown* at the Market Theatre also looks back at the township (Sophiatown) after which it was named which was also destroyed by the National government but his work is not a nostalgic reflection. It is a critical reflection. Much of the satire in South Africa, on the other hand, is reflexive work. It responds, bounces off and challenges the current political status quo in South Africa. At other times, theatre is not a reflective or reflexive mirror. It is a crystal ball. It allows us to re-envision our society. A young generation of artists who were born after 1994 is trying to do this kind of work.

Omphile Molusi: Yes. I think it mirrors in order to reflect and attempt to change perspective. The mirroring is also to define or redefine ourselves as a country. Examples; Phala O Phala's adaptation of Matsemela Manaka's *Egoli, Marikana - The Musical* by Aubrey Sekhabi, adapted from the book by a group of journalists "We Are Going To Kill Each Other Today", Mongi Mthombeni's *I see you*, Napo Masheane's *A New Song*, Philip Dikotla's *Skierlik*, amongst many others.

How do you develop political stories on stage? Theatre is not just for entertainment?

Yvette Hardie: Either you have a strong political consciousness – Pieter Dirk Uys, Mike van Graan and John Kani spring to mind – and you write with urgency towards the emerging themes in society, or you develop them in workshop with other artists. This latter process is probably more common and is one that comes relatively easily to South African artists who have often created theatre through experimentation on their feet – originally in response to what was happening at the time, and because literary theatre was not accessible to those involved, or because of an ideological concern to express voices which were commonly silenced.

The workshop process was one that allowed for some practice in democracy (although some would argue that this did not go far enough) and one which recognised a multiplicity of voices. An example in post-apartheid *South Africa is Truth* in Translation by Colonnades Theatre Lab SA, with a range of South African artists the piece recognised in its inconsistencies and contradictions, the multiple truths of ordinary South Africans who experienced and participated in the Truth and Reconciliation commission, and the translators who told these stories from the points of view of both perpetrator and victim...it asked the problematic question, is it possible to forgive the past to survive the future, and engaged its audiences in talk backs and workshops which allowed for a deeper exploration of how these themes impacted personally on those who had witnessed the piece.

Ismail Mahomed: At the heart of political stories is integrity, authenticity and conviction. Before 1994, political stories in South Africa were largely a protest against the apartheid state. This work had artistic integrity and political conviction. Immediately, after 1994, artists in South Africa struggled to write new political stories because the crutch of Protest Theatre had fallen away. Artists started writing celebratory stories because the Mandela era was a phase of euphoria. From about 1999, artists once again began writing political stories – this time the agenda was about HIV, gender and environment. Some of these stories worked and some failed hopelessly. The stories that worked were those that were written by artists with real conviction and who were activists working in these fields. The artists who created stories simply because of funding imperatives made work that lacked both artistic and political integrity.

Omphile Molusi: People often say politicians write scripts for us. This is also true for me to a certain extent. Inspiration for political stories is everywhere. It's in the state of the country for an example. But for me, I mainly develop stories from the point of view of those affected by political decisions our politicians make. The policies and laws that are debated in parliament affect everyone. If bad decisions/bad policies are made, this leads to a crisis in the country. And so I always look at ways to mirror this and reflect on what is, in order to challenge perspective and hopefully to affect change. On theatre as entertainment; yes, I think theatre should entertain. Even if we are issue driven, I don't think we should bore people, I think our entertainment should be about inspiring and not just entertaining for entertainment sake. I'm talking mainly about theatre that is considered to be political theatre. But theatre generally can definitely entertain however it likes. There are shows that are mainly just for that purpose.

How can theatre and art – singing, writing – shape our values?

Yvette Hardie: A production like *Woza Albert!* made the idea of liberation seem a possibility; while expressing forcefully and humorously the crushing realities of apartheid, the uplifting final scene provided hope and a sense of agency for those who experienced it... For some people, witnessing this production gave a sense of the totality of what apartheid was and the myriad methods it used to crush the human spirit; but also it demonstrated the fundamental power of the human spirit to survive despite these realities. And in so doing, it shaped values by providing a shift in consciousness. Of course there are also numerous examples of plays – and other art forms – which by supporting a lack of consciousness of present realities, shape values by supporting the status quo, or by paying attention to the insignificant, and do nothing to shift the consciousness of the audience. Perhaps these art forms are in the majority, and the examples which really serve to shift as opposed to shaping our values, are much fewer in number.

Ismail Mahomed: Theatre communicates with our hearts and minds. It allows us to step into the world of the other and to experience their histories, lives, fears and hopes. In order to achieve this it requires the audience to have an open mind; and to be prepared to engage both intellectually and emotionally with the work. South African playwright Mike van Graan's play *Rainbow Scars* is a good example of the kind of theatre that allows us to look at the issue of cross-racial adoptions in South Africa. It allows us to interrogate our personal prejudices about race; and then he challenges us to make up about our minds about the kind of society that he wants to build.

On the other hand, theatre can also entrench negative values, prejudices and attitudes. A writer, director and artists take risks when they put their work on stage. It is the right of the artist to respond to the work with love, hate or anger. It is however, the responsibility of festival directors and curators to position that work in a programme so that it can open a critical dialogue that will inform, challenge or change the values of our society. A festival director/curator is an agent who has the power to shape a society's values.

Omphile Molusi: We tell/sing/dance stories of people and about people or the human condition. Even if it's politics it's still about people. And so I think we tell stories of people to understand people and if we understand people we can learn to relate to each other and once we relate we can learn to live with each other, hopefully this will shape our values as people. When I did my play *Cadre*, which was based on my uncle's life, I got to spend a lot of time with him. Before writing the play I just saw him as an uncle who couldn't make life for himself and so depends on the family all the time. But during the process when I spent a lot of time with him I got to understand the man and this enabled me to relate with him, which helped change my perspective about him. What I now understood was that he doesn't have a life because he was busy making a life for us, fighting during the struggle. But now he is too damaged to make a life in the new South Africa. In writing a story about him, this is what I was hoping the audience would experience and look at unsung heroes with a different eye. I believe this is how theatre could make us better people.

Theatre for Young Audiences.
The Art of Education

Between Traditional Practise and Contemporary Forms

Theatre for Young Audiences in (South-) Africa

Yvette Hardie

African theatre for young audiences cannot be summarised in an article, and I don't pretend to have knowledge of all that happens on the vast and diverse African continent. However I will explore a few general themes about theatre for young audiences in Africa, which I hope will offer a window into the contexts, challenges and possibilities that exist.

African countries are by and large dealing (with different degrees of success) with a legacy of colonialism and oppression. Post-colonialism has brought with it new problems of corruption, dictatorships and conflicts between religious and ethnic grouping. There are often stark economic inequities within countries. In my own country, South Africa, these contrasts are extreme and inequality is rising; 41% of children live in the poorest 20% of households, while only 8% of children live in richest 20% of households. Alongside poverty come a host of deeply-rooted social problems, which are often interconnected.

Artistic Experiences and Commercial Interests

In South Africa, for example, we are dealing with rising youth unemployment, high levels of HIV-AIDS, endemic violence, gender inequality, cultural and religious intolerance, xenophobia, corruption, failing education, increasing abuse of drugs, alcoholism, and other forms of social dysfunction. While we have a progressive constitution of which we are very proud and great policies across many spheres of government, including education, we also see poor implementation of these policies on the ground. This is due to corruption, incapacity, and a lack of strategic thinking and planning. Education is faltering, and the success of children at school in terms of basic literacy and numeracy is very poor according to international standards. Most children in South Africa live with only one parent or grandparent, and there are many child-headed households as a result of HIV-AIDS.

How does this all affect TYA? Firstly, the agenda for TYA in my country, South Africa, can never simply be driven by artistic or commercial interests. In fact it is irresponsible to not consider this broader context of the life experience of the majority of children in our country. When 92% of the children and young people of South Africa are not in a position to afford theatre, then we have to make choices about who our audience is. Do we speak only to those who can afford the experience, or do we ensure that all children have access to theatre? This is true of most African countries, where access to theatre for children is a challenge.

However, giving children access to theatre brings with it economic challenges, and when there are so many other pressing social problems, theatre can be relegated to a position of least importance.

We see three inter-related drivers of TYA in much of Africa:

- the social driver – what are the needs of the society and of its children/ young people?
- the funding driver – who is funding and what are they funding, particularly with regards to children/young people?
- the artistic driver – what do I have to say as an artist to children/young people and how do I choose to express these ideas?

Theatre for Healing and Reconciliation

Much theatre for young audiences is driven by a response to the social factors and needs in the society. There has been a rise in dominance of theatre for social change/theatre for development, which tends to use forum theatre methodologies derived from Augusto Boal, and which focuses on the actual personal experiences of children/young people and their communities, as they deal with pressing current issues. We also see a great deal of theatre that deals with post-conflict issues and trauma – theatre for healing and reconciliation is much needed and practiced.

Since funding for this kind of theatre can often be accessed through international foundations or with the support of agencies with particular social transformation agendas, theatre for development and for healing tends to dominate also for pragmatic reasons. For many artists, the only way to survive is to make work that speaks to the agenda of a funding agency, whether it is theatre about the importance of sleeping under a mosquito net, or theatre that explores safe use of water, or theatre dealing with teenage pregnancy, or theatre dealing with reconciliation.

The problem with this emphasis is that while these forms of theatre can be empowering and are much needed, they do not always allow imaginative space for children to think metaphorically and transformatively about themselves and their societies. Also, the focus on issues can at times force children to confront certain things before they are ready to do so, contributing to their being forced to grow up too rapidly in an already overly-demanding world.

This is exacerbated by the fact that in Africa, few theatre pieces are designed to be age-specific, meaning that often a performing group or audience may comprise all young people from 2-18 and older. Often the dominant forms of theatre expose concrete problems, without prioritising the power of the imagination.

The Art of Storytelling

Another common factor, and one not restricted to Africa, is the tension that exists between traditional forms and contemporary forms of practice. In the context where the traditional practices were subjugated, oppressed and at times obliterated, there has in many African contexts been an attempt to revive the traditional arts.

But what are these traditional African theatre practices? In traditional African theatre performance is syncretic, combining music, dance, drama, riddling, poetry, costume, mask and storytelling to make one artistic experience. Disciplines are not separated out as often happens in the Western tradition. Storytelling traditions are probably the oldest continuous dramatic form in Africa, and the role of the storyteller in society is traditionally more multi-faceted than simply that of artist. It includes facets of priest, teacher, healer, historian, tradition-bearer, poet, community psychologist and philosopher. Oral African storytelling is a communal participatory experience, and an important part of children's traditional indigenous education.

However, with the influences of Western dramatic forms, these traditional approaches have been challenged and at times abandoned. As urbanisation and globalisation have affected children's socialisation, so we see traditional, communal approaches to theatre and storytelling being lost. Also, we have the problem that not all traditional stories are appropriate within the modern milieu. Many represent traditional ways of thinking which do not support human rights or the rights of the child. However, some of the most exciting examples of theatre for young audiences in South Africa have been where these traditional ideas have been brought together with a contemporary sensibility, which has reinvented the traditions and allowed for a performance, which unites past and present in powerful ways.

Cultural Diversity as a Challenge

A common misconception of Africa is that it is in some way homogenous. Nothing could be further from the truth. If we just look at the question of language, we see a vast range of languages sometimes in the same country (in

Nigeria, there are more than 450 languages; in South Africa, we have 11 official languages). This poses problems for the theatre maker working with or for the pre-school child, who has not yet come into contact with the lingua franca (English, French, Portuguese or German) taught in schools. Language can be both a strong cultural container, preserving ways of thinking and being, but also a polarising tool, separating and dividing artists and audiences. Theatre makers have to make choices about who they are talking to, in what language and for what purpose. One of the main questions we have in South Africa, is how do we prevent ourselves from falling into the separatist thinking of the apartheid period, while encouraging a celebration of those cultural and linguistic heritages, which were oppressed under apartheid.

Another issue is how we stay connected as artists on the continent. Travel on the continent is expensive and challenging, and connectivity by internet or other means cannot be taken for granted. In order to act in a unified way as African artists, to put pressure on our governments to prioritise the arts for children, we need to find ways to connect which move us out of the paradigm of dealing only with our own individual problems and allows us to think strategically as a sector on the continent.

"Changing the World, one Child at a Time"

As African artists there are many challenges, but there is also a huge potential. I see a theatre for young audiences in Africa, which creates a continuum between past and present, connecting African children with where they come from, while also allowing them a space in which to examine where they can find themselves and where they are going.

Etoundi Zeyang, Cameroonian director and ASSITEJ EC member, said recently, "If there is a continent that needs theatre for children, that continent certainly is Africa. Theatre touches all of life – it unrolls life for us to see it. The social pyramid is such that there are more children at the base, and we can make concrete changes to society by touching children first. If we want to save the world, we need to save children first." In South Africa, we have adopted the slogan, "Changing the world, one child at a time". This is what we see as the ultimate purpose of theatre for young audiences – allowing worlds of possibility to open up for children, so that they feel empowered and emboldened to change the world they live in.

The text was first published in the magazine "IXYPSILONZETT", Berlin 2013.

The ideal of a Rainbow Nation 1

What Theatre Arts and Cultural Policy in Europe can learn from Southern Africa

Julius Heinicke

"Don't talk, act!" This was the demand a young artist made of the directors of the Soweto Theatre, who, like many other ageing freedom fighters, represent a South African elite better known for its corruption than for its political successes. A generation of young artists are venting their frustrations in a theatre that was only opened four years ago in Johannesburg's South Western Township (Soweto). They see few prospects for the future of their art because of poor decisions on the part of the government. The theatre building itself seems to embody this failure. The colourful, modern building with multiple theatres comes across as a sterile, fenced-off foreign body, and seems to be little used by the local population.

South Africa is generally considered to be a model par excellence for the process of societal transformation. In 1994 the former apartheid state declared itself to be a Rainbow Nation, and quickly moved to introduce the world's most liberal constitution. The nation is not only the great hope of the entire continent but also represents the transformation of a society of victims and perpetrators into one of forgiving and forgiven citizens.

Everyone remembers the largely staged proceedings of the Truth and Reconciliation Commission, the impressive way that the country presented itself during the football World Cup and the dancing at the funeral of Nelson Mandela, who more than anyone personified the South African dream of a fair, multicultural society. So when it comes to "Theatre and Transformation", South Africa has to be where it happens. Directors, writers and artistic directors from the country's major theatres, including the Market Theatre in Johannesburg and the Baxter Theatre in Cape Town, came together with theatre educationalists, experts and staff of cultural organisations at the State Theatre in Pretoria, Tshwane University's theatre department and the Soweto Theatre. It was felt that this meeting would be a celebration of the huge importance of theatre for the process of transformation.

The failure of "pure" theatre

However, author and director Paul Mpumelelo Grootboom, who attracted international attention with his *Township Stories*, painted a gloomy picture of the impact of theatre with statements such as "Theatre is not the spirit of our time" and "We exaggerate the power of change through theatre". Ismail Mahomed, is the former artistic director of the famous Grahamstown National Arts Festival and since 2017 CEO of the Market Theatre Johannesburg, applied these sentiments to the nation as a whole, saying that instead of trying to present itself as a cosmopolitan Rainbow Nation, South Africa should focus more on its African origins. Such an argument reeks of the reactionary cultural policy of Robert Mugabe, the dictatorial president of neighbouring Zimbabwe.

The cosmopolitan freedom frenzy of the early post-apartheid years is over; the dream of a tolerant nation that protects every marginalised group has faded, along with the significance of "pure" theatre. Reductions in funding, rigid bureaucracies and structures and dwindling audiences are a reflection of the general sense of pessimism caused by the current situation in South Africa.

In Germany and Europe one should need to keep a close eye on these developments. Like South Africa, Germany and Europe are facing some major social, cultural and intercultural challenges. Theatre can and should address these challenges, rethink traditional structures and turn to different social and cultural groups while avoiding the mistake of simply echoing the ideals and hollow words of leading policy makers, or of trying to make a multicultural society more tangible without daring to present a more asymmetrical view, including representations of the unfamiliar and perhaps even the uncomfortable. The failure of "pure" theatre in South Africa seems to be partly due to the fact that it quickly allowed itself to be taken in by the wishful thinking of the post-apartheid government in a desire to be the location for and the creator of the Rainbow Nation's sense of community.

Applied theatre as a model?

In contrast, there is a much brighter outlook for a theatrical scene that likes to see itself as the opposite of "pure" theatre and indeed is often ignored by it. Remarkably, southern Africa's applied theatre explores the scope and potential of theatre much more deeply. Applied theatre includes projects where theatre is used for specific social, educational or political purposes that are clearly defined in advance. It has a long tradition going back to precolonial times in many parts of Africa. For example, Shona storytelling is consciously used for educational purposes, but the colonial powers also used "theatre for development" to achieve their own objectives, such as teaching agricultural techniques. It was also used to denigrate other ethnic groups and stigmatise them as "in need of development", as implied by the name of this kind of theatre. Applied Theatre is met with a critical eye because the term 'development' – and other concepts connected with it – is deeply implicated in (neo) colonial power structures.

Nevertheless, in the last few years, Applied Theatre and also theatre in education in southern Africa has departed significantly from typical international 'development' strategies, first and foremost in projects realized by local organisations, such as the Amakhosi Theatre in Bulawayo, Zimbabwe, ASSITEJ South Africa and Magnet Theatre in Cape Town. In the *Drama for Life* course at the University of Witwatersrand in Johannesburg, students address their Zulu-Xhosa or Boer past at different performative levels, which is not done without a certain amount of conflict. Projects at the Magnet Theatre in Cape Town help marginalised young people, often refugees from the Republic of the Congo, Zimbabwe or Somalia, to build their self-confidence and express it using the techniques of physical theatre. The approaches adopted by the applied theatre scene in South Africa seem promising because they are suited to a "rainbow" society and emphasise diversity without evoking dichotomous "us and them" stereotypes.

Some of these ideas from South Africa could be taken up in Germany as a way of facing up to some of today's challenges. In these cases, theatre practitioners develop new forms and methods that engage issues of concern to local children and teens and combine radically aesthetic strategies and techniques from different theatrical traditions that could be labelled democratic not in a Western political but rather in a broader social context. As African practitioners are deeply sensitised by the post-colonial discourse, they often detect (hidden) colonial and patriarchal hierarchies, norms and dichotomies with specific vigilance, trying to overcome and deconstruct them. And this seems to be democratic in the truest sense.

With this in mind, one can argue that these innovative techniques in theatre may give important impulses for the European context. In recent times European societies and their school systems are faced with intercultural challenges due to migratory flows, but also 'colonial' mechanisms – such as racism, homophobia and misogyny – have a long tradition in Europe and are still effective. Here, it might be promising to catch impulses from southern Africa and combine traditions of theatre and performance of various cultures without labelling them as 'the own' and 'the other', but rather to use them as a tool of performance techniques, which of course all have strength and weaknesses: For instance, Brazilian Theatre of the Oppressed focuses on marginalized groups but act in a very hierarchal way, American Playback theatre faces the problems of the youth, however, only the actors on stage have a voice to speak, and in German Pedagogical Theatre the role of the facilitator sometimes is quite dominant. In bringing together several of these techniques one can not only open the focus of the participants, but also detect and question dominant, often excluding and marginalizing strategies, provoking and hierarchizing cultural, racial and sexual categorisations and power structures.[1]

Postcolonial critique on intercultural theatre

In the 1990s, Indian theatre practitioner and theoretician Rustom Bharucha examined the causes of the dominance of Western theatre aesthetics vis-a-vis non-European performance traditions. He shows by way of intercultural works from figures like Peter Brooks that these works forced performative traditions of other cultures into a western theatre system, thereby exhibiting or exoticizing them (cf. Bharucha 1993). In "The Dilemma of the African Body as a site of Performance in the Context of Western Training", Samuel Ravengai argues that Western acting methods also reduced the complexity of non-European cultures:

"My hypothesis is that the psycho-technique is a culture-specific system that arose to deal with the heavy realism of Ibsen, Chekhov, Strindberg, Odets and others. I believe that there is a Western realism, which can be differentiated from an African realism. [...] Consequently the psycho-technique tends to favour a Western-groomed body and seems to disorientate any other differently embodied body." (Ravengai 2011: 35-36)

Ravengai criticizes above all the fact that even African acting schools teach an acting technique based exclusively on Stanislavsky's methods, one which conceals or even negates many of the expressive levels of the body, in particular those of African traditions. However, it is not just the dominance of Western theatre on the aesthetic plane that is a concern; the fields of theatre and cultural-management (financing, publicity work, organisation, and evaluation) also contribute to this colonial attitude. This has been frequently overlooked in the recent postcolonial critique of intercultural theatrical and cultural work; despite the fact that Helen Nicholson called attention to it in her book *Applied Drama: The Gift of Theatre* (2005). She argues that goals in the field of international cultural cooperation, such as the "freedom and autonomy of the subject", are fed by romantic notions of the European 18th and 19th centuries, while referring to Enlightenment values as if they were self-evident. As one example of this thesis, she shows that Augusto Boal's "Theatre of the Oppressed", which has been used for decades in intercultural praxis draws chiefly upon Enlightenment concepts: "Boal imbues his spectators with special qualities of creativity,

---

1 | Parts of the following paragraphs are already published in German, see Heinicke, Julius: "Koloniale Fallstricke erkennen und meiden: Perspektiven für die interkulturelle Theaterarbeit von der Finanzierung über die Ästhetik", in: Warstat, Matthias et al. (eds.): *Applied Theatre: Rahmen und Positionen.* Berlin 2017, 111-136.

autonomy, freedom and self-knowledge, and although his language and terminology is often Marxist in tone, it is on this idealist and Enlightenment construction of human nature that Boal depends for his vision of social change." (Nicholson 2005: 117)

This "Enlightenment Construction" emphasizes a universalizing conception of creative work that would be applicable and effective in any social space or culture, one in which artistic creation suffices to create a space for "free," "enlightened" thought. It also prescribes a political direction for cultural projects, one which also corresponds to European values. Nicholson sees here a risk that social, societal and cultural contexts may be downplayed in favour of European-western goals:

"This suggests that an uncritical reading of Boal's theories of creative exchange has the potential to obscure the significance of context to applied drama. It is left to those who use his techniques, therefore, to consider how the creative dialogue enabled by TO (Theatre of the Oppressed) strategies might illuminate different situations. Practitioners with a range of political perspective apply Boal's methods to many different situations and problems, and this means that developing a coherent and creative praxis involves recognising that all dramatic dialogues are not only contextually and contently located but also variously politically situated." (Ibid.: 119)

But it is not only Boal's theatre praxis that tends to simplify complex cultural contexts in favour of a promise of westernizing social-political effects. One should also heed Nicholson's advice with respect to the sponsorship conditions formulated by international cultural institutions like "AktionAfrika" of the German Foreign Office or the Dutch organisation Hivos. In cultural development collaborations, what are financed are above all projects that, even if they don't adopt the vocabulary of the European Enlightenment quite as obviously as Boal does, nonetheless call for development goals derived from "international consensus" and formulate the aims and promises of their work according to Western values. Examples include support for democracy, political enlightenment, the protection of minorities, etc.[2] Cultural projects financed in Africa

---

2 | Although UNESCO emphasizes time and again the equality of cultures, the agenda of the Ministry of the Exterior and the Ministry for international cooperation and development tends to have as its aim that the countries which receive financial assistance from western donors should make "cultural progress" toward democracy and the rule of law. During preliminary talks for the "Zimbabwe Arts Festival Berlin" that the author organized, which was financed by Aktion Africa of the German Foreign Office, precisely these points were addressed prominently.

Nonetheless, Kurt-Jürgen Maaß demands in "Rolle und Bedeutung von AuswärtigerKulturpolitik" less reticence from the Ministry of the Exterior in its use of evaluations.

by German, British or Dutch institutions have as their aim above all the establishment of a Western-democratic canon of values (cf. Heinicke 2013: 49-51). Although all of these sponsorships are for the most part worthy of support, the bold or vehement demand for the realization of the political agenda of the Western world is sometimes counterproductive, because it conceals specific contexts and cultural givens and is thus unable to link up with recent discussions of local context (cf. Warstat/Heinicke 2015: 60-67).

This attitude inherited from the colonial tradition reveals itself not just in financing guidelines; often, it is the leading figures themselves – the directors of the play and production, the organizers, cultural managers and division heads in the cultural institutions – who advance this way of thinking, often unconsciously. They may be fascinated by other countries and cultures, but as many of these projects reveal, their results show mostly forms of exoticism or dominate other cultural texts. This is because they often only possess only rudimentary knowledge – if any – of the political, societal, and cultural backgrounds of the latter, to say nothing of their ability to interpret them.[3] Even the publicity work of intercultural theatrical and project work frequently proclaims on its various platforms (websites, flyers, advertisements, etc.) the social-political aims of the sponsors, and less so the diverse cultural contexts and backgrounds of the potential participants.

The same holds for the evaluation of the projects. The financial situation of many cultural producers and independent theatre organisations in the intercultural context is precarious. Long-term support is rare; generally, those involved swing from one project to another. They commit themselves from the very

---

He argues that this enables international comparisons of German cultural politics, which would allow it to be reviewed. Vera Hennefeld and Reinhard Stockmann also give concrete examples of what a monitoring and evaluation system could look like. However, none of these three figures address the possibility of a "colonial attitude" toward aid-receiving countries in international cultural cooperations. See Maaß, Kurt-Jürgen: "Rolle und Bedeutung von Auswärtiger Kulturpolitik"; Stockmann; Reinhard: "Zur Methodik von Evaluationen in der Kultur und Kulturpolitik" and Hennefeld, Vera: "Zielvereinbarungen und Evaluation als Instrumente zur strategischen Steuerung der Mittelorganisationen in der Auswärtigem Kultur- und Bildungspolitik Deutschlands", in: Hennefeld, Vera/Stockmann, Reinhard: Evaluation in Kultur und Kulturpolitik, Münster 2013, p. 35 – 52, p. 53 – 86 und p. 137 – 162.

3 | Similarly, some reports of students who spent several months in other countries within the framework of the volunteer service "Kulturweit" demonstrate the conviction of German youths that they, although they had only just completed their secondary education, thought they could give all sorts of ideas for "foreign" countries further development, but had themselves never reflected on what they could have learned there from other cultures.

beginning, in their funding applications, to concrete effects, and must deliver results in their concluding reports if they are to receive further funds (cf. Warstat/ Heinicke 2015: 10).The criteria and possible schemas for evaluations in this area are the subject of controversy;1 (cf. Hennefeld/ Stockmann 2013) there are also individual voices that reject evaluation outright (cf. Hentschel 2008: 117-135; Reinwand-Weiss 2013: 111-136). Nonetheless, it is customary for the majority of projects that its social-political effects are discussed (at least in the project report), and one cannot reject out of hand that these, along with the funding guidelines, are oriented toward a canon of Western norms and values.[4]

Impulses from Southern Africa for avoiding colonial snares

In southern Africa there are theatre projects that continually strive to create structures and spaces in which colonial hierarchies disappear. The organisation ASSITEJ South Africa

"aims to promote and foster high quality theatre for children and young people, to raise standards within the industry, to increase access and awareness, to be an advocate for the right of every child to arts education in schools, and to build relationships within the sector locally, nationally, across the continent and globally" (ASSITEJ 2017).

The ASSITEJ Minifest 15 – part of the Harare International Festival of the Arts 2015 – presented two productions – one from Zimbabwe and the other one from South Africa – highlighting the "Rights of the Child" at Reps Theatre Upstairs. As both productions highlight the complex and divers setting of southern Africa theatre in education, I will analyse more deeply two of the plays presented during the festival in the following.

Although the venue, the day and the topic were the same, the aesthetics differ a lot and indicate to the artistic variety of African Theatre in Education and Applied Theatre. The South African production *Ilifa* (*The Inheritance*) stages the journey of the boy Themba extremely artistically designed. On his way looking for the Mzansi Tree, he has been caught by a couple, keeping children prisons to work for them. The storyline combines both African traditional tales and recent politics, also visible in the *mise-en-scène*, linking playing the ngoma (drums) to cause tension with clownish overacting in varying moods. Especially the wicked couple appears as a laughing stock. In doing so,

---

4 | In retrospect, in the concluding report for the German Foreign Office regarding the "Zimbabwe Arts Festival in Berlin", the author himself used unreflectedly slogans like "support for democracy in Zimbabwe" and "strengthening of a regime-critical, democratic public sphere" to discuss the required criteria.

the audience may laugh more about them than being afraid. Certainly, at the end the winners are the children who deliver themselves out of their captivity.

Also the Zimbabwean plays both highlights the rights of the child with current societal challenges. However, the aesthetic differs a lot from the former. *My Right is My Weapon* addresses child abuse claimed by a traditional healer, whom the family father contacted to come out if his non-win situation. Similar to the couple in *Ilifa* the healer was overacted and presented in a very stereotyping way that seems to be problematic in post-colonial patterns but also mirrors the discussions of younger generations in Zimbabwe, who want to distance themselves from spiritual traditions. As opposed to this, the plot is acted in a very realistic way. The play starts with the display of a regular morning routine at school in Zimbabwe. The pupils and the teacher sing the National Anthem; they act as if in real life. Also the ngoma is hidden behind the stage, not to disturb the realistic aesthetic. Even the abuse of the child is being staged in a realistic manner: The father opens his barn door, the girl is crying and weeping [...]. I cannot discuss here, whether this realistic acting makes sense on pedagogical terms. However, this dramaturgy is only one part of the play.

The plot is acted in a very natural way, but the director combined it with a lot of dances and songs, most of them very common in Zimbabwe. This technique looks back to a long tradition and offers a different aesthetical level and realm of experience, where the audience also plays an active part, because they are invited to sing and dance as well. Not only the storyline is acted in a realist mode, also the spectator became part of the "real" dances and songs. The line between reality and fiction seems to dissolve. Nevertheless, it is not possible to simply dismiss that the dances initiate a sphere the dialogues cannot create, but on the other hand, the truth – what happened to the girl – is unearthed in her dialogue with the teacher. In addition, *My Right Is My Weapon* underlines the "reality" of the plot, because due to the censorship and the political control of the public sphere by the government people are only "whispering" in recent Zimbabwe. The fear to speak loudly is especially relevant to children. Using theatrical techniques to unearth a truth against this backdrop seems to be a remarkable act. Both theatre plays not only highlight the variety of artistic and aesthetic techniques used in African Applied Theatre, also it portend to the gesture of current African theatre maker to use and combine various artistic tradition without differentiating them as pre-, post- and colonial. Moreover they argue, all of them are part of their history; so they overcome colonial hierarchies.

Amakhosi Cultural Centre in Zimbabwe between artistic traditions and societal communication

Also the Amakhosi Cultural Centre in Zimbabwe combines various performance techniques and supports marginalized people to find and raise their voice. Many playwrights, directors and spoken word artists learned their trade here at the Centre in Bulawayo. The Cultural Centre is located on the northern border of the city centre, bordering immediately on the township of Makokoba. A short access road leads to a spacious courtyard with trees, closed off by a large, open theatre rotunda, which is always filled with groups of young people, who sit there, discussing and working with one another, performing or dancing. In the theatre building, there are daily training courses in movement, rhythm, karate, music and acting. For these courses, Amakhosi draws upon a wide spectrum of artistic traditions, spanning the entire world. The artistic director Cont Mhalanga always emphasizes that theatre plays a significant role in Africa's history and is thus vital for societal communication:

"The concept is rooted belief that theatre, by its nature, is cultural as it involves song and dance, ceremonial rituals, the society and people and therefore becomes a way of life. It finds support from the fact that the continent of Africa has a long history of sending messages through drama and plays and through theatre performances, the work of African poets and actors has challenged policies and human right abuses." (Mhlanga)

The cultural centre's efforts to use the most diverse practices – borrowed from Ndebele, Shona, English or Chinese traditions – as expressive forms of equal value is remarkable. In a number of projects in which different cultural traditions and performance forms – for example, the Shona ritual dance *zvitamo nengoma* and karate – flowed into one another and were woven together.

Amakhosi's success, however, is founded in large part on the way that the centre organizes its cultural work. The youths there are not told by a director or a sponsor what themes they are to address artistically. Working against the political censorship of the Mugabe regime, which controls large portions of Zimbabwe's public sphere, the Amakhosi attempts to remain one of the last places where the young can develop artistically and express themselves freely (cf. Heinicke 2014: 160-162). This also includes Mhlanga's conscious decision to distance himself from international cultural sponsors, and to only work with local sponsors. He argues that this allows the projects to be developed more independently and freely (cf. Heinicke 2013: 35). Mhlanga too criticizes the relevant political financial support programs of the international donors and the non-sustainable financing of the centre through their project funds.[5]

Magnet Theatre in Cape Town provides professional training for talented youths

Further approaches for the sustainable management of inter- and transcultural projects are developed by Magnet Theatre in Cape Town. The Magnet Theatre, which has been working in the townships of Cape Town for more than 30 years and provides professional training to talented youths, focuses on long-term projects. The South African funding system, which consists of a mixture of private and public funding sources, offers opportunities to secure projects for many years, independently of larger cultural institutions and with relatively little effort spent navigating bureaucratic hurdles. Public sponsorships offer incentives for project development.[6] Then, these projects can apply for long-term financing from the private sector. The youths in the townships frequently possess little formal education, but are of great interest to the labour market. Thus, cultural projects with them are frequently financed by large firms and concerns.

The simple theatre building of the Magnet Theatre is located in the Observatory district, the new centre for art and culture. It stands next to a large parking lot, which is also used as a training space. During my last visit, a number of smaller groups of youths were working there on choreographies meant to portray a short biographical narrative. In a country with eleven national languages – not including the languages of immigrants – placing the focus on bodily representation is understandable. The trainer, Jenny Reznek, challenged the young people from the townships with differing immigration narratives to find gestures in which they could clearly express their story. In order to confront intercultural challenges, it is important for her to first create a space in which individuals with different cultural backgrounds can express themselves on an equal footing with one another. Before the process of reciprocal getting to know one another and negotiating diverse practices and traditions in intercultural

---

5 | In December of 2016, Amakhosi received for its independent cultural work the Prince Claus Award. In contrast to Hivos, also a Dutch funding organisation, the foundation poses no (social-)political conditions regarding the use of its financial means.

6 | Armin Klein also challenges the German-speaking cultural scene to take inspiration from other countries' models, such as the USA, which link together different funding types: Klein, Armin: *Der exzellente Kulturbetrieb*, Wiesbaden 2011 (3. Auflage), p. 207 – 276. Bernhard M. Hoppe and Thomas Heinze also provide suggestions regarding mixed forms of support: Hoppe, Bernhard M./Heinze, Thomas: *Einführung in das Kulturmanagement*, Wiesbaden 2016, p.103 – 146.

theatre can take place, one must have the ability to situate all of these on the same level – without hierarchy or degradation. Political aims and their agenda thus move to the background in Magnet Theatre, in favour of establishing spheres in which individuals with different cultural backgrounds and lifestyles can encounter one another at eye level. Apparently, those cultural projects are successful which do not place the emphasis upon pursuing some sort of inflated political agenda, but rather work in very flat hierarchies without the pressure for socio-political success or evaluation coming from their sponsors. This also makes it easier for the projects to accommodate themselves to the needs of potential participants and to "pick them up" where they happen to be at. Such cultural sensibility and flexibility are essential for the responsible management of intercultural projects.

Coming back to the conference *Theatre in Transformation* mentioned in the beginning, it was made clear a number of times the importance southern African cultural practitioners place upon the transcultural potential of their work. As for instance in the case of South Africa: While the dreams of a Rainbow Nation and its staging in art theatre stand on the verge of failure, the applied art scene in social, therapeutic, and societal contexts is experiencing a proper "boom" (cf. Heinicke 2016: 75-76). This is a result of the fact that societal challenges like refugee movements and migration – thousands of individuals flee from other African countries like Zimbabwe, the Democratic Republic of Congo, and Somalia to South Africa – can be countered with cultural and theatrical work in a number of ways, provided those carrying out this task and their management have been culturally sensitized. Moreover, because of the country's history of apartheid, they take great care to ensure that they do not trip over colonial snares.

Nonetheless, it should not mean to give the impression that there is some sort of schema by which everything European is colonial and everything southern African postcolonial. In Europe too there are a number of theatre forms that are pursuing innovative paths, sponsors who do not create rigid conditions for their support and of course alternative perspective or lifestyles which diverge from the societal norm. But these too, although perhaps not so obviously as in colonial-era Africa, are hindered by the symbolic societal order and its claim to universality, as is clear for example in the debates about gay marriage, blackface and the strengthening of right-wing organisations. At the same time, vast portions of the political elite in South Africa and Zimbabwe behave in a way that is anything but postcolonial. Instead, they formulate claims to power that are strikingly similar to those of former apartheid rulers.

Perspectives for Transcultural Theatre and Artistic Work

Inter- and transcultural challenges are growing across the world. As a result of refugee movements, migration processes and social upheavals, society are confronted with distinct cultural backgrounds and an increasing diversity of lifestyles, but also with tendencies toward partitioning and exclusion. Theatrical and cultural work are used with ever-increasing frequency as promising formats for creating spaces in which cultural diversity and difference can be shown, discussed and lived. As the preceding paragraphs have made clear, African theatrical and cultural artists have been engaging since the very beginning of decolonization with the challenges of cultural diversity, producing promising artistic techniques for intercultural communication. In their projects, many of them pursue an attitude which strives not to generate dichotomous differences between the "own" and the "other", but instead to emphasize that diversity is the symptom of a plural society. In his most recent book, the philosopher and sociologist Achille Mbembe described this approach as "care for the Open" and as a strategy of "unkinning" (désapparentement):

"This question of universal community is therefore by definition posed in terms of how we inhabit the Open, how we care for the Open – which is completely different from an approach that would aim first to enclose, to stay within the enclosure of what we call our own kin. This form of *unkinning* is the opposite of difference." (Mbembe 2017: 183)

Mbembe's understanding of "unkinning" (désapparentement) can also come across as the opposite of assimilation and points the way forward for a kind of artistic and cultural creation that pays tribute to the diversity of traditions and techniques, rather than forcing them into a construct and constraining them. In the artistic works from southern Africa that have been introduced above, an "aesthetics of care for the Open" is at work: in allowing artistic traditions of different cultures to meet one another on eye level, these works show in their artistic expression and their management strategies "care for the Open." The projects at the Amakhosi Theatre in particular show that an "aesthetic of désapparentement" – despite justified reservations about the concept of aesthetics, which is primarily a coinage of western cultural history[7] – may be a promising concept for transcultural theatrical work.

---

7 | Mbembe himself uses the concept of "aesthetics" in the context of artistic production in Africa, but other sources – for example, Rustom Bharucha and Shiva Brakasha – frequently object that aesthetics understands the effectiveness of art above all according to a western canon. Nonetheless, one should also keep in mind that "aesthetics" has also been conceived in diverse ways in European cultural history. See Bharucha, Rustom: Problematising Applied Theatre: A Search for Alternative Para-

For this reason, the Amakhosi Theatre was used as a source of inspiration for a workshop entitled "Creating Transcultural Spaces" that was held at the beginning of the conference "Action Art"[8], hosted by the Zurich Academy for the Arts. The workshop attempted to develop the participant's first conceptualisations for how one could create spaces for aesthetics of care for the Open. The goal was to deliberately create at the beginning of the conference a space for experiencing cultural diversity, since guests from Hong Kong, Indonesia and Ghana were taking part. Some of them have been asked before to present a short gestural sequence with a specific meaning in their culture, without however revealing this meaning. Participants were supposed to practice these short performances and reflect on what significance they ascribed to these gestures. Afterward, they were asked to develop their own, personal gestures, in which they expressed specific feelings like joy, fear, closeness or isolation. They were to present these to one another in groups of two. The requirement was that the reciprocal presentation and combination of gestures first took place nonverbally, followed by the presentation to one another of the respective personal meanings attached to them. Thus, the workshop sharpened their observational capacities with respect to one another and created in a space in which one could first observe others and their modes of expression, then imitate them and combine them with one's own gestures. However, in order to guarantee openness, this process also included phases of mutual reflection. The workshop was the first step in an attempt to create spaces in which diversity could be experienced, and in which tensions and differences between different cultural gestures would not be negated, but rather consciously permitted as part of the diversity of human expression in an "aesthetics of unkinning (désapparentement)."

Mbembe's principle of "care for the Open" can also provide valuable suggestions for the financing, management and evaluation of intercultural cultural projects. The preceding pages have shown that one essential problem lies in the fact that, with respect to the financing, the management and the evaluation of cultural development cooperation, the claim to universality of Western thought

---

digms. *Research in Drama Education: The Journal of Applied Theatre and Performance*, 2011, 3, S. 365-384. Warstat, Matthias/Heinicke, Julius (et al.): *Theater als Intervention: Politiken ästhetischer Praxis*, Berlin 2015, S. 7-24; Kolesch, Doris: Stichwort "Ästhetik", in: Fischer-Lichte, Erika (et al.): *Metzler Lexikon Theatertheorie*, Stuttgart 2014 (2nd Edition).

8 | The workshop was initiated and led by the author, the conference, which took place on the 4th and 5th of May, was conceived of by the project Foa Flux, under the direction of Dominique Lämmli and Annemarie Bucher. It was carried out in cooperation with the following master programs of the Zurich Academy of the Arts: "Transdisciplinary Studies", "Fine Arts", and the program "Connecting Spaces Hong Kong – Zurich."

is hardly questioned. Political demands of European-Occidental provenance, like democracy and the rule of law, are unthinkingly taken up into the agenda of cultural politics and turned into promises for the future. Thus, the political institutions decide not only about the financing, but also about the nature and course of cultural projects. The support, execution and evaluation of art projects in the intercultural context should thus take care that diversity is not destroyed, but rather guaranteed.

The text is a compilation of English language presentation given during the *Theatre in Transformation* Conference and a German article about the *Theatre in Transformation* Conference which was published in the magazine "Theater heute" ("Theatre today"), Berlin 2016.

Bibliography

ASSITEJ South Africa. Available: http://www.assitej.org.za/wmenu.php, Last Access: 6/12/2017.

Bharucha, Rustom (1993): Theatre and the world. Performance and the politics of culture. London, New York: Routledge.

Heinicke, Julius (2013): How to cook a country. Theater in Zimbabwe im politisch-ästhetischen Spannungsfeld. Zugl.: Berlin, Humboldt-Univ., Diss., 2012. Trier: WVT Wissenschaftlicher Verlag Trier (6).

Heinicke, Julius (2014): Performing the Public Sphere. In: KhālidAmīn und George F. Roberson (eds.): Intermediality, performance and the public sphere. Selected papers from recent meetings of the Tangier International Conferences. Denver: Collaborative Media International, International Centre for Performance Studies; in association with Crossroads Institute, Partners for International Collaboration and Education (International collaboration series, North Africa), p. 160-162.

Heinicke, Julius (2015): Zwischen Narrenfreiheit und neokolonialem Protektorat: Zur Frage des Schutzes in Afrikas Applied Theatre. In: Matthias Warstat, Julius Heinicke, Joy Kristin Kalu, Janina Möbius und Natasa Siuzulē (eds.): Theater als Intervention. Politiken ästhetischer Praxis. Berlin: Theater der Zeit (121), p. 60-67.

Heinicke, Julius (2016): Theatre in Transformation: Was Deutschland von Südafrika lernen kann. In: *Theater heute* 5, 2016, p. 75-76.

Hennefeld, Vera; Stockmann, Reinhard (eds.) (2013): Evaluation in Kultur und Kulturpolitik. Eine Bestandsaufnahme. Münster: Waxmann.

Hentschel, Ulrike (2008): Brauchen wir eine Kultur-Pisa? Möglichkeiten und Grenzen der Evaluation ästhetischer Bildung. In: Volker Jurké, Dieter Linck, Joachim Reiss und Matthias Mayer (eds.): Zukunft Schultheater. Das Fach Theater in der Bildungsdebatte. Hamburg: Ed. Körber-Stiftung, p. 117-135.

Mbembe, Achille: Critique of Black Reason, Durham 2017, p. 183, (Emphasis in original).

Mhlanga, Cont: "Theatre for Community Programme", http://www.amakhosi.org. Last Access 8/10/2015.

Nicholson, Helen (2005): Applied drama. The gift of theatre. Basingstoke: Palgrave Macmillan (Theatre and performance practices).

Ravengai, Samuel (2011): The Dilemma of the African body as a site of performance in the context of Western training. In: KenechukwuIgweonu (ed.): Trends in twenty-first century African theatre and performance. Amsterdam, New York, NY, s.l.: International Federation for Theatre Research, p. 35-36.

Reinwand-Weiss, Vanessa-Isabelle (2013): Wirkungsforschung in der Kulturellen Bildung. In: Vera Hennefeld und Reinhard Stockmann (eds.): Evaluation in Kultur und Kulturpolitik. Eine Bestandsaufnahme. Münster: Waxmann, p. 111-136.

Warstat, Matthias; Heinicke, Julius; Kalu, Joy Kristin; Möbius, Janina; Siuzulē, Natasa (eds.) (2015): Theater als Intervention. Politiken ästhetischer Praxis. Theater der Zeit GmbH. Berlin: Theater der Zeit (121).

Cradle of Creativity

Cape Town was the Capital of Theatre for Young Audiences

Wolfgang Schneider

They sing and dance, they scream and gesture, they imagine and defamiliarise, six actors in a piece directed by South African director Neil Copens. And they have something to say. George Orwell's *Animal Farm* creates a special theatre experience somewhere between musical and political thriller, tragic comedy and lecture performance, as it is adapted to a background of African history. It is no longer only about the patriarchal violence of Stalin's times, it is about the abuse of power, corruption and inhumanity in postcolonial Africa. The clichéd uniforms mark the superficial revolutionaries; the dirty scenography marks the fragility of authorities. The tale dating from 1945 and read by generations of school students in the West during the Cold War era, is newly interpreted in a new place. It relates to the disillusionment and disappointment especially of young people in many African countries today. The propaganda that claimed that all humans are equal has proven false. The cynical gang of pigs on stage knows better: some are more equal than others.

In May 2017 Cape Town was at the center of Theatre for Young Audiences, hosting an international theatre festival and the ASSITEJ World Congress which takes place every third year. The International Association of Theatre for Children and Young People renders this possible and the Congress has taken place 13 times in Europe, twice in North America, once in Australia and once in Asia. The 19th World Exhibition of young dramatic arts was hosted in Africa for the first time and the hosts presented a selection of inspiring surprises. Of the 63 shows presented, 29 are South African and of the 28 international performances, 11 have been produced in co-operation with partners from various African countries. Quantity and quality were both equally convincing, the stories staged and their aesthetics were State of the Art.

Far from an idyllic world, the audience was confronted with illusion, inner conflict and apocalypse – produced and presented without infrastructure for production and distribution and without a more than rudimentary system of public funding.

Rights of the Child

Yvette Hardie, president of ASSITEJ and the driving force behind the Congress, therefore does not tire of demanding a revision of cultural policy whenever she speaks in public, whether it be welcoming words, speeches or statements on a podium. Her motto "Cradle of Creativity" refers to the fact that the ten countries with the youngest population are all to be found on the African continent, that more than 40% of the South African population are children and young people, 10% of them are homeless, tenth of thousands HIV positive, many girls victims of rape. In Cape Town, the Convention of the Rights of the Child is a frequently quoted reference.

The right to take part in the arts and culture is also central to an international conference that links several disciplines and all those who do research in the field of Theatre for Young Audiences. Wolfgang Sting, professor of performance studies in Hamburg, Julius Heinicke, professor of applied cultural studies in Coburg as well as Annika Hampel, Katharina Schroeck and Aaron Weigl, all doing research at the University of Hildesheim, were contributors from Germany. Weigl presented his research on cultural education as theatre pedagogy and its implementation in schools and elsewhere. Schroeck discussed a reform of regional networks for presenting theatre in order to ensure access to culture in rural areas and beyond city life. Hampel presented the results of her research on international co-operations and how they can succeed as "Fair Cooperation".

"Youngsters are the future of theatre!"

Intercultural exchange was also at the heart of an artistic platform organized by the Goethe-Institute South Africa. Lien Heidenreich and Francois Venter initiated an exchange of theatre makers from Germany and their potential partners from several African countries. Carla Lever's article sums up some of the participant's insights: Carole Karemara from Ishyo Arts Center in Kigali (Rwanda) and Barbara Koelling (Helios Theater Hamm) presented the co-production *Our House* and summed up the experience: "Of course, homes are like memory: the dark basement is always there. But in Rwanda, our memory is open for all to see: you are never a stranger in your own home. I think the Germans found that an interesting approach." (Lever 2017)

The role of institutions like the Goethe-Institute was also reflected upon. Actor Joshua Alabi from Lagos (Nigeria) thought it "strange" that there had to be an initiative by a foreign institution to "bring African countries closer together". The co-production-platform funded with German tax money, sees the necessity of a dialogue in both directions. Kirstin Hess, Junges Schauspielhaus Duesseldorf, has experienced this in the process of co-producing the

German-Nigerian production *Obisike*: "Our audiences are always very diverse, but our actors are much less so. When we performed our co-production, one little girl spontaneously shouted 'AFRICA!' – She was so happy to see herself represented on a German stage. This might be why we do this whole thing."

For ten days, Cape Town was the Capital of Theatre for Young Audiences and from Germany alone there were more than 60 delegates and artists present. ASSITEJ as a worldwide network, active in more than 90 countries all over the world, has shown how influential the performing arts can be, how co-producing is a two-way-communication where all involved benefit and how all this contributes to the development of TYA. Against this backdrop, the African Independent's headline can only be confirmed: "Youngsters are the future of theatre!" (Mohlomi 2017).

Translated into English by Meike Fechner.

The text was first published in German in the magazine "Politik&Kultur" ("Politics&Culture"), Regensburg 2017.

Bibliography

Lever, Carla (2017): Creativity Without Borders: a Perspective on the Goethe Coproduction Platform. In: *IXYPSILONZETT. Das Magazin für Kinder- und Jugendtheater* (English – not yet published) (2), p. 15-17.

Mohlomi, Setumo-Thebe (2017): Youngsters are the future of theatre. African Independent. Available: https://www.africanindy.com/culture/youngsters-are-the-future-of-theatre-9204349, Last Access: 3/8/2018.

Who's saying what about whom?

South Africa's next generation is on a quest for its own identity

Theresa Frey, Petra Jeroma and Johanna Kraft

"There are very few occasions that the South African leadership of theatre is in one room. You know most of the time when you find [this] is when you are in Europe [...]. And again today Europe has brought the leadership of the South African theatre together in this room. And so you ask yourselves, what has really transformed? So as we talk about this issue of transformation those are some of the issues that we must really engage. Who is really telling our [South African] narratives and how do we want our narratives to be told?" (Sekhabi 2016)

These were the words with which Aubrey Sekhabi, Artistic Director of the State Theatre in Pretoria, opened the *Theatre in Transformation* conference. He immediately addressed one of the key questions of post-apartheid South Africa: How are South African narratives being told? *Who* is saying *what* and from *which perspective?* Sekhabi's words highlight South Africa's desire for its own narrative, one that is detached from the colonial and post-colonial attributions of others. So it is all the more important to ask: who we are, the writers of this article?

Our four-month internship at ASSITEJ South Africa (the South African branch of the International Association of Theatre for Children and Young People) provided us with valuable insights into the South African theatre scene. We watched numerous productions, talked to their creators and audiences and experienced how all kinds of different people are working together to give young people access to art and creativity. We spent time in Cape Town, Johannesburg, Pretoria and rural areas, particularly two villages in Hammanskraal.

This article looks at the contemporary theatre landscape for young audiences, supplemented by observations and quotations from the *Theatre in Transformation* conference. When reading this article, we hope you will join us in considering what problems – but perhaps also what opportunities – arise from taking this outsiders' view?

Creating opportunities: a social component of contemporary theatre

The end of apartheid in 1994 ushered in a period of hope in South Africa. The Rainbow Nation, with one of the most tolerant constitutions in the world, was convinced that it could quickly dismantle the legacy of apartheid. Today it is clear that racist and/or corrupt structures are far from being dismantled, but are being constantly reproduced. The legacy of apartheid, which oppressed whole sections of the population for decades, is now expressed in extreme income inequality and people who still live in segregated areas. Many Blacks still live in remote townships, often with no running water and with poor access to the cities. Most children and young people have limited cultural and educational opportunities. At the same time, the art and culture of the townships remains invisible to the rest of the population, who rarely visit the townships. Ismail Mahomed (Chief Executive Officer of the Market Theatre in Johannesburg and Artistic Director of the National Art Festival from 2008-2016) describes this structural separation as "the ghettorization of the arts".

How do people involved in contemporary theatre for young audiences tackle these circumstances and challenges? How does it affect their theatre practice? And what social and political demands are placed on them (including with regard to cultural policy)?

Few props, everyday clothes plus one or two costume parts, self-written scripts that deal with people's everyday concerns – family, love, violence, alcohol addiction. In Hammanskraal, theatre is a simple affair. It plays out in semi-closed and open air venues; one of which is a homemade wooden stage at Othampo Drama School in Kekana Gardens, as well as open ground in Marokolong village. "Besides drama, I also teach these young stars script writing for radio and TV and theatre performance. My aim is to make sure that they reach their dreams and I want to create job opportunities in the performing arts industry." (Sibanyoni 2012) This is how founder Buti Morake stresses the importance of theatre for young people in rural areas. In Hammanskraal, theatre opens up new perspectives. This was Buti Morake's belief until he was killed in 2017 at his hometown, Leboneng, Hammanskraal (cf. Masilela 2016: 8).

Who is doing the talking? Language creates identity

The productions in Hammanskraal were in the local languages. But this is not always the case in multilingual South Africa. For a long time, English was the dominant language also in the theatre space, but it is changing. One example is *Phefumla (Breathe)*, produced by director Thando Doni together with four former prison inmates from various townships outside Cape Town. *Phefumla* is a multilingual production. The performers switch between English and isiXhosa. The use of the two languages mainly has an artistic purpose; it is not merely for translation. Besides the strongly physical and narrative influence, the specific use of language is a fundamental feature of contemporary theatre for young audiences in South Africa. Young South Africans speak one of the country's eleven official national languages. They often only learn English at school, but it remains the dominant language in education and working life. This means that the majority of South Africans do not use their mother tongue in their day-to-day lives. Warren Nebe, founder and director of *Drama for Life* at the University of the Witwatersrand in Johannesburg, describes this as a process of dehumanisation. The dominance of the English language leads to dual identities that can be compared to schizophrenia. Living in a country where your mother tongue is not the dominant language leads to communication problems that are more than just linguistic. For many people, it restricts their freedom and ability to express themselves and makes it more difficult to access cultural and educational programmes.

Nebe's colleague Faith Busika, whose mother tongue is isiXhosa, tackles this problem by using traditional Xhosa narrative methods in her theatre work. In this way, she is trying to involve children and young people more directly; to capture and reproduce their stories without a filter. She repeatedly calls for a critical questioning of the responsibility that lies behind creating art and whether young people are really perceived and taken seriously: "Are we really allowing the voices of the children and the youth to come out? Yes, we're provoking their thinking, asking them certain questions and showing certain scenes. But are we really allowing them to use their own voices?" Above all, this applies to community theatre, which works with young people in the townships. After so many years of being defined *as something* by others, from the outside, it is now time for South Africans to define *themselves*. The use of different languages on stage helps to build South Africa's cultural identities.

No red curtain on the loamy floor

After the performances in Kekana Gardens, Hammanskraal, we talk to the players. They apologise, saying the place isn't really a theatre. It doesn't have a proper stage, a red curtain or a set of spotlights. We feel quite upset. To us, this place, with its beaten earth floor and the dust that glistens in the bright midday sun, seems too romantic and peaceful. But the young people who grew up here see it as a symbol of their poverty.

The image of theatre that prevails in South Africa also shapes its artistic education – and vice versa. They are both largely a legacy of colonial structures. The representative of the National Department of Arts and Culture, Mpho Molepo, is critical of the fact that European content and values continue to shape the education system: "So the outcome of the students at the moment is an Euro-trained Black artist whose interpretations and references are based somewhere else in some book in Europe." The cultural identity of young South Africans is a mixed identity, mainly drawn from a range of traditional South African and Western influences. He calls for greater diversity and the inclusion of other cultures and traditions in education.

Janine Lewis, theatre lecturer at Tshwane University of Technology, believes the potential for change in South Africa lies with her students themselves. They are "the next generation of theatre" and have to learn to tell their own stories – beginning with each and every one of them. Nebe also sees this as a tool of decolonisation. The play no longer revolves around the words written by a British author but around the personalities of the performers themselves.

Yvette Hardie, President of ASSITEJ South Africa, addresses the subject of children's and youth theatre in South Africa. Looking back over the past ten years, she says that the theatre landscape of children's and young people's theatre was a divided field when ASSITEJ South Africa was set up in 2007. On the one side was commercial children's theatre with Disney aesthetics, far removed from any South African context, while on the other side, theatre was a learning tool with its index finger raised. The reason for this remains today – financial dependence on government funding programmes, which pre-scribe specific topics and thus prevent the free development of theatre makers. Many theatre projects have an educational purpose but little artistic ambition: "Theatre for young audiences often becomes a bad version of teaching. It takes all the worst attributes of a teacher that you can imagine and puts them into a theatre piece." (Hardie 2016)

Transformation processes in South African TYA

To counteract this and promote high-quality artistic theatre for young audi-ences, ASSITEJ has established specific support programmes such as *The-atre4Youth* and *Inspiring a Generation*. These programmes help young groups, playwrights, directors and actors to learn their trade with the aid of workshops, mentoring and liaison with schools and festivals. At the same time, projects such as *Kickstarter* are working with teachers to anchor theatre and drama studies firmly in the school curriculum, even in remote regions.

TAAC (Theatre Arts Admin Collective) is a key partner in Cape Town. Together with ASSITEJ Cape Town, it organises the Obs Family Festival and every year shows many new productions by young theatre makers. The Zabalaza Festival, hosted by the Baxter Theatre in Cape Town, also serves as an important platform and springboard for up-and-coming artists from the Cape Town townships. This gives theatre makers from the townships an opportunity to present their work in more mainstream venues in an attempt to counter "the ghettorization of the arts", at least to some extent.

These platforms provide a stage for different cultural identities and the performers can focus on topics with personal relevance. We were struck by the way audiences are still segregated. At the Afrikaans Festival KKNK in Oudtshoorn we were surrounded by an almost exclusively White audience. When we attended the Zabalaza performances, we were the only Whites there. Sekhabi comments: "Afrikaans-speaking people are just going to go to an Afrikaans play. You gonna find a few White people that are coming to see Black art. Same as you gonna find very few Black people that are going to see [White art]. So it's a divided audience and this is the legacy." (Sekhabi 2016)

Contemporary theatre for young audiences in South Africa affords different cultures equal respect and appreciation. It displays social and political relevance by addressing people's keen desire to speak their own language and present their own culture and stories, both thematically and structurally. Perhaps this is precisely where the potential of young people's active participation in cultural life lies. Now they have their own voice and can create a mix of traditional and modern art forms. It is important to prevent a return to the segregation of apartheid while promoting and strengthening the cultures that have been oppressed. Enabling diversity on stage must also entail a focus on audience diversity. Children's and young people's theatre has the task of representing the diversity of people and cultures in South Africa and strengthening their cultural identities – not only on the stage: "What we need is to invite children to give their own interpretation of things, bring their own stories, bring their own experiences and then find a way to empower these." (Hardie 2016)

Translated into English by Gill McKay.

Unless otherwise referenced, quotes are taken from panel discussions at the *Theatre in Transformation* conference held in Pretoria form 11 – 13 March 2016.

Bibliography

Masilela, Thapelo (2016): Versatile dramatist laid to rest. In: Sosh Times, p. 8. Available: http://www.soshtimes.co.za/.

Sibanyoni, T. (2012). The beat. Available: http://thebeat.linmedia.co.za/articles/news/14274/2012-08-03/drama-school-now-in-bela-bela, Last Access: 12/5/2018.

Township Theatre Making

An Ethnographic Study about a Developmental Tool
for Khayelitsha Youth

Ongezwa Mbele

In 2013, I worked with a Khayelitsha[1] theatre youth group called *Qina n Divas* to embark my research project. In this study, all members of *Qina n Divas* are referred to by a pseudonym, in place of their given name, so that the reader is clear about when I am referring to a member of the group. From here onwards, I will refer to *Qina n Divas* collectively as youth. The work process with the youth was for three months. The study was ethnographic[2] in that in the duration of the fieldwork, I stayed with my aunt in Khayelitsha. However, I have unresolved thoughts about the study being framed within ethnography because I share values, cultural practices and ways of understanding with the Khayelitsha community. I therefore do believe that the study cannot be considered entirely ethnographic, but can be also viewed as a community member's reflection and engagement on how township young people navigate theatre as a form of resistances from the inherent and ongoing injustices in embedded within the structures of the township.

The youth and I met after school at 16h00 in a shipping container located in Ntoshi's backyard. During the day, Ntoshiran a crèche in the container. The youth's theatre making encompassed, singing, improvisation, contemporary, Tswana and Xhosa cultural dances and various songs. They used minimal props. When I wrote my thesis about the work with the youth, I proposed that

---

1 | Machapondwa (2010: 334) draws upon (Ndingaye 2005, Maverick 358 cc 2006, Médecins Sans Frontières 2010) who describe Khayelitsha as one of the largest townships that is an impoverished area, which was created in 1985 during the apartheid era for Black people.

2 | "Ethnography is interested in the realm of ordinary life, which portrays the experience of particular subjectivities and their identities within scales of organization and historic events." (Marcus 2007: 1130)

Khayelitsha youth use township theatre as a youth developmental[3] tool. The young people engage with each other to create, discuss and review their realities of living and growing up in Khayelitsha.

The South Africa theatre making scene consists of township young people that make theatre and participate in various theatre festivals. As a South African theatre community member, I have observed that township young people's theatre work at times seeks to identify and address the problems in their communities. These problems range from violence, governmental issues, human immune deficiency virus (HIV) and drugs. Mattes states that many young Black South Africans born post-apartheid still face almost insurmountable hurdles to securing decent education, housing, health and a decent quality of life. The intersection of poverty, corrupt governance structures and the devastating impacts of the HIV epidemic have impacted on the life span and prospects of an entire generation (cf. Mattes 2012: 140). This complex unjustly existence for young people is inherent from apartheid and sustained through South Africa's capitalist and neoliberal systems. Thus, to an extent, theatre enables the youth to resist the socio-political and economic challenges that attempt to stifle their development.

Youth development is a study of the human developmental processes that identifies and discusses the social, political and economic systems that shape and influence the lifespan of young people. In the case of the youth, the theatre provided them with an opportunity to rehearse how to negotiate their realities of Khayelitsha. These were their relationship with their parents, guardians and peers. Boal states that in *theatre of the oppressed*, the theatre participant is the subject. The participants' abilities to improvise enable them to use their human ability and experience to create and review stories which are inform by their reality. This process allows the participants to attempt to imagine and offer new possibilities to their reality through their theatrical choices (cf. Boal 1995: xx-xxi). Even though, the youth didn't overtly embark on theatre of oppressed techniques, making theatre offered them a moment to explore and attempt to imagine possibilities about their lived realities.

---

3 | The study of youth development seems pertinent in psychology and sociology discourse. Psychology theorists Urie Bronfenbrenner and Pamela Morris, youth development can be viewed through the ecological system theory, which means that is a human development process which takes place within a relevant and conditions (Bronfenbrenner, U.; Morris P. 1998: 993).

Township theatre is the hope

The youth's ability to imagine and tell their stories can conjure hope for them. Morris states that township dwellers enjoy watching theatre and making theatre. Traditional ceremonies such as funerals consist of poetry, dancing and singing. This participation of township people leads them to believe that performativity is a revolutionary act for their lives (cf. Morris 2013: 7). Morris's account implies that theatre making and performing elements in traditional ceremonies have commonalities, which provide a rehearsal for change and urgency for the township people. This perceived revolutionary act of theatre is the hope.

The young people informed me that they participated in theatre making to stay away from the streets of Khayelitsha, teenage pregnancy and gangster activities. The young people said the streets were dangerous for them. Participation in dangerous activities was influence by peer-pressure. It seemed that theatre became a prevention tool and 'safe' space for them. "However, despite the absence of infrastructural amenities and financial backing, theatre in the townships continues to thrive, impelled by its determined practitioners." (Morris 2017: 146) The youth's use of shipping container was not only a creative choice, but it was a means of survival. The youth's ability to organize themselves and use their imagination is not a means of glorifying their oppression entrenched township existence, but to acknowledge their theatre making is a resistance to the spatial oppression.

Inception of theatre making

The young people would start their rehearsal exploration day with a prayer led by one person as we held each other's hands while we stood in a circle. The prayer was about gratitude and well wishes for the day's rehearsal. I have never asked the youth why they chose prayer as a starting point. The prayer indicated preparation, cultural or religious practice for transcending into this theatre space or practice of theatre making.

In the first week of working with the youth, I played games with the youth so as to get closer to know them and know them better. For instance, I asked them to mime their daily duties. This was done with the group while I am standing in a circle and miming the daily duties. The aim was to be introduced to the youth and also use what they showcased to formulate and plan theatre exercises that were relevant to the youth. The outcomes of miming varied for everyone. Sisi, mimed drinking alcohol at a shebeen and a friend convincing them to join a theatre group. Athandwa, mimed a classroom sitting on a desk and writing something in a book. One person mimed learning their lines for a play. Nosipho mimed washing and drying the dishes. I mimed reading a book.

The youth showed courage and vulnerability in coming to the centre of the circle sharing their daily duties. The daily activities indicated that the young people have fun in their lives. They also engaged in responsible activities by going to school and helping with chores at home. Some of them showed moments where they changed their behaviour with having peers that influenced them to change their behaviour. This microscope view of the young people would be the through line of us working together.

Rehearsing culture

I attempted to facilitate the youth in improvising scenes with the intention that the scenes would form a play that we would present for my Master's research project. However, the youth had performance calls that required us to stop the improvising scenes. The two performance calls were performing dance in a birthday party and showcasing choral music at a community event. The dance performance which gave them remuneration and music performance in which their received musical instruments as a prize. The youth started to rehearse contemporary and Xhosa, Tswana cultural dancing. They asked me to give them feedback on their rehearsals. "Cultures, according to Victor Turner, are most fully expressed and made conscious of themselves through their rituals and theatrical performances." (Okagbue 2007: 3) The youth rehearsed and affirmed their various South African cultures in their performances, which offered them to practice their cultural identity. The performance venue was in the suburbs of Goodwood. The youth's ability to perform in the suburbs navigated the inherit apartheid spatial injustices. The youth also engaged with lucrative opportunities and healthy performance competition, which contributed in their growth process of responsibility and achieving a task of performance. This process highlighted that youth's theatre making became business opportunities and they could engage in positive activities.

The challenging moment

After the performance at the birthday party, the youth and I continued to rehearse for my Master's research play. Sipho, one of the young people, wanted us to make a play about the subject of rape. I found this challenging because I did not have the skills and confident to handle any repercussion the play might bring during the rehearsal process. I consulted with my supervisor Gay Morris about this challenge. She suggested that I offered the youth a script. I chose to offer them a script by Gcina Mhlophe called *Have you seen Zandile?*[4]. I nego-

---

4 | Gcina Mhlophe's 1986 play *Have You Seen Zandile?* is the story of a young South African girl kidnapped by her estranged mother and separated from her loving grand-

tiated with the youth to assemble previous performances such as the dances, singing, unfinished improvised scenes within improvising scenarios of the play. For instance, the classroom scene in Zandile was drawn from Athandwa's mime of being in the classroom, when she had portrayed her daily duty. Zandile's grandmother's character was played by a boy who went to the school and around the neighbourhood to look and call for Zandile. Abhuti who played the grandmother's character, showcased the character with slow walk. We decided to make him wear a headwrap to enhance the grandmother character. The neighbourhood was represented with a tableau in the form of window frames. This was done with the youth's arms on the side of their faces. The youth decided to set the play within Khayelitsha. The youth ended the play with a dance performance, which was the dance they had performed at the birthday party. The songs that the youth had sung for their singing competition were rendered in the play to enhance the mood or indicate scene changes. The youth performed the adaptation of *Have you Seen Zandile?* at the Masibambisane theatre youth festival[5] at the Baxter theatre[6].

Theatre is embodied

The youth improvised using their bodies and cognitive abilities. The body became a resource of rehearsing and investing their development through theatre making.

"The first principle Boal articulates is that the human being is a unity, an indivisible whole. Ideas, emotions, sensations and actions are interwoven. A bodily movement is a thought and a thought expresses itself through body." (Linds 1998: 73)The young people's bodies that were immersed through theatre enabled them to create characters, stories and images through imagination, decision making and thinking and reflecting about their realities. The body as a resource afforded the young people to engage cost effective means of making theatre. This addressed youth's challenges of financial resources. The young

---

mother, and is based on the playwright's own childhood experiences. (cf. Delisle 2006: 387)

5 | Masibambisane Festival was a festival run by "Masibambisane youth organization that opens opportunities for the young people who are interested in Art and Cultural Activities." (Mbele 2015: 3)

6 | The Baxter Theatre Centre is a vibrant, multicultural entertainment hub in the Southern Suburbs of Cape Town. Nestled under the striking Devil's Peak Mountain and at the foot of the University of Cape Town, the Baxter boasts a world-class theatre and concert hall, as well as a studio stage, rehearsal rooms, offices, a restaurant and bars and an impressive spacious foyer. (http://www.baxter.co.za/about/about-us/)

people's means to gain profit from their theatre making displays entrepreneurship thinking and skills, which can be an attempt to alleviate their poverty.

Theatre making enables the youth to engage in decision making about characters, storyline and themes. This displayed that the youth were concerned about their future and made an effort to engage with a theatre practice and community. They were contributors to the South African theatre making. This reveals that the young people can contribute to the macro systems, by engaging in decision about their future. "Youth opinion must be invited and allowed to shape the policy and intervention plans. This is vital in South Africa with its history of indifference to youth opinion." (Theron 2007: 373) This is a positive outcome of youth development, which can encourage responsibility, harness negotiating skills and active citizenship amongst the youth.

Community building

The youth of Khayelitsha taught me theatre that serves young people and engages relationships. I still communicate with the various youth members. The reflexivity process of the work with the youth is ongoing for me. Our partnership affirmed that theatre was revolutionary in that it offerseach young person the opportunity to dream and imagine himself or herself into existence with his or her own body and cognitive ability. The youth unconsciously and consciously use theatre to negotiate their realities.

This paper attempts to unpack and reflect on my Master's applied theatre fieldwork project.

Bibliography

Baxter Theatre Centre. Available: http://www.baxter.co.za/2017, Last Access: 1/7/2017.

Boal, Augusto (1995): The rainbow of desire. The Boal method of theatre and therapy. London, New York: Routledge.

Delisle, Jennifer (2006): Finding the Future in the Past: Nostalgia and Community-Building in Mhlophe's Have You Seen Zandile? In: *Journal of Southern African Studies* 32 (2), p. 387-401.

Linds, Warren (1998): A journey in metaxis: theatre of the oppressed as enactivist praxis. In: *NADIE Journal 22.2*, p. 71-86.

Marcus, G.E (2007): Ethnography two decades after writing culture: From the experimental to the baroque. In: *Anthropological Quarterly* (Vol 80, Fall 2007), p. 133-153.

Mattes, Robert (2012): The 'Born Frees': The Prospects for Generational Change in Post-apartheid South Africa. In: *Australian Journal of Political Science* 47 (1), p. 133-153.

Mbele, Ongezwa: Township theatre-making as a developmental tool for Khayelitsha youth: an applied theatre study from an ethnographic perspective. Dissertation. University of Cape Town, Cape Town.

Morris, Gay (2013): Flexible weaving: investigating the teaching and learning opportunities in the practices of theatre-makers and performers from selected townships in Cape Town. In: *Research in Drama Education: The Journal of Applied Theatre and Performance* 18 (1), p. 4-24.

Morris, Gay (2017): Dinosaurs Become Birds: Changing Cultural Values in Cape Town Theatre. In: *Theatre Research International* 42 (02), p. 146-162.

Muchapondwa, E., (2010): A cost-effectiveness analysis of options for reducing pollution in Khayelitsha township, South Africa. TD: The Journal for Transdisciplinary Research in Southern Africa, 6 (2), pp. 333-358.

Okagbue, Osita (2013): African Theatres & Performances. Hoboken: Taylor and Francis (Theatres of the world).

Theron, Linda C. (2007): Uphenyongokwazikwentshayasemalokishiniukum elananesimoesinzima: a South African study of resilience among township youth. In: *Child and adolescent psychiatric clinics of North America* 16 (2), 357-75, ix.

**Freedom of Expression.
Perspectives on the Performing Arts**

From "Playing" to "Working"

Arresting systemic labour regression in the creative economy of Theatre in South Africa

Motsumi Makhene

The International Federation of Actors (FIA), in articulating policy on the Status of Artists, asserts that

"What defines the status of artists is the consideration that society holds them in and the recognition by society of the liberties and rights, including moral, economic and social rights, with particular reference to income and social security, which artists should enjoy." (FIA 2014)

For the South African artists, particularly the performer, the liberties, rights and privileges expressed may be defined as luxuries in the context of the progressive decline of the artist from being a 'cultural worker' to an 'independent contractor.'

As a contractor, the artist has no recognition under the country's comprehensive and constitutionally robust Labour Relations Act (LRA). The contractor is a trader who provides products and services to willing buyers on the basis of a civil contract, devoid of work rights, protection of intellectual property or social security. That is why in 2015, the de-registered Creative Workers Union of South Africa (CWUSA), then affiliated to the federation, the Congress of South African Trade Unions (COSATU), began to 'regroup' towards the re-establishment of the minimum status of the protection artists' rights and the promotion of their economic interests. Noting at the time that there existed no policy and legal framework for the protection of creative workers, apart from the dated Copyright Law as amended and poorly implemented, in line with the much lauded post-apartheid Constitution of the Republic of South Africa. CWUSA in turn lost a war of recognition by the Department of Labour. Thus there is no 'measure' of fairness to define, protect or promote the interests and welfare of

South African cultural workers other than the Copyright Law of South Africa and its weak attendant institutions.

When FIA regards as a minimum 'measure' of fairness, the "upholding freedom of expression and association; promoting education and training in all artistic disciplines, as well as contract, social, tax, intellectual property laws and regulations that are tailored to the atypical and intermittent nature of their work" (ibid.).

Even after two attempts to define creative work as 'atypical' due to its seasonal or project nature, creative work and its requirements for the protection of practitioners' rights continues to elude policy makers and legislators. The closest attempt was in 2003 when the understanding of 'the atypical and intermittent nature of (artistic) work' could make sense in the agriculture and domestic work occupations, and by extension, perhaps to benefit creative workers. But the challenge proved greater than anticipated, as the problem of resolving 'atypical' work unearthed deep structural labour inequalities and injustices inherited from the previous apartheid political economy.

The struggle for legal recognition of artists' formations is less about legal provisions and protection of a dying class of unemployable theatre practitioners. This dying class of theatre practitioners of forty to seventy years represents one of the two main streams of apartheid theatre experience. One is the main stream 'theatre of privilege,' has produced by state theatres (city, provincial and national) and various commercial enterprises, emulating the Broadway traditional influences and/or venturing into the theatre worlds of Grotowski and Kafka. The other is the world of the theatre of resistance and development, whose social commentary and mobilisation asserted the need for the promotion of new forms of theatrical expression. Township-based theatre that expresses emerging urban Black experience of cultural fusions of rural-urban languages, social prisms and individual aspirations that produced a community of theatre activists of the working class that formed the first artist unions to promote institutional transformation and mitigate marginalisation. Progressively, the theatre of resistance movement was overshadowed by the euphoria of the post-liberation era and the consolidation of the Americanisation of South African theatre.

Creative Industry Employment

In the 2003, the National Institute for Economic Policy (NIEP) concludes that 'casualisation' and 'externalisation' of labour in the post-apartheid South Africa, constitutes the institutionalisation of apartheid political economy and labour patterns that consolidate labour marginalisation and exposure to unjust labour practices. NIEP observes that

"A broad finding of the study was that there were only certain categories in which casualisation had increased, in the period from 1999 to 2003. In other categories it had
declined. As one would expect, females, Africans and Coloureds were significantly
less likely to be in 'typical'yor standard employment compared to whites and males...
Similarly, highly skilled workers are more likely to be 'typically'yemployed than skilled
workers. Unskilled workers are less likely to be 'typically'yemployed." (NIEP 2003)

The gravity of this labour dispensation lies in the further observation by the
NIEP that

"Perhaps the most robust finding concerns the increase in self-employment, in both
the formal and informal economies. In particular, there was a consistent increase in the
number of unskilled workers who were self-employed in the informal economy across a
four-year period, from 1999 to 2001. The number of informal, self-employed persons
in agriculture also increased significantly over the same period. It is also of interest
that the number of skilled and highly-skilled workers is increasing, whilst the number of
unskilled workers is remaining constant but is being displaced from formal to informal
employment. There is also an increase in the number of home workers from 460 000
to 520 000 between 2000 and 2002 (although the increase is not consistent)." (Ibid.)

Underlying these observations is the lack of awareness and omission of reference to the arts as an economic sector. This includes the recognition of the
skilled and high skilled nature of artistic practice, the unknown growth of
creative workers as a result of youth participation and the serious social impact
of unemployment on artists as a result of the non-provision of the Unemployment Insurance Fund (UIF), as demonstrated in the negative impact of the post
2008 collapse of the global economy. This exposed the stark social security vul-
nerabilities of arts practitioners at all levels, particularly Black creative workers.
The extent of equity deficit for the historically marginalised is illustrated by
NIEP's recommendation that was short of relevance, that the 'atypical employment' scenario as researched "Suggests re-training programmes to assist
informal, unskilled workers get into formal employment. It also suggests that
the employment of females, Africans and Coloureds be incentivised, to address
their apparent disadvantage in securing standard employment." (Ibid.)
    Not only does this scenario exclude artists in related creative industries, it
also highlights that South Africa does not have the creative industries as a non
designated economic indicator to track the employment of artists, reinforcing
their lack of labour status in the Department of Labour.
    To compound the picture, South Africa's unemployment rate increased to
24.9% in 2009 and progressively grew to 26.7% in June 2016, representing an
estimated 5.7 million workers (Stats SA). In the labour monitoring system, the

creative industries and its workers remain invisible and even their social and development impact progressively less palpable.

The Imperative to act

Mabutho "Kid" Sithole, the former CWUSA President of and champion of the effort to remobilise creative workers to regroup and lead the transformation of South Africa's creative industry, asserts that artists must insist on being:

"Referred to as cultural workers and not celebrities, because I can't be seen to be celebrating poverty...We tend to take for granted that we are not working. Often I hear artists saying that 'siyadlalae Market Theatre. Si-'a-dla-la (We-are-PLAYING)'. When the stage is actually a workplace and many people have taken advantage of that. My wish for theatre is that all of us who are practitioners must understand that when you strum your guitar, when you pound your drum, when you take to your flute or saxophone, when you take to the script and run your lines, you are on duty. There is no difference from a person who is a teacher in classroom, as a policeman in a police station and so on. My wish is for young who are here to become change agents in this regard." (Sithole 2016)

The imperative to act was triggered in late 2015 by the outrageous prospect of the Sarah Baartman Story; a complex epic and extremely sensitive colonial story that was announced to be filmed by American producers. To crown it all, the lead actor and co-writer was to be none but the multi-award American musician, Beyoncé Knowles. This prospect triggered a local radio public debate on the SABC's SAFM, but also highlighted a plethora of issues that remain 'under the carpet' as the crises in the South African cultural and creative industries quietly deepens. The Sarah Baartman Story triggered three core policy issues, that reminded practitioners of unresolved matters of cultural and economic justice: (1) the appropriation of Sarah Baartman as one of South Africa's indigenous icons, testing the Protection, Promotion, Development and Management of Indigenous Knowledge Systems Bill currently under discussion, particularly from the question of who should own indigenous Intellectual Property and/or fictionalise heritage resources?; (2) the local content regulation debate since the mid-nineties, as a measure of who controls access to live and audio-visual media experience and therefore employment opportunities and the dominant cultural narrative, in spite of South Africa being signatory to various cultural conventions for cultural diversity, rights protection, heritage promotion and social justice; (3) the defunct Artists Work Permit Committee of the Department of Home Affairs that regulated access to local employment markets by international artists and producers, particularly the export of rands that resulted from lucrative theatre circuits and festivals following the impact of the lifting of the then Cultural Boycott on South Africa.

The call, led by Sithole, assembled an Artists Caucus of experienced and seasoned practitioners, including leading actors (e.g. John Kani and Owen Sejake), musicians (Sibongile Khumalo) and promoters, which had a series of workshops to define and analyse root causes, from policy gaps, poor solidarity formations and to weak institutions in the current political economy. The goal was to organise a national convention on the creative industry involving stakeholders and leaders of arts practitioners, industry and government to build consensus on the transformation of South Africa's nascent creative economy on the basis of a comprehensive Industry Charter. The convention would define the industry transformation agenda to achieve a move away from

"a celebrity and awards culture that derails creative arts leadership to focus on individual wants and interests – creating a vacuum of solidarity that renders young artists vulnerable to exploitation and seasoned practitioners marginalised. We are here to shape a compelling business case for change from being marginalised to being central to economic change and social development." (Ibid.)

The then newly elected FIA President, Ferne Downey, a Canadian actress, expressed the view that

"It's quite a journey that we undergo individually as artists. As performers we share many challenges because the life of an artist is never an easy path. It's a precarious career filled with uncertain work opportunities and fluctuating pay-cheques; it's built on taking risks, embracing change and reinventing oneself. Despite our contribution to our cultures, societies and economies, too many of us are forced to work in despicable working conditions, to fight for the recognition of our social status and the respect of our core labour rights. I am privileged to have a strong union behind me; fighting for my rights and helping me make an honest living from my work. As the President of FIA, it will be my mission to ensure that other fellow performers may equally rely on solid unions to protect their legitimate rights in the workplace." (FIA 2012)

Although FIA has been at the forefront of this global recognition and strongly campaigned with sister organisations in the early 80's (including the participation of South Africa's Performing Arts Workers Equity [PAWE]) for the adoption of the UNESCO's recommendations concerning the Status of the Artist. This document is still very relevant today, despite the years, as few countries have taken comprehensive steps so far to acknowledge the role of creative workers in society other than with statements of principle (cf. FIA 2016), and although the PAWE signed milestone agreement with the SABC, as a public broadcaster, on performers rights in the 1990s and the employer body, the Theatre Managements of South Africa (TMSA) in 2000 respectively, the Status of the Artist in South Africa remains moribund and industry injustice rampant.

"Everyone has the right to fair labour practices"

In 2014, further in the establishment of the South Africa's new democracy as a constitutional democracy, it is stated:

"The imminent screening of the new look *Generations* TV series, which has been off the air since its producer fired the cast last month, should sound an ominous knell for every Black creative in South Africa. The 16 fired actors held talks at the CCMA last week with the production house owned by Mfundi Vundla who axed the actors, after they went on strike for residual payments (which they should have been getting all along), and for three year contracts (which were promised to them by the SABC in the first place)." (Majavu 2014)

The article summarises the nub of the problem as:

"*Generations* is essentially a publicly funded production. Although it is produced by a private company, it is purchased by the SABC...on a regular basis, year after year. As such, the SABC should make sure that the actors on *Generations* are afforded the same standard conditions as actors in the rest of the world, instead of letting the producer – in this case, Vundla – drag down working conditions and basic rights across the industry... It has become a cliché of sorts to blame the government for everything, but the governance of the South African screen industry is inconsistent at best and chaotic at worst. It makes no sense for the Department of Trade and Industry (DTI) to be coming up with new plans to support Black filmmakers, while leaving others out in the cold. At the same time, the SABC's endorsement of the oppressive and heavy handed axing of some of the country's best known Black actors further undermines the advancement of creative Black South Africans." (Ibid.)

The most striking conclusion to the above case lies in two statements by Bulelani Mzamo, an Advisor from the Commission for Conciliation, Mediation and Arbitration (CCMA), established in terms of the LRA, and the SABC's key spokesman, Kaizer Kganyago. Although their stances could be said to be legally correct, they fall far short of promoting the provisions of the South African Bill of Rights. In the following statements, the SABC and CCMA, as vital organs of state, show the propensity for corporatism rather than for being public service institutions under the much lauded South African Constitution: The actors' legal adviser, Bulelani Mzamo, was quoted as saying, "The CCMA is not a one-step process. There is a considerable amount of work that needs to go into demonstrating the basis of this claim to the CCMA." (Ndlovu 2014) The SABC's Kaizer Kganyago was quoted thus: "I did not have any mandate to settle anything. We don't know what they want us to settle, because they are independent contractors, so we could not settle anything with them. It's up to them whether they want to take it to arbitration." (Ibid.)

Indeed, the CCMA is charged with the mandate to promote and mediate the implementation of the LRA. The condition for its involvement lies in the recognition of the striking actors as workers by the Department of Labour, following correct definition of creative worker as 'atypical' and economically fluid. Section 23 of the Bill of Rights provides asserts that: "Everyone has the right to fair labour practices. Every worker has the right to (a) form and join a trade union; (b) participate in the activities and programmes of a trade union; and (c) to strike." (Constitution of the Republic of South Africa 1996: Section. 23)

Therefore, the folly of the actors was to imagine that they are undertaking creative work under the protection of the Constitution and the Labour Relations Act – hence their exercise of 'the right to strike' in terms of the Labour Law. Benjamin further provides context that underscores the acute extent of exposure of South Africa's cultural workers. He notes that, although a research project by Department of Labour on the changing nature of work and atypical forms of employment 2004 showed that the growth of non-standard employment has eroded the quality of labour protection and that there is a need for a reappraisal of polices and legislative provisions, 'casualisation and externalisation of employment' has deepened to the extent of employment regulated by a commercial contract rather than by a contract of employment. In their extreme form, both types of workers experience 'Informalisation' of employment where there is nominal protection by labour law but are not even able to enforce their rights as well as those who are not employees because they have the legal status of independent contractors (cf. Benjamin 2006).

According to the CCMA, the actors have no basis of claim to even approach the CCMA for conflict resolution. By way of absolving itself, the SABC clarifies the precarious Status of the Artist by reminding the actors that "because they are independent contractors, so we could not settle anything with them" (Majavu 2014). Again, the SABC does not regard itself as the employer, in spite of signing a broadcast collective agreement with PAWE in the 1990s to "giving actors the right to share a pool of 2% of total revenues generated by repeat broadcast fees" (ibid). Does it mean that with the collapse of CWUSA (successor of PAWE), the SABC is no longer morally committed to the PAWE-SABC agreement, notwithstanding their imposed legal status as independent contractor?

Inverting Marginality

In a bizarre way, the SABC has recently (2016) experimented on an unexplained unilateral declaration of raising the local content quotas from 60% to 90% on public broadcast stations (radio and television), triggering a torrent of social media confusion and/or excitement about intention, commitment or even potential negative impact on the broadcast industry. The myth was in the increase of opportunities for independent contractors by stimulating content demand through higher quotas. Implementation was announced to immediately start with radio and culminate in a proclamation on targets for the audio visual industry at the end of three months later. Prior to being challenged by musicians, the SABC response to the new targets proposed by the Independent Communications Authority of South Africa (ICASA), it agreed with the proposed SA music quota of 35% for commercial radio whilst it objects the 70% quota for public radio, arguing that "Increases of the local music quota should be based on music research with the public thereby ensuring that radio stations respond to listener needs... 70% is high and will lead to loss of audiences. This proposed quota will hinder the growth of the public broadcaster." (Independent Communications Authority of South Africa 2016)

What was initially seen as the enemy of local content made a quick two months turn-around to support a fifteen year artists' campaign for equitable quotas they would guarantee demand for creative production, increase in employment and the recognition of the creative economy as a vital part of South Africa's future GDP. Apart from the unfulfilled promise of a three months review of the 90% local content decision (May to July 2016) and the deafening silence on the announcement of the audio visual broadcast quotation more than six months down the line, the advent of the 90% theatre of the unlikely, has re-focused attention on the social-cultural and economic potential of the arts and thus the question the Status of the Artist.

South Africa's Bill of Rights, Section 16(1)(a)(b)(c) provides that "everyone has the right to freedom of expression, which includes (a) freedom of the press and other media; (b) freedom to receive or impart information or ideas and freedom of artistic creativity" (Constitution of the Republic of South Africa 1996). The Caucus of Artists regards the convergence of conventional platforms of live and electronic media performance as THE answer to South Africa's dilemma of how the creative economy could be organised to benefit the theatre (live and electronic), music and visual arts worlds. At the moment, a lot confusion and opportunism surrounds the questions of the Status of the Arts, yet, the solution lies in the comprehensive Canadian State of the Artist Act that has successfully reconciled the notion of the artist as an

"independent contractor' with a comprehensive legislative provision that caters for (1) the atypical nature of creative work relative other conventional employment; (2) collective bargaining that is essential to a framework and protocol for defining and outline conditions of employment and (3) the establishment of special ombudsman office with dedicated ability to understand and process unique employment relations and conflict dynamics that are typical of a fluid creative industry" (Canadian Status of the Artists Act: Section 5 and 6).

To realise the demands of knowledge-based creative industry in Africa, the reconstruction of theatre and performance industry is essential. In this era when Information and Communication Technology (ICT) dictates the direction of 'the fourth industrial revolution,' the leveraging of live arts infrastructure, ICT social expression and media, the emerging audio-visual of broadcasting and the infusion and centralisation of the arts in the emerging knowledge economy is central to the forging of creative as the new determinant of knowledge and skills formation. In the end, the remedy to the problem lies in fostering an honest national consensus among strategic stakeholders across live and audio-visual industry platforms, to set aside the narrow apartheid incentivised interests and shape a symbiotic partnership between the colonially divided South African creative industries to build a new globally interactive creative industry ethos that is based on rural, urban and international re-imagination of the creative industries as a unifying force of human expression.

Bibliography

Benjamin, Paul (2006): Beyond 'Lean' Social Democracy: Labour Law and the Challenge of Social Protection. In: *Transformation: Critical Perspectives on Southern Africa* 60 (1), p. 32-57.

Canadian Status of the Artists Act. Section 5 and 6. Available: http://laws-lois. justice.gc.ca/eng/acts/S-19.6/, Last Access: 29/6/2018.

Constitution of the Republic of South Africa (1996).

FIA, International Federation of International Actors (2012): President's Message. Available: http://fia-actors.com/about-fia/introduction/presidents-message/, Last Access: 28/6/2018.

FIA, International Federation of International Actors (2014): Policy Document and Presidential Speech. Available: http://fia-actors.com/policy-work/working-conditions/status-of-the-artist/, Last Access: 28/6/2018.

Majavu, Anna (2014): Black Actors and Filmmakers Face Enormous Obstacles in South Africa. Available: http://sacsis.org.za/site/article/2175, Last Access: 29/6/2018.

National Institute for Economic Policy (NIEP) (2013): Changing Nature of work and "Atypical" forms and employment in South Africa. Available: https:// niep.org.za/, Last Access: 24/6/2018.

Ndlovu, Andile (2015): CCMA fails to bridge 'Generations' gap. In: *Times Live*, October 2015. Available: https://www.africanewshub.com/news/2062993-ccma-fails-to-bridge-generations-gap, Last Access: 29/6/2018.

Staring Dispassionately into the Abyss

Director and Author Mpumelelo Paul Grootboom from Soweto

Rolf C. Hemke

No South African author and director has attracted the kind of attention drawn by Mpumelelo Paul Grootboom since the days of Athol Fugard and William Kentridge. He is young and Black, innovative and provocative, and he tells the kind of stories from the townships that one might expect: sex, crime and violence. It's no wonder he's well on his way to becoming a shooting star, his productions like *A Portrait* at the State Theatre Pretoria are being passed around all the big festivals in Central Europe, between Amsterdam and Brussels, Vienna and Zurich.

He has been hailed as the young genius of South African theatre. But the South African critics have boycotted him for the last two years. Once again he does not feature in the main programme of Grahamstown National Arts Festival. He has been accused by White South Africans of being racist. He has a reputation for being notoriously unreliable: for missing appointments, constantly turning up late to rehearsals and making his actors' lives hell. And in his personal dealings, he is said to be rather awkward and quick to lose patience.

So it is quite a surprise when Paul Grootboom arrives five minutes early for our meeting. Later he admits he does find it very hard to keep morning meetings. He simply can't get out of bed, "I enjoy the night-time, I like to make as much of the night as I can. I read, I watch films, I write. I'm a night-owl." But that is not why he self-critically perceives himself as 'socially weak' in his dealings. He says that stems from the fact he was raised in a very authoritarian and religious manner. He was not allowed to play with other children, so that in the end he just observed others' behaviour. He says he used to be just shy, though that is not how he would describe himself today. But he finds it hard to follow conversations unless he is directly involved. After five minutes, he loses interest in what others have to say.

Controversial hate tirade

He says there is a funny story behind the accusation of racism, and laughs. "I was actually putting on a mixed-race piece called *Interracial*, but I couldn't find any White actors in South Africa to take part in it. I found that very odd because all the great films that had inspired me had White actors. Whenever I develop ideas out of this, they are totally unrelated to skin colour." He had of course spoken a lot to White actors in preparing for the play, but he came up against a lot of resistance and so maybe he had then been rather arrogant. Anyway, in the end, his Black actors had also had to take on the roles of the White actors.

"I wrote a monologue for the end of the play, in which the play's director vents his frustration with the situation in the new South Africa because he can't find any White actors. In this monologue he says, 'Fuck the Whites'. Gra-hamstown Festival-goers did not take kindly to that. They thought it was a hate tirade. But in fact it was just an accurate description of how things are between people in this country." Since then Grootboom has not been included in the official programming and he has had to stage his current productions, *Foreplay* based on Schnitzler's *La Ronde* (*Der Reigen*) and the premiere of *Cats and Dogs*, as part of the Grahamstown Fringe. They cannot prevent him from putting on his productions there. However, the new Festival Director recently announced a revision of this exclusion to the motto: "Theatre must provoke, this is also and especially the case in South Africa".

"Township Tarantino"

He presented his latest coup d'état in Grahamstown under the working title of *Cats and Dogs*. He says: "I want to create a township comic-strip." But the work-in-progress he recently presented in Grahamstown was more like a neo film noir. It's a bit like a cryptic gangster ballad, a game of cat-and-mouse between township gangs and cops. Even more than in his previous productions, he uses strong clichés in story and character while utilising stylistic mechanisms like slow motion. The story revolves around a furry-faced man whom everyone calls "King Kong" – a thoroughly honest young boy with bear-like strength who has hair growing all over one side of his face. When he starts dating the girlfriend of a well-respected gang member, he gets caught up in the bloody battle between the underworld and a corrupt police force.

Grootboom has been dubbed the 'Township Tarantino' because of his skill in staging fast-paced scenes of violence, but he's not keen on this label. He likes Tarantino's work far too much to want to be compared with him. He says that the comparison is not made on the basis of their supposedly similar genius, but purely because of the violent aspect of their work. He feels this is to misunder-stand both his and Tarantino's work.

Fight in slow motion

As an artist he is clear where he stands in South African society. One reason he is in theatre is because of the audience. "I want to encourage the audience to think differently about the use of violence. I try to achieve that in the way I stage my plays rather than through the texts of the plays. For example, when I stage a very long and violent fight – drawing out scenes is a technique I like using a lot – then the audience ends up wondering: 'Why is the scene so long? Why do we have to watch this for so long?' That's when it suddenly stops being routine entertainment, because the audience asks why the director is inflicting this brutal scene on them for so long. That's how I try to affect the audience."

His own intuition is a key factor for him when working on a production. He learned this from watching American films. Grootboom, born in the Mead-owlands township, Soweto, in 1975, holds no academic qualification in drama. When he was 18 he wanted to make films, to become an actor. He dropped out of a private screen writing course in exasperation and sent his attempts at a screenplay to dozens of film producers. He received just one reply. The TV producer John Rogers phoned him and said, "Just about everything is wrong with it, there's no structure, no drama, no narrative arc. It's a dreadful screen-play but your dialogue is impressive". On this basis, Rogers offered to tutor him privately and Grootboom accepted. To do so, he dropped out of his degree at Wits University, Johannesburg, and fell out with his family. After a short period of homelessness, he moved in with his mentor. Through John Rogers he got to know Aubrey Sekhabi who was Theatre Director in Mafikeng at the time and is now Artistic Director at the State Theatre, Pretoria, and has been Grootboom's producer, friend and mentor ever since. He first got him to work on didactic educational plays and Grootboom still regularly puts on youth and school productions.

"I've never had my intuition trained out of me", laughs Grootboom. One example of this, the assured and compelling choice of music in his productions is based purely on feeling. Either he has an idea or one of his actors or assistants bring their favourite music along. They try it out and then he quickly gets a feel for whether the music fits. "It's a bit stupid to rely on intuition, but it's more or less how it is", he says coyly.

Raw violence

He works in a similar way with his actors. "The scene in my *Township Stories* where the pregnant girl is beaten by her boyfriend came more from a feeling than a concept. I simply had the feeling that the actors should get into a proper fight with each other. I didn't want them to just pretend or to choreograph it. And then the actor brought to her acting all her frustration she felt at having actually been hit. This fight scene was a bit of a miracle, when you think how this girl dealt with all the crap that I demanded of her. At first she just howled when I said she had to play it. She really didn't want to do it and I had to practically beg her. I can't really say why it was so important for me for her to do it like that. But it led to her really hitting back hard at the guy because she was so mad that he was always beating her. And so the scene developed into something I was really happy with."

He laughs in response to the question whether some of the actors wouldn't hate him for this. "Some of them see me as a slave driver. To be honest, I really don't know if I enjoy other people's suffering, but I always find the time of 'stress rehearsals' one of the best." If you talk to his actors around rehearsals you soon notice that on either side of the extremely difficulty rehearsals reigns great admiration for this young, slightly inhibited, but completely unpretentious, and in the end rather radical young director. "He pushes his actors to the limit", says Aubrey Sekhabi. "And that's why we love him."

Township Stories has intensity, power and an anarchistic rawness that stunned audiences as much in Germany, Austria and Switzerland as in England or Australia. The audience cannot help but be gripped by the shocking opening scene. In blind panic a desperate woman runs for her life round the stage, screaming for help, stumbling and finally collapsing as she struggles with an invisible attacker who goes on to rape and murder her. In their portrayal of the underbelly of township life at the end of apartheid, Grootboom and co-author Presley Chweneyagae include just about every horror imaginable, from robbery and murder, to rape and child abuse. At the heart of it is the hunt for the so-called G-string strangler. The threat of him makes life hell for the township women. And by the time the audience have realised that a piece of clothing from every murder victim is pegged to the washing line above the stage, it is clear that few of the cast will survive.

Racy sex merry-go-round

Grootboom's fourth professional production, *Foreplay*, a radical South African adaptation of Schnitzler's *La Ronde* (*Der Reigen*), premiered in Amsterdam last autumn. He developed the idea after seeing Kubrick's *Eyes Wide Shut*, which was based on Schnitzler's *Dream Story* (*Traumnovelle*). After that he started to research the Austrian writer. "I always wanted to do Schnitzler. When I first read the play I thought how universal it is and how well it fits the South African situation. I wanted to try and transfer it to the South African situation. One of the main problems was translating the language into a modern Black South African English. The actors had to read the English translation of Schnitzler out loud to me so I could identify what problems they had with it. And then that's how I adapted the text."

Grootboom has exploited his actors' wealth of experience in all his productions. *Township Stories* with all their radicalism are based on his actors' (not necessarily autobiographical) tales, as is the creation of the characters in *Foreplay*: "When I decided to transform one of Schnitzler's characters into a preacher, I came up against the problem of not having been to church for ages. I didn't have much of an idea about it. So my actors had to tell me how preachers behave. What preacher would say to a pretty girl and how would she react. Based on their experiences I was thus able to create the scene and the character anew."

Foreplay is a racy sex merry-go-round. The sultry atmosphere of the European salon at the end of the 19th century is replaced once again by the dirt and sweat of South African townships. The play again begins with a chase that leads to a bloody shooting only at the end of the evening. Like Schnitzler's original the evening is made up of ten scenes; each dealing with a sexual encounter, and linked by dint of a character re-appearing in the following scene. Only when one of the characters from the very first scene re-appears does the circle close and the merry-go-round stop.

Many of Grootboom's characters echo Schnitzler's although they are taken from South African society: a soldier, a thief, a prostitute, a bar maid, a spoilt young man, a teacher, a schoolgirl, a politician, the politician's wife. Grootboom's stylistic devices are overtly explicit rather than subtle and that is also true of the language he uses. Sex is shown openly and is raw and sometimes graphic in its choreography. All the actors chew bubble gum. The bubbles symbolise orgasm. The bubble gum crops up in scene after scene – as if being passed from one character to the next – like a sexually transmitted disease. In this, Grootboom is very close to his beginnings of didactic educational theatre again. But it is this very directness, this immediacy and the performers' correspondingly physical presence that makes the production so strikingly powerful.

The final scene in which the politician rapes the prostitute, who is blackmailing him with compromising photos, is extremely realistic, brutal and deliberately drawn out under Grootboom's direction. No one in the audience can be unaffected by it. But it is only when we see the composure with which the prostitute analyses her role as a victim in the closing monologue that the mundaneness of this atrocity is exposed, and suddenly the audience is made to stare dispassionately into the abyss.

Translated into English by Rosi Jillett.

The text was first published in the magazine "Dawn in a land of cages. New Theatre in South Africa" as part of "Theater der Zeit" ("Theatre of the time"), Berlin 2009.

Theatre Development and Cultural Policy in Rural Areas

A grassroots perspective from North West Province, South Africa

Sefako Bethuel Mohlomi

To many rural artists in South Africa, the word *theatre* is an abstract concept in a sense that there are no such facilities in many environs. When the word is mentioned, what immediately come to the minds of rural artists are images of big buildings with hi-tech equipment meant exclusively for certain class of actors from urban areas like town and cities. Not even business people in rural areas think about constructing theatres. The same applies to the arts and culture departments at all spheres of government, including but not limited to especially the Human Settlement Ministry that is mandated to provide such infrastructure to effect positive impact on the society, community and socio-welfare of young people and upcoming generations. Theatre is but one of the many things that are ignored or overlooked in many efforts and/or attempts to combat poverty and aid rural development.

Indeed, theatre can provide a platform for integration and unity in diversity as rural areas are now gradually becoming multinational in that Asian traders, especially from countries like Pakistan and Bangladesh, are establishing businesses there. In fact, in most cases, they have literally taken over business entities that originally belonged to the locals. Theatre can get youth off the streets and into an environment where they can learn, grow and achieve manageable goals. Through music, drama, storytelling, poetry, and all other genres of the arts found at almost every rural community, theatre can play a critical role generating awareness to social issues like HIV/AIDS awareness, substance abuse, life skills, domestic violence, poverty and all other relevant youth/community issues.

In five sections to follow below, I deliberate on many different angles of rural theatre development in a ground breaking journey towards theatre development in rural areas. The views expressed here are usually canvassed in discussions by the North West Cultural Policy Reading Group (CPRG), though they do not officially represent the stance of the collective. Prior to the sections, however, it becomes prudent to contextualise the locations and operations of crucial interest groups.

Based in Mahikeng, CPRG was formed in 2014 by a crop of young writers in the North West Province after a series of discussion led by Mike van Graan and Sophia Sanaan from the African Arts Institute (AFAI). It was during these deliberations that local artists noticed a huge gap in the province on knowledge of cultural policies and how they affect them with the view to remedy the situation. Among other documents discussed were: United Nations Educational and Scientific Commission (UNESCO)'s 2005 Convention on the Protection and Promotion of the Diversity of Cultural Expressions; African Union Plan of Action on the Cultural and Creative Industries; Belgrade Recommendation on the Status of the Artist; Agenda 21, International Federation of Arts Councils and Culture Agencies (IFFACA), International Federation of Coalitions for Cultural Diversity (IFCD) Statement on Culture in a Post-2015 Development Agenda; Arterial Network's position paper on culture in a Post-2015 Development Agenda called *Adapting the Wheel, Cultural Policies for Africa*; South African White Paper on Arts and Culture (1996); and the South African White Paper on Arts and Culture (2013).

CPRG was offered an office by the provincial government's department of Culture, Arts and Traditional Affairs (CATA) at 17 South Street Mahikeng. This is the major service point for Arts, Culture and Heritage in Mahikeng. Since then, the group has written several documents on cultural policies for rural areas from personal experiences in the province's rural landscape as cultural practitioners.[1]

In 2015, CPRG further partnered with Reaipela Cultural Group at Ratlou District in the formulation of arts and culture policy for that district. The group specialise in the performing arts and crafts that include dance, poetry, music, storytelling and drama. They also do beadwork and fine arts. The Group is in partnership with NetSquared; a San Francisco based Non-Profit-Organisation specialising with Technology Education worldwide.

---

1 | The documents published online include: http://www.academia.edu/34034669/ Arts_and_Culture_for_Socio-Economic_Development_of_Rural_Areas; http://www. worldculturesconnect.com/?referreruserid=120396&fileid=-20674; http://www.world culturesconnect.com/?referreruserid=120396&fileid=-20595.

Why Theatre Development?

According to Google Translation, development is the process of developing or being developed. Synonyms: evolution, growth, maturing, expansion, enlargement, spread, build out, progress, success, blossoming, blooming, burgeoning, headway. Wikipedia defines theatre as a collaborative form of fine art that uses live performers, typically actors or actresses, to present the experience of a real or imagined event before a live audience in a specific place, often on stage. The performers may communicate this experience to the audience through combinations of gesture, speech, song, music, and dance. Elements of art, such as painted scenery and stagecraft such as lighting are used to enhance the physicality, presence and immediacy of the experience. The word "theatre" is derived from the Ancient Greek θέατρον (théatron, "a place for viewing"), itself from θεάομαι (theáomai, "to see", "to watch", "to observe").

Nowhere in the definitions is mention of building infrastructure in reference to where the activities are usually held. In this sense, theatre is based on human capacity than infrastructure. Since theatre exists in the people (the artists), it qualifies to be regarded as folk art. In SeTswana culture, theatre is associated with mantlwane and serala. Mantlwane is house-playing by children mimicking adult experiences from their homesteads. Serala/Seraleng simply means a performance space. Unlike Mantlwane that is played during the day, Seraleng is a place for evening-based entertainment mostly. However, it was switched to daylight performances after missionaries built churches and church buildings in which to host such artistic events. Hence in rural context, Seraleng can be regarded as the professional stage and Mantlwaneng the theatre academy.

As mentioned earlier, Community Halls in many rural areas are not theatre venues and the politics surrounding them often denies the artists opportunities to utilise them. As part of government intervention in the distribution of cultural facilities, I advocate for the construction of at least 1 theatre per 1 village. That way, rural area will be able to retain talent and grow their own creative and cultural economy.

How can we develop theatres in rural areas?

Development is multidimensional. Theatre development for rural areas must explore all other dimensions of rural development. It must be able to generate its own money and not depend on funding applications for survival. All rural traditional and cultural economy methods must form part of the strategy and planning.

There are many good and talented artists looking for a space for self-expression in rural areas. And to use their talents to impact positively on society, such spaces can be the beginning of a journey towards the love of theatre by local community, a breeding of cultural entrepreneurship and talent retention as well as creation of rural creative economy. Neighbourhood can buzz with economic spin-offs from the performances to the benefits of communities. Fine artists can be employed to paint the neighbourhood with creative information, draw/paint directions to other arts locations using creative flair and artistic temptations on walls, houses, gates, poles to take a tourist or client though a stare and gleam walk to every corner of arts business in the neighbourhood. The entire village can turn into Arts Spaces inspired by theatre, where dreams and aspirations are realised.

Construction of new theatres is a mountainous task for every government as the arts generally competes with much needed basic needs such as water and electricity in the national budget. While waiting for government to build theatres, rural areas can in the meantime utilise available community halls as they usually have stages, change rooms, and sometimes sound equipment. In villages, there are also other dilapidated buildings like schools, beer halls, churches and shops that can be converted into theatre spaces. In addition, there are some abandoned community projects with huge storage buildings and unrented/unused government buildings that can be transformed into mini and mega theatres. The other notion of theatre development can take the form of utilising available vehicle garages in our homestead as theatre rehearsal spaces instead of renting them all out to the Asian traders to convert them into tuck shops.

Get Set, Ready, and Go strategy!

Once local theatre practitioners are set and ready to go, they may call for auditions for resident theatre companies for purposes of attracting actors trained at universities and other institutions to teach and transfer skills to emerging rural theatre artists as well as collaborating with them and expand the network to provincial, national and ultimately international level. There is no point of getting professionals to go to rural areas to hosts workshops, seminars, summits and conferences and leave thereafter without establishing any future working collaboration to show the outcome of training or capacity building. Rural theatre development should follow such method for quality assurance.

Sustainable economic development, poverty reduction, moral regeneration and African renaissance are important issues of the century, and theatre can play an important role in addressing them. To develop theatre at rural areas, rural communities must be included in the planning, design and implementation stages of development to enable them to propose strategies that could be deployed to effectively develop them. For them to be more effective they must not be made to depend entirely on the creativity of professional artists, for this could easily translate into exploitation and the perpetuation of dominance by powers that be. This is in line with Karl Marx's theory that "spectators receive knowledge according to the perspective of the artist or of the social sector in which he is rooted, or which sponsors him, pays him, that sector of society which holds the economic power, controlling with it all the other powers and establishing the directives of all creativity" (Boal 1979: 53). Therefore, theatre should be a way of giving a voice to the voiceless within communities; not something with which to silence them or strip them their identities in the name of global trends/standards.

Arts incubators could also be created within communities to train or breed all theatre workers in sustainable manner. Outputs of these would be the showcasing of talents, skills, and styles locally, nationally and internationally as proactive agents of change. In the process, artists would brand themselves individually or collectively so as to be easily recognisable by art connoisseurs. Branding helps artists to market themselves, describe their work, and create or expand networks with their counterparts world-wide. Our theatre model should be part of community development and social welfare of the people rather than for the promotion of the arts only. Although generally rural artists prefer the entertainment element of theatre, they must model their theatre development such that the educational imperatives are accommodated.

Funding for Rural Theatre Development

Considerable amount of money is required to set up a community theatre and also to monitor and evaluate it. Securing funding to support community theatre activities is not easy. In North West Province we have the great Mmabana Arts Centres that have theatres and the financial struggles in those centres have led to rumours of them shutting down. Irrespective of how great and positive is impact of theatre in a community; it's still not easy to solicit funding for it. Theatre is often a threat to corrupt and oppressive leaders, which makes it unfavoured development as its activities may raise the consciousness of civil groups and expose corruption and oppression through the arts by sensitising the community to be vigilant.

This section highlights what seems to have worked overtime in rural areas in terms of income generation for our arts and culture programs and activities. There is a need to reflect on these in order to open further windows of opportunity by modifying or expanding them to maximise funding catchment for rural theatre development.

The cost of living in rural areas is not as expensive as in the urban counterparts. For instance, a certain financial allocation to an individual Playwright or Art Director in the city can cover many theatre workers at rural areas who would be content in sharing not because they don't value money but that they are content to leave within their means, as well as the spirit of *Botho/Ubuntu* which calls for collective solidarity. In this sense rural people can be the biggest drivers for socio-economic development of our country especially that many own the vacant land from which new Cultural Meccas and even cities could be created.

For generations, rural people have built own schools, clinics, churches and so forth from fundraising schemes like letsema and mogodisano (stokvels). Similar efforts could be applied in the arts world whereby funds raised could be managed and invested into property trusts towards building rural theatres. The success of the above require support, financial capacity building, good governance or organising bodies, organisational management training, financial policies, global, national, provincial and regional partnerships with businesses, local governments, tribal councils, arts, culture and heritage institutions, donors, sponsors and the community. Though not exhaustive, the above could serve as both features and standards for rural cultural policies in the context of the national cultural policy as discussed in the next section.

Rural Theatre Development in relation to South Africa's Arts White Paper

For us in rural areas, when looking at the South African White Paper on Arts and Culture, one question that lingers on is: Does policy actually matter in the arts? Why we should care about something that doesn't include us, something that marginalises and makes decisions for us without us? Many of us as rural inhabitants never cared about policies as I mentioned in the beginning about the formation of CPRG. Such perspectives make us to be more of hustlepreneurs concerned mostly about our own creativity, distribution of our creative work and how this will help us to pay the rent at the end of the month than being active participants in cultural policy formulation which unfortunately bears no mercy as to whether we participated in it, are aware of it or not, whether we like it or not, decisions taken at a macro political level do have direct impact on what is funded, who may access funds, how funds are distributed and ultimately then on the viability and sustainability of artistic practice.

Here we have a policy that affirms the constitutional right to freedom of expression yet it gives the arts and culture minister and the deputy exclusive powers for final approval of funding despite the fact that either or both are politically appointed officials with no understanding of the value or role of the arts. How are they going to develop guidelines for the remuneration of performing arts practitioners and perhaps emulate the South African Defence Force by recognising individuals who have over the years made significant contribution to the theatre sector and are no longer employed but can still add value to the sector? Over and above this, the Ministerial powers are extended to make unilateral decisions of sensitive macro issues such as naming or renaming of geographical places. Sometimes politicians further stoke instead of healing the wounds of the historically violated fraction of the society by turning down their applications to appease the minority in the name of racial reconciliation. This is political self-hatred and betrayal of the worst kind!

The current revised White Paper seems to be backed by colonial influence in that it's not aligned with the Freedom Charter and somehow it gives preference to the elites while on the other side it preaches the proverbial Moses's promise of land of honey and milk by simply citing the delivery of arts, culture and heritage to all towards the creation of better life for all without supportive systems and structures. This is like – to stretch the analogy further – government bring milk to the people without the bees for honey because they fear to be stung yet are more than eager to suck the cows dry. The impact of apartheid on arts, culture and heritage is aptly captured in the African National Congress's (ANC) Draft National Cultural Policy which states that:

"Colonialism and apartheid neglected, distorted and suppressed the culture of the majority of South Africans. The freedom of expression was destroyed and systematic efforts were made at stifling creativity. Communities were denied resources and facilities to develop their own cultural expressions, unless they coincided with the aims of the colonial masters. The absence of an effective educational system, high rates of illiteracy and extreme poverty compounded the cultural deprivation of the majority." (Department of Arts and Culture 2013: 11)

As alluded earlier, it is regrettable that the current White Paper still perpetuates the same thing. The theatre sector in South Africa still perpetuates the colonial legacy of benefiting a minority, though this time around it's more around class than race which is incidentally still a powerful variable that even determines class. In the North West Province, particularly the city of Mahikeng, there is only one independent theatre at Majemantsho village owned by the Mosekaphofu Cultural Ensemble. The theatre was built/funded by National Lotteries. Apart from that, only Mmabana'sMmabatho Arts Centre has a theatre which must be hired for use by local communities. In far west of Mahikeng at Dr Ruth Mompati district, there is mini versions of 2 theatres located in community arts centres; Monamodi Freedom Square and Atamelang CAC. There is very little known about them apart from the fact that they've somehow been supported by local provincial arts and culture department and the currently troubled North West Federation of Community Arts Centres. The Province itself boasts with theatres located in Mmabana Arts Centres in Lehurutshe, Taung and Rustenburg which are legacies of former Bophuthatswana homeland and are currently almost dysfunctional due to financial constraints and lack of access by local communities due to a variety of factors including exorbitant entrance fees.

We should avoid a deaf museum policy that will not be implemented

The Department of Arts and Culture (DAC) should consider different subsectors, genres and theatre value chain. Since government is one of the largest investors in the arts, the changes in funding structure have serious implications for all arts practitioners (everyone will need to compete for the same funds). DAC should develop a theatre strategy working with all key role players and stakeholders in creation of new markets and audience development by opening up of theatre facilities and resources to a wider community of arts practitioners including rural areas. This can be achieved through development of new programmes to mobilise the cultural, social and economic potential of the country and to revitalise community theatre at previously disadvantaged/ underserved areas. It must ensure that there is access to the use by communities, the physical infrastructure particularly of the large publicly-funded theatre infrastructure like Mmabana Arts Centres.

In all theatre development initiatives, we should avoid a deaf museum policy that will only sit in government offices without been implemented. We should encourage DAC to have implementation and monitoring task teams that reports to the theatre sector not to government. That way the task teams can be held accountable for all matters of policy in relation to implementation and monitoring. The revised White Paper should be taken to far regions of rural areas for genuine public participation. The last consultation session in Mahikeng was at Mmabatho Palms Hotel; an excluded upper 5 star hotel that is not even easily reachable with public transport. The notification about the meeting was not sent across the city; only few people who happen to be friends knew about that. So in a broader view, whatever is reflected in the revised paper is still going to continue to marginalise rural areas.

The revised draft White Paper still fails to deliver a more broadly transformative vision for the theatre sector. There is no clear indication of investment on theatre infrastructure at rural areas. It still looks like there is a conflict between the aim to ensure that arts and culture are available and accessible to all and the aim to harness/utilise the arts as a form of job creation and a driver of economic development. There is a need to remind ourselves as arts and culture nation that the human and social value of the arts needs to be defended especially in light of the naturalisation of development discourses. We need to contemplate on this:

"The concept of a developmental state means that government can, and will, directly support and get involved in actual delivery where this may either be lacking; not happening at all; happening but needs to be reinforced and strengthened; and is happening but at too slow a pace." (Department of Arts and Culture 2013: 14)

Gilles Ste-Croix states:

"Since human beings started to gather in groups and communities, they sensed the necessity to transmit their experiences and knowledge- fundamentally- through story-telling. The transmission of these stories, through the ages moved from shamanism to modern forms of art on and off stage. Theatre is a tool that has existed for thousands of years. I imagine that from the first moments people wanted to transmit their experiences of the hunt, or their father and grandfather. It is both the wish and necessity of human beings to tell stories." (Ste-Croix 2016)

South Africa is endowed with theatre not in the form of physical buildings but actors, playwrights, storytellers, dancers, singers, comedians etc. They are some of the motive forces for theatre development. Working towards the achievement of rural theatre that will be self-sustainable, the right course is for each of us to reflect, articulate and share our own ideas across artistic turfs. We should always remind us as human beings that "none of us is better than the rest of us." In SeTswana culture we say "Ditiro di kgonwakamatsema" which means team work is the only way to go.

To realise the achievement of a socio-economic viable rural theatre, we must involve every stakeholder from idea stage up to the last nail on the roof and the day we officially open the door. The project manager must be someone educated in the field of theatre, must know community culture, and be able to deal with people of all ages and personalities. Must understand the concept of *Botho/Ubuntu* above everything as that will be a guide to him/her to achieve the project. The SeTswana proverb says that "Motho ke motho ka batho," which means a person is somebody through other people (*I am because we are*). People in rural areas don't like arrogance, they don't like to be undermined or disregarded – it's our culture. If they feel undermined or looked down upon them on the basis of their rurality and impose things on them, they are likely to ignore them or even vandalise them through violent protest actions. Thus it is important for government to genuinely involve people in their development plans.

Bibliography

Boal, Augusto (1979): Theater of the oppressed. London: Pluto Press.
Department of Arts and Culture (2013): 2nd Version of the Revised White Paper on Arts, Culture and Heritage.
Ste-Croix, Gilles: Articles and interviews by VikasShambe/@mrvikas. Available: https://thoughteconomics.com/theatre-performance-and-society/, Last Access: 23/6/2016.

Are we actually deeply enough...

...with these socio-political questions in our theatres?

Khayelihle Dom Gumede

We come from a theatre history that is very emphatic in its political agenda. It had very clear political messaging around the struggle against apartheid. However part of our current task as a theatre community, is to collate and create a new voice or voices against an emerging identity. This is difficult because of the particularly mercurial sense of a South African social identity in 2016. Given the myriad of political questions that have been violently thrust forward in our society, it is the most interesting time to be asking this question and to be interrogating, the now seemingly, fraught notion of the promise of the Rainbow Nation.

22 years into our democracy, as we find ourselves in very trying economic and social conditions, many South African's conditions haven't moved. Many communities feel that they have been left out of this new socio-political order. They feel excluded from the ANC government's development agenda. Whether this is true or not, I am sure is debatable. This seems to be a rapidly growing sentiment though, especially in the urban centres. There are many who feel that they've been over look and they are still waiting for their promised RDP house and for the education scheme and economic policies of the government to transform their lives.

From my perspective, there also seems to be a hardening of racial lines between groups of people within the country. Take for instance the clashes between supporters and students at Free State University.[1] When I saw the Free State University video I got chills because all of a sudden you had people physically attacking each other over essentially what is transformation and race issue that came to a head at a rugby game.

The #FeesMustFall movement also seems to be producing a binary between students of privilege, labelled mainly as White, and students who feel economi-

---

1 | See Whittles: 2016 - http://ewn.co.za/2016/02/23/UFS-suspends-classes-after-black-vs-white-brawl.

cally excluded, labelled mainly as Black. Then there is also the fact that, Janusz Walus, Chris Hani's murder, has been granted parole. The amount of socio-political friction that has cause is astounding. Individuals have been picketing outside of the courtroom and there has been fierce debate in the media about it. Chris Hani's widow, Limpho Hani, was also extreme vocal about her opposition to not only the parole but also the insensitive manner in which Judge, Nicolene Janse van Nieuwenhuizen, addressed the matter.[2]

There has also been the Rhodes Must Fall Movement that has raised an important public debate about socio-political symbolism in a new South Africa. We need to ask ourselves if students would attack these historical symbols if they felt that they bare less consequence in their lived conditions. In other words, if students felt socially included and economically secure would these historic or colonial symbols feel like such an imposition in their lives?

I mention all of this because we currently have this completely turbulent political circumstance and one wonders if the plays that are being produced in the playhouses or funded theatre complexes are adequately reflective of this. Have they cordoning onto these current political moment? Are we having that dialogue? Are we actually engaging deeply enough with these socio-political questions in our theatres?

Struggling to find what a new social voice looks and sounds

I think in some instances there are isolated circumstances like Paul Grootboom has said in the conference in Pretoria. But I think on the whole, in my own preparations and thoughts for this discussion, why do we keep going back to the classics then. Why is it that every year we will see staging of several *Sizwe Banz's*, several *Woza Albert's*, several of the quintessential Protest Theatre works within our cannon (our new cannon of Protest Theatre works that is). I also think that part of that question is that somewhere in there we are trying to dig out an essence that will help us move forward as a society.

I don't think it's only about theatre houses wanting to be safe or having something bankable or an agenda for just reinvigorating an archive. I think a big part of it is that we are actually struggling to find what a new social voice looks and sounds like within our contemporary theatre. How do we probe these questions? How do we attack it? There are some wonderful illustrations of this in the satirical work of a Jeff Tshabalala and what he has created. I think of what Omphile has done with *Cadre*, I think of *Silent Voices*, *The Man in the Green Jacket* and more recently *Animal Farm*. There are also those plays that deal with a politics of aesthetics but are not overtly political plays; politics in

---

2 | See TMG Digital: 2016 - http://www.timeslive.co.za/local/2016/03/10/Chris-Ha nis-widow-slams-judge-over-decision-to-parole-Walus.

the sense of party politics. *A Voice I cannot Silence* is a recent one that carries a politics of aesthetics in unpacking the legacy of one of our greatest novelists, Alan Paton. There are also plays that have started to hone in on the alternative lived experience, seen through plays like Phillip Dekotla's *Skierlik*, there is also more famously Paul's *Relativity* and *Cards*. Then obviously, we know Mr Purkey and many of the works he oversaw as Artistic Director, *Girl in the Yellow Dress*, *Dream of the Dog, Songs of Migration, Ten Bush* and many others. We are aware that this history with Malcolm traces back to Junction Avenue. These works have really begun a different conversation. It's also great that we are having this conversation after *Crepuscule* has closed at the Market and *Sophiatown* is about to open at the same theatre. Because the subject matter and the worlds are the same (50's *Sophiatown*), but the works have very different sensibilities. There seems to be an interesting intergenerational dialogue being had between the two works though. *Sophiatown* in its context, in its time, carried a very different aesthetic and political sensibility to *Crepuscule* for instance.

The dependency on funded theatres is a problem

So I think more and more we need to be in a space where it is not an either or. Where we are not continually rehashing our classics as ways of trying to read into our current social dynamics as South Africans but rather that these works are in dialogue with a contemporary theatre that resonates as deeply. We need new works that are not only trying to speak back to that canon but also about where we are at right now. It seems that it is also indicative of the funding climate. The dependency on funded theatres is a problem. One knows they've got to depend on the Market theatre, or state theatre or the funded festivals to try and get their pieces of work out there. Whereas the robustness of making work independently and making work in multiple areas outside of the main-stream theatres feels very limited, people aren't able to commit themselves to that way of working because they have to live off this. Whereas before, they might be supported by a day job and make a piece of work part time.

I think of particular interventions that look at facilitating a current socio-political debate, Warren's *Drama for Life* festival being one of those. However if it is not prodded I seldom, even at places like a POPArt, feel as though these subjects are being adequately broached. To be fare POPArt is quite a mixed bag, some work there is very commercially palatable ventures, while some work is very unsafe, like Tau for instance. In the middle of this urban pocket, that is essentially a kind of wonderland for the middle class and above, you get this very weird mix of works that tries to bridge that conversation. There is also The Platform and the like who are still trying to find their space and we will see how they fare.

So it's an interesting conversation to ask how if we are trying to really engage with our context. Part of what we have to be honest about is that we don't fully know where we are as South Africans. We are forming ourselves. However ours is to go into that vacuum and embrace the fact that we don't know who we are as a nation. We are still dealing with the fractures of a society that is attempting to find it's healing, to find what it's trying to be about. And that's why these frustrations are surfacing in the way in which they are. These are marginalised conversations that we haven't been having for over 20 years.

If one thinks of the University space as a microcosm of a society for instance, a university and the #FeesMustFall campaign is an absolute essential conversation around how our society is marginalizing certain forms of conversation and people. And those individuals are not allowing it to happen anymore. I identify deeply with this, as a student I experience any of the same problems and often felt vulnerable and angry because of it. It's a highly schizophrenic experience. One feels under prepared as a student and only access the affluence afford them on campus. Then you feel disavowed by the pedagogical imperatives of the teaching and learning process and the content you are studying.

The politics of aesthetics and the language of physicality

I think our theatres are at a loss as to how to deal with questions such as these. The mainstream almost seems entirely fixated with the plans stipulated in the funding proposal to retain subsidy leaving little space for flexibility. It's a conditioning from the state-funding climate. There are independent and fringe works that survive this though. If I think of the work I saw recently at the workers museum, Nhlanhla Mahlangu's *The Worker's Chant*. It's the first performance piece that has been in the workers museum, according to the management there which is significant but also the way in which it was beginning to open up a dialogue experienced by the working and lower classes at the coal face. For me it asked how we deal with the social anxiety, the anger and marginalization of the mass of our people.

There is a definite moments of shift and marked evolution in the aesthetic landscape of our theatre, within the theatre language itself. We are starting to see the shoots of a very interesting language in our physicality that is sometimes more sophisticated that the dialogue driven drama. Because we have multiple languages in our country it is often difficult for us to broach what we are really trying to say to each other, in the minutia. Yet we have a physical intelligence to the work we have created. Whether it is a Sylvaine Strike, Christinaan Olwagen or Nhlanhla Mahlangu, Khutjo Green, Neil Coppen and the like. I feel my own work has a very big physicality to it because there is always a lack in the dialogue that frustrates. I feel there is something I am constantly trying to probe that I never quite get to in words. You want a body to carry it.

And when the body does carry it, it opens another level of politics. The politics of aesthetics as Black and White bodies move in the space. What are those relationships between those bodies what is in the unsaid? I feel there is more space for the audience to negotiate their own sense of meaning there. Personally I feel we do badly with the dialogue we often craft within our theatre. We try and insert too much of our own political rationale for the characters we create.

I think there is a more sophisticated physical language, at least for me, than much of the dialogue heavy drama we are able to broach. Even when there is a combination I find that the playmakers, Phillip Dekotla, Jeff Tshabalala, Khutjo Green, Neil Coppen, and Omphile like the use of physical sense that marries the body and spoken word in an interesting way.

I think of the early Dadaist and post world war II Butoh in Japan and how it embraced the dislocation of works and a dislocated sensibility. They didn't fear that milieu they entered it. Yet it seems we are afraid to play with those aesthetics because it is dangerous for us as a society. We are a nation that has a lot of post-traumatic stress. So to begin to engage that conversation and not know where it will go or how to cap it makes us feel comfortable.

The theatrical moment is now negotiating the history of history

In my honours research I was dealing with an Arts and transformation project which was starting to talk or think about what happens in this imaginative space. There is the real and raw instant in life, a moment of historical biography, often attached to a particular politics. The question became what happens when you take that piece of biography into an imaginative space and begin to negotiate it.

A big reference for me was Phillip Miller's *Rewind Cantata* and how for those that aren't familiar, he used all the sounds that were around the testimony that were recorded as part of the special hearing as the sources from which he created a musical score, a clearing of throats, scratching of papers, vacuous sounds, feedback from a microphone. Then he introduced notions such as the scratching of tape. He then took moments of spoken testimony. Mam' Nomonde's Calata's testimony was one of those moments. Then Mam' Sibongile Khumalo sings an Aria over the testimony from the moment Mam' Nomonde breaks down and cries. From the time that she cries there is an Operatic whale that begins to take over and for me that is the moment of hand over into the imaginative space. Mam' Nomonde in her reflection over the years about that moment, talks about not understanding why, but somehow feeling lighter after witnessing that play and that moment.

That is because the moment, or at least in my interpretation, the theatrical moment is now negotiating the history of history, the archive the real, the raw biographical instant, the so called immovable. We as a society have a history, an archive, an 'immovable' that sits on top of us which is our dark and discriminatory history. So our theatre I feel, needs to negotiate more, how we can take ourselves from underneath that history and put ourselves next to it. So we can negotiate it. So we can make decisions against it, with it, as opposed to it simply suffer its imposition on top of us.

The full text was published in the book "Social Work Artfully: Beyond Borders and Boudaries" by Christina Sinding, Hazel Barnes (eds.), Waterloo 2015.

Scratching the Wounds of the Past

A Playwright-Director's Note on the Play – *Silent Scars*

Calvin Ratladi

In the South African theatre context, there is a need to engage and translate "the body that is embattled through being immersed in social and political environments that are systemically violent, and the body that is subject to classical dualisms that leave it somehow subordinate to the animating intentions of the mind" (Grosz 1994: vii), considering the discourse of patriarchy emanating from the country's history.

The Witwatersrand University scholar Achille Mbembe declares that "there is, truly, no memory except in the body of commands and demands that the past not only transmits to us but also requires us to contemplate" (Mbembe 2008/2006: 11). And it is through the reflection of my previous works where I seem to "contemplate" much around the legacy of patriarchy and colonialism in relation to our bodies. The rationale to this idea is evident in the fact that history still defines our social lives even in the post-apartheid South Africa. Thus, this suggests that theatre today has more role to play in changing perceptions about stereotypes. And part of that role is to investigate the influence, effects and contributions that the South Africa's violent history has had onto our psyche and bodies. The prejudice of apartheid and colonialism has effectively espoused our collective histories and left whatever remains severely distorted in our bodies.

Bodies are the material through which theatre researchers most often discuss performance; they are scrutinised, critiqued, displayed, transformed, gendered controlled and determined in critical reviews, historical accounts and theorisations of practices [...]. Whether performing or spectating, bodies are often the means for understanding how performance operates and makes meaning (cf. Kershaw & Nicholson, 2012: 210). For instance, if the body is the place where apartheid and other forms of violence make their mark, then the body also becomes the site for the damage to be responded to through training and for the possibility of the reclamation of identity and creative power (cf. Scarry 1985). Thus, this paper contributes to the body of knowledge, on the sociology of the body, by reflecting on my own theatrical production, *Silent Scars*.

Silent Scars was initially part of the Mzansi Fela Festival's 2016 Community Arts Dramaturgy Outreach (CADO) Programme, but has subsequently won the following awards at The South African State Theatre and the Baxter Theatre, respectively:

Best Director (2016 SA State Theatre CADO Awards)
Best Production (2016 SA State Theatre CADO Awards)
Best Actress (2016 SA State Theatre CADO Awards)
Most Promising Actor (2016 SA State Theatre CADO Awards)
Best Director (Baxter Theatre 2017 Zabalaza Festival)
Best Visiting Production (Baxter Theatre 2017 Zabalaza Festival)
Best Musical Director (Baxter Theatre 2017 Zabalaza Festival)

More notably, the play was staged at the prestigious Standard National Arts Festival in Grahamstown in July 2017 where it scooped the *Standard Bank Silver Ovation Award* in the event's Fringe Programme. It subsequently also had a successful run in 2017 (19 July-06 August) at the South African State Theatre.

Excavate and reclaim everyone's unspeakable stolen memories

The production is an interrogation of the performer's body that remains at risk and requiring to be rescued from systematic violation in order to reclaim its voice and narrative. The crafting of the work was bold, brave and in conversation with personal wounds through movement, dance, live music and dialogue. It is within this context, whereby I facilitated my cast to journey back to excavate and reclaim everyone's unspeakable stolen memories with hope to heal those alike. The story is set in an expressive impoverished and imaginary place in South Africa. The authenticity of the production lies at the heart of storytelling, physical metaphors, mesmeric song and symbols to communicate what many may consider as an inter-generational 'damage' of patriarchy. A very disturbing realisation of the production was the impact the performances had on the audiences every night. I do not recall a single night whereby nobody neither approached me nor any of the performers to share personal stories that they had kept in silence. This was indeed an affirmation of how repressed and harmed we are as a society institutionalised by patriarchal systems.

The concept of patriarchy is defined by different thinkers in different ways. Patriarchy refers to the male domination both in public and private spheres. Feminists mainly use the term 'patriarchy' to describe the power relationship between men and women. Thus, patriarchy is more than just a term; feminists use it like a concept, and like all other concepts it is a tool to help us understand women's realities. Mitchell, a feminist psychologist, uses the word patriarchy "to refer to kinship systems in which men exchange women" (Mitchell 1971: 24). Walby defines "patriarchy as a system of social structures and practices in which men dominate, oppress and exploit women" (Walby 1990: 20). She explains patriarchy as a system because this helps us to reject the notion of biological determinism which suggests that men and women are naturally different because of their biology or bodies and, are, therefore assigned different roles, or "the notion that every individual man is always in a dominant position and every woman in a subordinate one" (ibid).

Literally, the word 'patriarchy' means the rule of the father or the 'patriarch', and it was originally used to describe a specific type of 'male-dominated family' – the large household of the 'patriarch' which included women, junior men, children, slaves and domestic servants all under the rule of this dominant male. Now it is used more generally "to refer to male domination, to the power relationships by which men dominate women, and to characterise a system whereby women are kept subordinate in a number of ways" (Bhasin 2006: 3). Thus, patriarchy describes the institutionalised system of male dominance. So we can usefully define patriarchy as a set of social relations between men and women, which have a material base, and which, though hierarchical, establish or create independence and solidarity among men that enable them to dominate women (cf. Jagger and Rosenberg 1984). Patriarchal ideology exaggerates biological differences between men and women, making certain that men always have the dominant, or masculine, roles and women always have the subordinate or feminine ones. This ideology is so powerful that men are usually able to secure the apparent consent of the very women they oppress. They do this "through institutions such as the academy, the church, and the family, each of which justifies and reinforces women's subordination to men" (Millett 1977: 35).

Power, dominance, hierarchy, and competition of the patriarchal system

The patriarchal system is characterised by power, dominance, hierarchy, and competition. So patriarchy is a system of social structures and practices, in which men dominate, oppress and exploit women. Patriarchy, in its wider definition, means the manifestation and institutionalisation of male dominance over women and children in the family and the extension of male dominance over women in society in general. It implies that "men hold power in all the important institutions of society" and that "women are deprived of access to such power" (Lerner 1989: 239).

Antagonistically, feminist theory is directly and predominantly political. Its purpose is to struggle against the oppression of women as women. This oppression, which is seen to be historically extremely common and widespread, is the result of patriarchy, the supremacy of masculine power and authority most firmly entrenched in the figure of the father (thus the strong relations between feminism and psychoanalytic work). Feminism, therefore, works toward the unravelling and overthrowing of patriarchy. Judith Fetterley asserts that feminism posits the feminist as a 'resisting reader' in the face of patriarchal cultural domination (cf. Fortier 2005: 108).

There is a recognition that traditionally, when women have been allowed to partake of the dominant culture, they have been indoctrinated in masculine values and ways of seeing (identifying with male heroes while viewing female characters at a distance, for example), what Fetterley calls the 'emasculation' of the woman reader (cf. Austin 1990: 27). Feminism attempts to create a woman reader who sees as a woman and thereby brings a different and other perspective to bear on culture.

The African academic, Ama Ato Aidoo expresses a vision of feminism for Africa that is both pan-African and nationalist, thus:

"When people ask me rather bluntly every now and then whether I am a feminist, I not only answer yes, but I go on to insist that every woman and every man should be a feminist — especially if they believe that Africans should take charge of African land, African wealth, African lives, and the burden of African development. It is not possible to advocate the independence for the African continent without also believing that African women must have the best that the environment can offer. For some of us, this is the crucial element in our feminism." (Aidoo 1998: 47)

Aidoo's vision can only be realised, by addressing the many struggles and obstacles that continue to affect the lives of African women as in *Silent Scars*. Adichie unpacks this dilemma practically in that: "We teach girls to shrink themselves, to make themselves smaller. We say to girls: you can have ambition, but not too much. You should aim to be successful but not too successful. Otherwise you will threaten the man." (Adichie 2014: 26)

Adichie's dilemma is also evident in Tracey Saunders review of the play in the newspaper, *Weekend Special*: "The piece was a meditative reflection on masculinity and the roles that men are expected to perform and those that they fail miserably at." (Saunders 2017) This review simply shifts the central tenet that the work was created for – reclaiming Black female bodies that had widely been used and accepted as a site of fragmentation, distortion and degradation. The review asserts how the dominant ideology of patriarchy is found in all areas, and that includes how arts journalists and audiences view performances. Thus, to raise women's position, it is urgent to protect women from patriarchal subordination. It is patriarchal "Ideological Status Apparatuses" (Althusser 2001: 35) which makes us feminine and masculine; it assigns us different roles, rights and responsibilities. This shift recognises the erasure and neglect of a female body in performance. Similarly, arts practitioners living with disabilities are not insulated from special experiences. I should know better: I am part of that community due to some misfortune of my birth!

Even though the issue of disability was not dramatised in the play, it is a matter that warrants urgent and serious attention in the country's cultural arena where artists with physical challenges are seldom seen on stage and screen. Their appearance is rare and far in between. The relevance of this topic is that it is a sub-theme of the paper's discourse of the body as a laboratory of scientific inquiry, artistic instrument, and site of political struggle. Therefore, the matter qualifies for special mention in this text, as well as concerted efforts in future endeavours for me personally, as well as for my compatriots.

Stereotypes are a barrier to understanding the reality of disability

In recent years, persons with disabilities have claimed individual and collective rights and sought to change their circumstances in part by changing the words used to describe them. But often, their efforts were either solos or unsustained when organised. Negative words and stereotypes are a barrier to understanding the reality of disability. Misguided language and many prevailing attitudes promote outdated beliefs that persons with disabilities are suffering, sick, disadvantaged, needy, and, in general, not like "us", and have juxtaposed persons with disabilities with those who are 'able-bodied' (cf. Department of Social Development, 2015: 23).

The struggle to define disability which accurately and realistically encompasses the lived experience of persons with disabilities is a historical one; symptomatic of power dynamics, prejudice and social exclusion of those who do not 'belong'. This struggle is best described by Soudien and Baxen:

"Each definition is embedded within the broader constructs of how society works, who is in and who is out, and under what conditions decisions are made. How definitions work to frame, organise and create policies and the social practices that flow from them, is nowhere clearer than in the field of education. It is crucial, therefore, that these definitions be understood as emergent from particular histories and discursive formations." (Soudien/Baxen 2006: Chapter 12)

I raise this definition to argue how South Africa's national cultural policy, the White Paper on Arts, Culture and Heritage (WPACH), inadequately addresses the inclusion of people living with disabilities within the cultural arena. As alluded to earlier, the scarcity of artists with physical disabilities on scripts, screens and scores in South Africa mirrors their invisibility in the national cultural policy panorama. The White Paper has been reviewed thrice since its inception in 1996. It is now on its third review, which incidentally is currently going through the third draft. In all the occasions, the doctrine fails to focus on the abilities or capacities of people with disabilities rather than their differentness. Not once does the doctrine refer to any issue related to people with disabilities in any way whatsoever, including for instance, in the provision of braille for the visually-impaired artists or access to cultural facilities for people experiencing difficulties with physical mobility.

The 3rd draft of the current revised White Paper seeks "to transform the historically exclusive and authoritarian system into an inclusive, democratic, deliberative and participatory dispensation" (Department of Arts and Culture, 2017: 5). Yet excludes the mainstreaming of disability into the arts sphere. Exclusion refers to the act of socially isolating or marginalising individuals or groups on the basis of discrimination by not allowing or enabling them to fully participate and be included in society and enjoy the same rights and privileges. This devaluation of and exclusion of individuals or groups results in keeping "others" outside from the prevailing social system and thus restricting their access to material, social, economic and political resources and rights (cf. Department of Arts and Culture, 2015: 7). Disability Mainstreaming requires a systematic integration of the priorities and requirements of persons with disabilities across all sectors and built into new and existing legislation, standards, policies, strategies, their implementation, monitoring and evaluation. Barriers to participation must be identified and removed. Mainstreaming therefore requires effective planning, adequate human resources, and sufficient financial investment – accompanied by specific measures such as targeted programmes and services (cf. ibid.: 5).

Inclusion – the need for broader systemic and attitude changes in society

Surprisingly, South Africa's arts White Paper disability deficit is not identical to its twin, the 2015 White Paper on the Rights of Persons with Disabilities (Department of Social Development, 2015), in which Article 30 of the United Nations Convention on the Rights of Persons with Disabilities (UNCRPD) unequivocally accords full rights to people with disabilities to participate in cultural life, recreation, leisure and sport. The article list five obligations, with concomitant sub-divisions, to which member States must uphold in fulfilment of these rights (cf. ibid.). Yet, regrettably, the reality is different in South Africa. In the next edition of the White Paper, the Department of Arts and Culture needs to adopt the WPRPD social model to addressing disability. The social model acknowledges that disability is a social construct and assesses the socio-economic environment and the impact that barriers have on the full participation, inclusion and acceptance of persons with disabilities as part of mainstream society. It is a model that focuses on the abilities of persons with disabilities rather than their differences, that fosters respect for inability and that recognises persons with disabilities as equal citizens with full political, social, economic and human rights (cf. ibid.: 21).

The social model does not locate the "problem" within the person with impairment; rather, it acknowledges and emphasises barriers in the environment which disable the person with the impairment aimed at inclusion rather than exclusion of persons with disabilities from mainstream life. It emphasises the need for broader systemic and attitude changes in society; the provision of accessible services and activities; and the mainstreaming of disability to ensure full inclusion of persons with disabilities as equals. The model further encourages that persons with disabilities must actively participate in transformation processes that impact on their lives. Also it does not deny the reality of "impairment", (an incident of human diversity), nor the impact this may have on the individual (cf. ibid.: 21).

In conclusion, gone must be the days when people living with disabilities are treated in the society in general, and as caricatures on stage, for amusement, sympathy, and ticking policy statements and annual reports. In fact, artists living with these conditions should realise that they have a big contribution to make in the country's nation-building project. Apart from the fact that the country's Constitution confers them full political, social, economic and human rights as ordinary citizens, they must also enjoy privileges and protect from rights specifically prescribed for artists. For starters, artists living with any sort of physical challenge should adopt the slogan: *Nothing about me, without me, and not by me!* Thus, I have made a personal commitment as a theatre maker to produce a body of works that reclaim stolen memories, and stand for activism in issues about gender, identity, and politics of the body.

Bibliography

Adichie, Chimamanda Ngozi (2014): We Should All be Feminists. London: Knopf Doubled.

Aidoo, Ama Ata (1998): The African Woman Today. In: Obioma Nnaemeka (ed.): Sisterhood, feminisms and power. From Africa to the diaspora. 1. print. Trenton, NJ: Africa World Press.

Althusser, Louis (2001): Ideology and Ideological Status Apparatuses: Notes towards an investigation. In: Louis Althusser (ed.): Lenin and philosophy, and other essays. New York: Monthly Review Press.

Austin, Gayle (1991): Feminist Theories for Dramatic Criticism. Ann Arbor, MI: University of Michigan Press.

Bhasin, Kamla (2006): What Is Patriarchy. In: Women Unlimited. New Dehli.

Department of Arts and Culture: White Paper on Arts, Culture and Heritage. Available: http://www.dac.gov.za/content/white-paper-arts-culture-and-heritage-0., Last Access: 8/4/2018.

Department of Arts and Culture: Third Draft: Revised White Paper on Arts, Culture and Heritage. Available: http://www.dac.gov.za/content/third-draft-revised-white-paper-arts-culture-and-heritage, Last Access: 8/4/2018.

Department of Social Development: White Paper on the Rights of Persons with Disabilities. Available: http://www.dsd.gov.za/index2.php?option=com_do cman&task=doc_view&gid=654&Itemid=39, Last Access: 8/4/2018.

Fortier, Mark (2005): Theory/Theatre. An introduction. 2. ed., repr. London: Routledge. Available: www.eBookstore.tandf.co.uk, Last Access: 8/9/2017.

Grosz, Elizabeth (1994): Volatile bodies. Toward a corporeal feminism. Bloomington: Indiana Univ. Press.

Jaggar, Alison M.; Rosenberg, Paula S. (eds.) (1984): Feminist frameworks. New York: McGraw-Hill.

Kershaw, Baz; Nicholson, Helen (2013): Research methods in theatre and performance. Edinburgh: Edinburgh University Press.

Lerner, Gerda (1989): The Creation of Patriarchy. New York: Oxford University Press.

Mbembe, Achille (2008): What Is postcolonial thinking? An Interview with Achille Mbembe. Eurozine. Available: http://www.eurozine.com/articles/ 2008-01-09-mbembe-en.html, zuletzt aktualisiert am 9/1/2008, Last Access: 12/20/2011.

Millett, Kate (1977): Sexual politics. London: Virago Press.

Mitchell, Juliet (1971): Women's Estate. Harmondsworth: Penguin.

Saunders, Tracey (2017): Zabalaza: All the winners. WeekendSpecial. Available: https://weekendspecial.co.za/zabalaza-all-thr-winners, Last Access: 31/3/2017.

Scarry, Elaine (1985): The Body in Pain. The Making and Unmaking of the World. First issued as paperback. New York, NY: Oxford Univ. Press (Oxford paperback).

Soudien C.; Baxen, J. (2006): Disability and schooling in South Africa. In: Brian Watermeyer, Leslie Swartz, Theresa Lorenzo, Marguerite Schneider und Priestley. Mark (eds.): Disability and social change. A South African agenda. Cape Town, South Africa: HSRC Press.

Walby, Sylvia (1990): Theorizing patriarchy. 1. publ. Oxford, UK, Cambridge USA: Blackwell Publishers Ltd.

Application of indigenous performance techniques in South African theatre

The case of Mmabana Arts Culture Sports and Foundation, North West Province

Obakeng Kgwasi

Replacing action with text in SeTswana[1] drama and theatre by applying traditional dance images and gestures in a performance through the performer's body shows that the genres draw its physical element of performance
from some African rituals. This shows that indeed theatre is an experience
which has existed in Africa before colonialism and it should not be observed
and analysed from western aesthetic as the only criteria for determining what
African theatre is. This article seeks to demonstrate that both theatre and
drama are mutually inclusive categories in the African tradition because of,
according to Chinyowa, the fusion of particular elements of drama such as role-
playing, costume, dialogue, song, dance, symbolic gestures, movement, mime
and other historic signals into the fabric of the ritual (cf. Chinyowa 2001: 3-13).

Enekwe adds that African drama is more than storytelling due to the notion
that it is more of a ritual experience that seeks to recreate and, in the process,
affirm desirable models of community life. In my opinion, this gives a descrip-
tive analysis on how BaTswana storytelling, idioms and taboos (*meila and
maele*) function and are utilised for appropriateness through dramatisation in
SeTswana ritual dance, choral music and poetry. Thus it should be understood
that ritual performativity aspects are not only valued in terms of entertainment
but also for their didactic values within the society. This shows that these form

---

1 | BaTswana are one of South Africa's ethnic groups belonging to the Sotho languages
cluster. In singular form it is MoTswana. BaTswana are spread in the Gauteng and North
West provinces, though they are concentrated in the latter. They also form a single
nation in BoTswana, South Africa's neighbouring country. Their language, SeTswana, is
one of the biggest languages in Southern Africa up to Zambia. Their customs, traditions
and culture are also simply referred to as SeTswana; after the language and customs.

of art, which forms part of 'total theatre'; they can be adapted and intertwined successfully into performance for presentation to the audience. It should be emphasised that African performative aspects have similar performative elements but differ in their individual presentational styles. That said, it is not necessary to dwell on those performativity aspects but rather illustrate how a performance could be conceptualised through applying and intertwining drama, SeTswana ritual dance and choral music utilising indigenous physical theatricality of African theatre (cf. Enekwe 1981: 155).

To teach the young about tribal life

Originally, stories, idioms and taboos among BaTswana were used to teach the young about tribal life and acceptable modes of behaviour for group members. Such stories give us an opportunity to view the idea of what African theatre performances stands for in a unique stylised form through the physical application of the body linked with text.

  These stories, idioms and taboos can be used not only in play production but for storytelling, reader's theatre, improvisation or individual reading (cf. Green 1981: 8). Since there are many Tswana storytelling, idioms and taboos, it will be highly impossible to apply them all in this setting. Thus, I examine only those which have been selected and used within the production, *Identity,* in order to reflect and highlight the artistic viability of these Tswana storytelling, idioms and taboos which seeks literary resources from their own cultural performances.

  For the purpose of this article the theme identity (in SeTswana: *maikitso ka setho sa botho*) is the same-titled production, which means to know and understand the significance one's cultural roots, shall be explored. The theme will be elaborated in details on how it was conceptualised and developed for a performance through SeTswana storytelling, idioms and taboos in collaboration with choral music. The author's posture is influenced by Enekwe's argument that theatre is not the discovery and reinterpretation of meaning because theatre is first and foremost an experience (cf. Enekwe 1981: 155). From this line of thinking, drama arouse out of fundamental human needs in the dawn of human civilisation and has continued to express those needs ever since. This is to say that drama originated within the people of the society (cf. Ogunbiyi, 1981: 3). According to Ogunbiyi:

"In the course of history, man learnt to make nature work according to his needs and soon learnt that he could achieve his desire by acting and dancing them out in the form of rites. Through producing different gestures acquired from experience, these dramatic presentations are over-whelming interwoven with songs, drumming, extensive improvisation and dancing." (Ibid.: 11)

In the production, *Identity*, I (as both playwright and performer) holistically utilise performativity aspects of (storytelling, idioms and taboos) as a significant or figurative mode of communicating or promoting dramatic intention. Story-telling, idioms and taboos jointly become the narrative form to be articulated to the audience in a very noteworthy artistic format, and choral music becomes the vehicle of sound and songs applied within the performance. Therefore, this becomes clear that African drama is/was not an isolated event, but part and parcel of the rhythm of people's communal life, which included other aspects where performers transform themselves into things of the natural world that invest them with strength and vision. Performers receive power through their songs and through utilisation of dance they touch unknown and invisible elements, which they sense in the world around them.

Furthermore, this demonstrates the notion that within indigenous African performance, there is no separation of art forms (acting, dance, singing and mime) as in European theatre. Instead, the performance utilises the use of movements, images, nods and gestures as a form of communication, rather than verbal language being the main objective within the performance. Clearly this reflects that African performances had always functioned together in totality, rather than the misconception which has been fostered by European theatre practitioners like Michael Etherton through separating and naming various forms of African performances (cf. Etherton 1982, 56; 57).

The process of performances

The following analysis is going to unpack the dynamic processes of perfor-mance making in which concrete experiences are integrated into an order of concepts and discourse, due to the notion that the performance draws its performativity from cultural stories and experiences. This is the type of work which will result from the unique creative integrity and informed by indig-enous cultural artistic practices, therefore, theatre does not reflect society in an objective manner. An objective reality does not really exist. Theatre is an instrument by which actors, dancers, singers, narrators and writers interpret their own ideas of reality. This assignment is divided into five sections below.

The first initiative plan is to set down, discuss and explore the theme based on the social, political and economical issues surrounding the society in Taung; which gives the cast the direction and general idea of what is requested from them, and plan scenes to develop it for performance purposes. This is achieved through selecting material chosen by the cast working collectively because communal decisions are the secret of unit. This will suit the cast's sense of what is appropriate from a very diverse broader perspective based on theatrical tradition (cf. Beik 1987: 131).

After selection is made, exploration of the theme with the cast begin by selecting stories, idioms and taboos which are relevant to the theme and combined them in a very unique way and formulate the performance by interpreting stories, idioms and taboos through drama, SeTswana dance and choral music. It should be noted that all these specific genres of performance draw their roots of performance from African theatre which demonstrate an effective significant ability to convey the performer/creator's idea.

Performers gather potential material from each other, from observation of others and from everyday life, trying new ideas in rehearsal and polishing them through interaction and discussing with other members of the group. The group's cohesion and long experience of working together is essential to this ability to improve the performance. The rehearsals are devoted and intended to ensure that all participants are sufficiently disciplined in their actions before appearing in public. The theme chosen should reflect news and the events that concern people around the society and the country as a whole. In the final stage, the working experience should be integrated appropriately into the main theme (Identity) within the performance (cf. Darah 1981: 506).

To structure the plot

The first draft of application is a sequence of images, actions and dialogue with a beginning, middle and ending. But before undertaking that it is very necessary to choose a plot structure, meaning structuring the performance from where to begin and where to end. Because the plot might start at the end of the story or half way in, a nutshell this is the process which reflects how the performance should unfold.

Culturally, stories, idioms and taboos explored are not applied for entertainment but are used to convey messages because they are common to the people. Furthermore, they are applied to enlighten the audience to know and understand that, the use of oral history has become a popular form of contemporary theatre and it is crafted into a theatrical work of art. Performance of this nature also makes us aware that African theatre contains a plot structure in which there is no rule which stipulate how to structure the plot because it depend on the creativity based on how to apply the theatrical work to be experienced.

Characters in action

Characterisation refers to individual performers assigned to play roles complimenting each other. This incipient specialisation, added with experience of each new performance, allow individual performers develop their own repertoires of skills. The performers should know their roles thoroughly and perform with care, as everything in the performance should be integrated appropriately into the main theme.

After the selection process of the material is accomplished, the director sets out and arranges how the scenes are intertwined and improvisation takes place. When asking performers to draw from personal experience it is only logically to be sure that they are also prepared psychologically and talk about the need for confidentiality within the group and be able to refer them for further support if it is needed. This is influenced by the idea that performers express their emotions behind a specific experience or idea using his/her body and visual elements through the use of songs, poetry and action which adds value to them psychological.

Exploration of characters is influenced by repetition because repetition itself is the master of learning in a sense that such style of performance which combines drama, traditional dance and choral music 'total theatre' will need performers to develop their characters to master the style of performance which demand lots of physicality.

Knowing and understanding their characters will reflect through physical appearance as each performer will be assigned to their roles. Performers set an intention for the character before the actual performance so as to recognise his/her utmost ability, skill and demonstrate the unique and emergent quality in performance. The objective of characterisation leads performers to become familiar of each other and it takes a character of the performers to keep audience's attention as attentive as possible.

The design of setting

The stage as a physical environment for presenting an artistic display is nothing new to the theatre sensibility of any human society. The setting and structure of stage implies not only the physical venue but equally the concept, style and content of what goes on in it. Traditional mats utilised within the performance create traditional environments such as receiving audience or visitors in a compound. The conventions of these settings are simple but nonetheless convey a sense of real SeTswana milieu (cf. Nzewi 1981: 437).

The structural setting communicates directly and confronts the audience and gives life to the performance, because the performance is not based on western model of theatre, where auditorium separate spectators from performers due to the fact that this physical structuring affects the form of performance. So the physical structure out-side the conventional of European theatrical structure which is an open space, is very familiar to the whole cast due to the notion that within their Tswana culture they are very much aware that a performance can take place anywhere; for example, be it any space in the community, sports fields and chief's kraal (*kgotla*).

The use of SeTswana cultural songs and choral music are applied in a performance in such a way that, they create artistic mood and atmosphere within the performance, which also draw the audience's attention. Furthermore, these songs are accompanied by the use of drum which is perceived and understood as an instrument which is utilised for many activities, so it is very relevant to make use of drum to create the great mood and atmosphere within the performance and it is considered also as an indigenous instrument to Africans (cf. Green 1981: 63).

Performances are often staged outdoors because they establish continuity of everyday life which is the product of interplay of many factors, including setting, act sequence. These will consist of the set of cultural themes and ethical and social-interactional organising principles that govern the conduct of performance (cf. Bauman 1977: 28). Also, the basic structures of performance are the participants, performers and audience. It should be self-evident that performance cannot occur in isolation, but are mutually interactive and interdependent. In the index are the scene work, bits and pieces of the story, characters, and actions, different ideas about genre and acting style, images, ideas about set, props and costumes. Floor plan is done by the director to reflect the moment to make choices, select the material and arrange it in a way which is appropriate. It is where the director starts to take more creative control over the process of theatricality (cf. Twijnstra/Durden 2013: 203).

The art of our cultures reflect who we are

The main reason for the exploration of this concept is influenced by the thought that, there is lack of transformation in terms of productivity and creativity within Mmabana Arts Culture and Sports Foundation (MACSF). This begs these questions: Are we not capable to work with what we have within our cultures to establish a proper approach in terms of enlightening and awakening people around the society about their cultural forms of theatre and establish a better living for a better society through the work of arts? What do we need in order to experience performances that will attract our people within the societies to theatre?

I have come across many cases whereby it is claimed that Mmabana institutions are no longer serving the purposes for which they were established i.e. to serve the society. That said, members of the society need to understand that they have the ability to stand and represent the impact on making these institutions to grow and develop rather than to rely on government. Members of the society need to understand that the art of our cultures reflect who we are. Therefore, I want to highlight the importance of how artists can come together and produce performances without big budget. In my opinion, we live in a world that is very versatile and we need to learn to utilise what surround us within the societies, where working hard collectively proves that communal decisions are secrets of unity.

In BaTswana culture, the ability to tell a story was acquired through listening to elders of the society camp around the fire in the evening when everyone had completed their daily errands. Stories and idioms were shared by boys during the day (*komadisong*) while looking after livestock. The boys would give each other chances to tell stories told by their grandparents, uncles, aunts, elder brothers and sisters during the evening. The medium of instruction was verbal text incorporated with songs and dance. There were no pens and papers. This method helped them to pay attention attentively to focus and concentration on what was to take place or unfold. Such medium of instruction have a direct link or interaction between body, imagination and memory. For example, if one's attention was on the sensations of body, that awareness will definitely elicit memories, feelings and imagination. The most enlightening factor is that the story, whether successful or not, relies on how the storyteller's voice projection and body manipulation. For me, the attention was always on the utilisation of the body by replacing text with action and reflects how the story would take place by replacing specific part of text with action. This technique is learned mostly from observing and mimicking animals.

Choral group and indigenous dance are integral part of rhythm and sound of life

Generally, in African societies, stories not only revolve around people but also around animals and natural events. Stories were spontaneously re-created by storytellers through application of unique individual vocal and physical styles. According to Green:

"The African style of storytelling is a composite of several skills of the teller himself as he recreates his characters, impersonates all of them and fills in the background, describes the scenes and builds the plot. With gestures, facial expressions and varying intonation of voice that can create a patterned fabric embodying all of the story's tension, mood and atmosphere." (Green 1981: 79)

African storytelling is not static. It moves with the times, adapts to new conditions and change to new dimensions. According to Nawa "indigenous African culture is not sensitive or allergic to influences from other cultures. Actually, it thrives on and evolves around them, subject to reciprocity based on mutual respect, humanity and humility and never ever superiority, arrogance, antagonism and appropriation" (Nawa 2016).

Against this background, I have blended my cultural upbringing with western orientated tutelage at the Tshwane University of Technology (TUT) where I specialised in physical theatre and other performance techniques. This experience has polished my artistic skills and abilities in terms of understanding performance and terminologies applied within the performance. The incorporation of drama, choral group and traditional dance is influenced by the idea that all of these genres are an integral part of the rhythm, sound and cycle of life around the society and also form part of all consuming modes of communication, which is characterised by skill, agility, strength, gracefulness and energy. For example, among BaTswana, drama and dance are often jointly classified as 'play' (literally, *motshameko*) because they have a dramatic form of representation which is complex in form yet rendered in childlike playfulness (cf. Green 1981: 63). Such performances bring these genres together in culture-specific and variable ways, ways that are to be discovered ethnographically within each culture and community. Close observation of this type of performance is the significant aspects of patterning of performance within the societies. The performance becomes the integral component due to the fact that cultural performance tends to be the most prominent performance contexts within a community.

Knowledge from the past, communication with the future

The sustainability of indigenous theatre hinges on the extent of the familiarity of topics or subjects on the part of the audience. Performances of this kind show that African audience understand the logic of the African way of thinking. The nature of the performance also allow to remember that modes of learning were oral which also shows and reflect that knowledge comes from the past. Hence the appropriate approach is to apply the most popular art forms such as repetition of indigenous games which carry powerful messages, stillness and nods and gestures as a tool of communication within the performance. The holistic idea is to move from artistic texts by simply looking at how such texts are rendered in action by approaching phenomena whose primary aim lies in the nature of oral communication in terms of the abstracted textual products of the communicative process. This allows interpreting what we do rather than what we say due to the notion that "the body knows things which about the mind is ignorant too" (Lecoq 2000: 9).

The rationale behind the examination of the subject is better clarification, explanation and demonstration that when we are about to move into something new, it is sensible to first take a stock of what we already have, if only so that the distance travelled can later be measured. It should not be ignored that theatre faces challenges whereby we have to attract and excite audience into theatre. By so doing, it means we have to compete with the relentlessly visual realms of film and television which have replaced oral storytelling. Hence I often record my work so that I employ and reference cinematic devices where younger generation have access to technology and be able to experience the performance through video recording. Through this medium, the indigenous theatrical performance lives on into future generations, and channels or podiums.

Bibliography

Bauman, Richard (1977): Verbal art as performance. Illinois: Waveland Press.

Beik, J. (1987): Play Structure. Lagos.

Chinyowa, Kennedy (2001): The Context, Performance and Meaning of Shona Ritual Drama. In: Lokangaka Losambe und Devi Sarinjeive (eds.): Pre-colonial and post-colonial drama and theatre in Africa. Trenton, NJ: Africa World Press, p. 3-13.

Darah, G. G. (1981): Dramatic Presentation in Udje Dance Performance of the Urhobo. In: Yemi Ogunbiyi (ed.): Drama and theatre in Nigeria. A critical source book. Lagos, Nigeria: Nigeria Magazine.

Enekwe, Ossie (1981): Nigerian Theatre and Drama. Lagos.

Green, L. L. (1981): A Description of Makonde Oral Narratives as Theatre. PhD Thesis. Green State University, Bowling Green.

Lecoq, Jacques; Carasso, Jean-Gabriel; Lallias, Jean-Claude; Bradby, David (2000): The moving body. Teaching creative theatre. London: Bloomsbury.

Nawa, Lebogang L. (2016). Hammanskraal, 2/12/2016. Personal Conversation Obakeng Kgwasi.

Nzewi, M. (1981): Music, Dance, Drama and the Stage in Nigeria. In: Yemi Ogunbiyi (ed.): Drama and theatre in Nigeria. A critical source book. Lagos, Nigeria: Nigeria Magazine.

Ogunbiyi, Yemi (ed.) (1981): Drama and theatre in Nigeria. A critical source book. Lagos, Nigeria: Nigeria Magazine.

Twijnstra, R.; Durden, E. (2014): Theatre Directing in South Africa. Skills and Inspiration. Johannesburg.

Unleashing the caged power of the Black girl
South Africa's sociological theatre landscape

Refilwe Madumo

"A Black woman combines the dual stigmas of being both female and black in a society that devalues both." (Myers 1975: 240) In a world where a young Black womxn's strength is equated to that of a proverbial *'imbokodo'* (a rock/ boulder), how could she know that the pulpy joyfulness she feels inside her chest matters? In a world that requires her to figuratively *'tshwara thipa ka bogaleng'* (hold the sharp edge of a knife), how could she know the value of her blood? In a world where mothers' comforting words are *"bontle bo a itshokelwa"* (beauty can only be real if it came through pain), how would she know that she was born beautiful? In a world where the constant reminder is *'monna ke selepe' (a man is an axe)* – he can cut down any tree he chooses – how could she aspire to be anything besides out of his way? SHE is *the* tree: thick, an unmoving trunk begging to be mowed down. Conveniently omitting that the tree is the source of the air we breathe.

From a very young age, it is planted in the girl-child's head that her ability to dream is limited to the patriarchal structures under which she exists. Fordham says: "In a socially, culturally, racially stratified society, cultural-specific routes to womanhood are inevitable." (Fordham 1993: 3-32) Girl-children are therefore *'Othered'* if they attempt to make sense of their lives away from the male gaze. According to Holland, Ramazanoglu, Sharpe and Thomson the male gaze breeds in girl-children a constant struggle with conformity, agency and resistance (cf. Holland et al. 1998: 1-14). Adichie unpacks this dilemma by saying:

"We teach girls to shrink themselves, to make themselves smaller. We say to girls: you can have ambition, but not too much. You should aim to be successful but not too successful; otherwise you will threaten the man. We raise girls to see each other as competitors – not for jobs or for accomplishments, which I think can be a good thing, but for the attention of men. The problem with gender is that it prescribes how we should be rather than recognising who we are." (Adichie 2014: 26)

Gilroy warns that there is a tendency to envisage the crisis of Blackness as the crisis of Black masculinity alone (cf. Gilroy 1993: 7). He unpacks this further by arguing that: "The integrity of the race is denned primarily as the integrity of its men-folk and secondarily through the patriarchically ordered nature of the families over which they would proudly and justly preside if white supremacy did not intervene and create catastrophe." (Ibid.)

According to Gherardi and Poggio, the relationship between male and female is expounded by the positions the respective genders are assigned according to a situated discourse (cf. Gherardi/Poggio 2002: 247). In the rural spaces of South Africa, there is a tug-of-war between patriarchal practices and the African cultural traditions that govern society. Both sides inflict constricting rules on girl-children even before they have an awareness of who they are. In the poorest spaces, the lack of resources makes it difficult for people to progress. When one's daily worry is confined to whether there will be food on the table, one's future view is reduced to the prospect of the next meal. This is even truer for the girl-children. Their primary purpose in their community is to serve in and around the home for the benefit of the male figures in their lives.

Troublesome transition into dissembling

Bem theorises that gender bias is used to organise and direct behaviour based on a society's gender norms and expectations (cf. Bem 1993: 80-83). For girl-children, the social conditions under which they live limit their hopes of escaping their hardships. The transition from girlhood to womxnhood proves to be troublesome. Simply because the transition from being a girl to being a womxn is so vast and requires a kind of morphing into something else. Brown and Gilligan postulate that the passage out of girlhood can be one into silence, disconnection and dissembling. "A kind of troubled crossing that culture has plotted with dead-ends and detours." (Brown/ Gilligan 1992: 17)

Girls who are outspoken and opinionated in their childhood, often grow up to be reserved because "ladies" are not supposed to be confrontational – therefore, denoting that the label of 'lady' be ascribed to social requisites and conditioning. Young womxn give up their feelings, thoughts and opinions for the chance to create more secure relationships for themselves within their communities. Woolf calls this phenomenon the "adultery of the mind" because young women learn to silence their inner voices in order to become 'good' (cf. Woolf 1938).

I am one of those girls who grew up under societal structural constraints. I come from Taung, a village in the North West Province of South Africa. My parents gave birth to three sweet princesses before I came along. I was born with too much spirit and, as a result, was a hassle. I was constantly being told to pull down my dress; to sit with my legs closed; to watch the level of my voice; to look away when an elder addresses me. My innate fascination with other human beings began to suffer because all these constrictions denied me access to people on equal footing. I grew up thinking there was something wrong with me. I could not possibly be a good girl because I did not know how not to make these mistakes. I found a little more freedom running with the boys because they were allowed to be more abrasive. The notion of the perfect little girl made me feel broken.

I didn't have language to articulate these things but I could feel them. I could feel a lump in my throat before I needed to scream. I could feel the stirring in my fingers that caused me to loop them around the hem of my dress. I could feel the weight of my arms that could only be released by dragging the linen off my bed and rolling it into a tight ball. I could feel the itch in my feet that caused me to walk until I felt nothing but the shuffle of my flip-flops hitting my heels. Long before I had words to speak, my body knew.

Singing and dancing that healed

The only thing that gave me respite was make-belief. If I stayed away long enough in my fictitious world, analysing the things happening around me was less frightening. I could set the rules and pace at which my world turned. I could reproduce confusing emotions at a gradient conducive to how I could make sense of things. Singing and dancing with myself was the only balm that healed. I didn't know what it was called but it was the only tool I had to survive the turmoil of not being good enough.

Soon enough, I saw a student recital at a school where my mother taught English and for the first time, I recognised what I had been doing, albeit it be by myself. I watched in awe as young womxn in traditional dress created tapestries of ideas, challenging the narratives that up until then had been the norm for me. I realised then the power of what my body could do. It could perform. This was my language. That was how I made sense of the world. That was what my body had been trying to tell me all along. My body could reincarnate and embody so many lives. It could challenge everything I had been taught and reflect it back to the people who had taught it to me. The power to create became the method to my madness. It gave me the power to say 'no' with conviction. The power to say this is my truth and own it. It taught me that I am at the center of my universe and I control the narrative. It gave me the ability to let go and trust that my body will always know what to do. It gave me the courage to walk alone if I needed to. It helped me to recognise the power of my choices. From childhood, performance had been my first positive action.

O'Toole and Donelan contend that the power of performance and theatre to interrogate social conditions (cf. O'Toole/Donelan 1996: 11). Theatre provides a cultural space for dialogue and exchange of ideas in real life. It also provides the potential to assist in the genuine empowerment of young people. Some young people live in geo-political war zones, others within wars at community and family level (cf. Ahmed 2004). However, according to Bretherton young people anywhere can call up the natural and universal human quality of make-believe to suspend the apparent social reality and its imperatives. From there they can create and project themselves into fictitious worlds where the rules can be changed and new possibilities can appear (cf. Bretherton 1989: 24).

Theatre empowers the society

Furthermore, theatre empowers the society by affecting the personal, cultural, communal and socio-political realms (cf. O'Toole/Donelan 1996). For the personal, through using and engaging with theatre one's sense of self is transformed. Learning about genres, histories and a range of choices is an important part of personal empowerment. For the cultural, theatre is the means of making the invisible influences of culture visible and discussable. Theatre acts as a mirror of how we are made and of who we might become. For the communal, theatre can be used as an act of community in which we actively participate in the making of communal representation. Theatre can be the social and aesthetic expression of a community's hopes, fears and dreams. For the socio/political, theatre can be a rehearsal for change and an arena for radical dialogue.

But the experience is not without obstacles because the theatre landscape is not immune to sociological determinants that are cruel to the Black experience. But the relevant point for now is: in spite of inherent limitations, theatre helped me, as a Black womxn, to learn how to carve out my own space in the world. This is how I learnt that I am not a *boulder*. Theatre taught me that I am malleable. That my spirit may be knocked, pressed and hammered but my body will know exactly where to store that pain and release it on a stage – I could do it alone or with as many people as I wished. I also learnt that, though, my body may house many truths; it is not a temple. It is a forest with thick canopies of trees and sweet scented wildflowers sprouting in the under-wood. With theatre, I have grown back over and over despite my devastations.

Bibliography

Adichie, Chimamanda Ngozi (2014): We should all be feminists. 1st published. London: Fourth Estate.

Ahmed, Sara (2004): The cultural politics of emotion. London.

Bem, Sandra L. (1993): The lenses of gender. Transforming the debate on sexual inequality. New York. Available: http://www.jstor.org/stable/10.2307/j.cttın q86n.

Bretherton, Inge (1989): Pretense: The form and function of make-believe play. In: Developmental Review 9 (4), p. 383-401.

Brown, Lyn Mikel; Gilligan, Carol (1992): Meeting at the Crossroads. Women's Psychology and Girls' Development.

Fordham, Signithia (1993): "Those Loud Black Girls": (Black) Women, Silence, and Gender "Passing" in the Academy. In: Anthropology & Education Quarterly 24 (1), p. 3-32.

Gherardi, Silvia; Poggio, Barbara: Creating and recreating gender order in organizations. In: Journal of World Business, 36 (3), p. 245-259.

Gilroy, Paul (1993): The black Atlantic. Modernity and double consciousness. Cambridge, Mass.: Harvard Univ. Press.

Holland, Janet; Ramazanoglu, Caroline; Sharpe, Sue; Thomso, Rachel (1998): The male in the head. Young people, heterosexuality and power. London: Tufnell Press.

O'Toole, John; Donelan, Kate (1996): Reflections in the River. Drama, culture and empowerment. The IDEA dialogues. Brisbane: International Drama/ Theatre & Education Association.

Woolf, Virginia (1938): Three Guineas. London.

Wright Myers, Lena (1975): Black Women and Self-esteem. In: Sociological Inquiry 45 (2-3), p. 240-250, Last Access: 6/28/2018.

Epilogue:
Theatre and the post-apartheid condition

Towards a new vision

Mike van Graan

Theatre – like all other sectors of South African society – reflects the structural legacies of our apartheid past and will continue to do so, unless structural interventions are effected at policy and implementation levels. This short paper will provide proposals as to how this might happen.

Divisions within the theatre sector

Notwithstanding twenty-four years of post-apartheid transformation, key divides persist and in some cases, have been exacerbated since 1994.

These divides include the following:

Infrastructural divisions
Nationally-subsidised theatre infrastructure exists only in the cities in which they existed during the apartheid era. Artscape in Cape Town, PACOFS in Bloemfontein, Durban's Playhouse Theatre and the State Theatre in Pretoria – all former performing arts councils of the apartheid era – have been joined by the Market Theatre (which now includes the Windybrow Theatre) – as recipients of more than a R200 million per year. Despite the 1996 White Paper's vision to ensure that "everyone has the right to participate in the cultural life of the community and to enjoy the arts", some of the country's poorer provinces – Limpopo, North West, Eastern Cape, Mpumalanga and Northern Cape – do not have theatres (or similar performing arts infrastructure) that are subsidised by national government. Accordingly, the theatre industry continues to be concentrated in the major cities, theatre markets remain underdeveloped in less-resourced provinces and theatre makers in those provinces have limited access to infrastructure to create and distribute their work, and little access to funding and markets with disposable income to sustain their work.

Urban-Rural divisions

This infrastructural divide also contributes to the perpetuation of the urban-rural divides regarding who has access to theatre, who produces theatre and are able to build national brands, and the content and interests that theatre serves.

Economic divisions

There is a growing Black middle-class, reflected in the audiences at theatres such as the Market Theatre in Johannesburg and the State Theatre in Pretoria. More Black theatre makers are now able to access funding to create and distribute their work through state-subsidised theatres and the National Arts Council and its provincial equivalents, where such exist and are functional. But the economic divisions rooted in apartheid's maldistribution of opportunities, technical skills and resources are no more starkly reflected than in the Afrikaans-language festivals and other parts of the South African theatre sector. The Klein Karoo National Arts Festival, Woordfees, Vryfees, Aardklop and Inniebos Festival are generally supported by private sector sponsorship, with some being linked to universities where Afrikaans was the dominant language, and the resourced White Afrikaans community is able to pay higher theatre ticket prices (R80-R150) to sustain the work produced at these festivals.

Language divisions

Despite there being eleven official languages, most professional theatre continues to be produced in the apartheid-era official languages i.e. English, with the Afrikaans festivals producing theatre in Afrikaans, with the support of the National Afrikaans Theatre Initiative (NATI). This impacts on whose stories are told, who has access to these stories (the Afrikaans festivals rarely have access to theatre produced by Black South Africans and Black audiences seldom have access to Afrikaans theatre) and on the reviewing and judging of theatre (judges in the major theatre awards in the country and reviewers generally do not speak nor understanding indigenous languages).

Audience divisions

Infrastructure, economics and language contribute to the divisions between audiences, but in addition, different audiences – defined in apartheid's terms – demand theatre and stories in which they are reflected, with theatre that seeks to cross racial boundaries attracting smaller audiences than audiences that consciously play to "ethnic" audiences.

Gender divides

There are many more Black actors who are prominent on South African stages, but the gender divides continue, particularly in the disciplines of playwriting and directing. There have been initiatives to address this, but these have borne little fruit, particularly with regard to Black women playwrights and directors.

Technical skills

The two major theatre regions are Gauteng and the Western Cape, but while significant progress has been made in Gauteng with regard to developing and providing opportunities for costume and set designers, lighting designers and other technical skills, the as reflected in the annual Fleur du Cap theatre awards, little transformation has taken place in these areas in the Western Cape theatre industry.

"Professional" and "community"

The apartheid era nomenclatures that referenced "professional theatre" as mainly White, mainstream theatre and "community theatre" being a label for theatre made by Black theatre makers, with much greater Black participation in mainstream theatre, the divides would appear to have "professional" mean that which happens in established theatres, dealing with "universal" issues and generally reasonably paid from box office income, while "community theatre" is associated with non-formal spaces, social issues and funded or low-income theatre.

In summary, post-apartheid policy and practice have

- placed an inappropriate "creative industries" policy burden on theatre to sustain itself largely in the market place, favouring those who have skills, reputation and resources
- allocated huge sums of public funding to infrastructure that serves an urban elite and continues to deny access to theatre to the majority of SA's citizens
- largely failed to provide the vision, the strategies and the funding fundamentally to transform the industry and the role of the industry within SA, other than through superficial demographic institutional "transformation"
- failed to put practical "social cohesion" strategies into place so that racial, urban-rural, gender and other divides persist
- while there has been much demographic change – particularly in the governance and management of publicly-funded theatres – there has been little structural change so that awards, festivals and the country's stages continue to reflect historical privilege.

Towards an alternate vision

As part of the revision of the White Paper on Arts, Culture and Heritage, I produced a Discussion Document – *Towards a Vision and Strategies for the development of the South African dance and theatre sectors* – which outlined the following proposals that would be would be features of an ideal theatre (and dance) sector. These would go some way to addressing the structural issues that hold back the industry.

1. One nationally-subsidised theatre in Polokwane, Nelspruit, Mahikeng, Kimberley, Pretoria, Johannesburg, Bloemfontein, Durban, Pietermaritz-burg, East London, Port Elizabeth and Cape Town, with these comprising a national circuit of theatres, able to support national tours by theatre and dance companies, and with production budgets to purchase, commission and co-produce work.
2. Artistic directors are to serve a maximum of five years at state-subsidised theatres, allowing for fresh blood to be injected and to prevent long-term gatekeeping.
3. An independent theatre company of 10 and an independent dance company of 12, each at least 80% Black and 50% women, resident at each of the nationally-subsidised theatres (i.e. one per province); such companies are to be assured of 3-year core funding.
4. A resident director and/or playwright and/or choreographer based at each of the nationally-subsidised theatres on 1 to 3-year contracts.
5. At least one education and training institution per province offering diploma, degree and certificate courses in dance, theatre, entrepreneur-ship, marketing, administration, policy, etc.
6. At least 50 multi-functional art centres located throughout all nine prov-inces, with highly skilled administrators/managers (rather than political deployees) running them.
7. A network of 10-15 festivals meeting with the managers of the national circuit of venues to plan, co-produce national tours by dance and theatre productions.
8. A touring agency with at least ten theatre and ten dance productions trav-elling abroad each year.
9. A national database of at least 5000 people making their living in the dance and theatre sectors, each receiving a monthly newsletter about devel-opments in their sector.
10. An online archive of all theatre and dance productions of the previous two years.
11. Nine provincial (primary and secondary) schools' dance and theatre festi-vals.

12. Legislated minimum wages for dance and theatre workers and approved remuneration scales used by all theatres, festivals and independent companies.

13. Social security for dancers and theatres with customized medical, pension and unemployment schemes.

14. A Code of Conduct adopted across the dance and theatre sectors, with a Labour Ombudsman and a Protector-type agency in place to take up issues on behalf of those who are abused within the sector.

15. An annual national theatre and/or dance conference, with monthly public forums and a national dance and theatre publication.

16. A politically non-partisan national theatre and dance structure that actively monitors, helps to implement and evaluates policies and strategies affecting the dance and theatre sectors.

17. Publicity and marketing entrepreneurs and companies in each of the nine provinces to build audiences and sustainable markets.

18. 150-200 theatre productions and 50-100 dance productions competing for excellence awards on an annual basis.

19. Funding structures and strategies in place that recognize the different functions of theatre and dance, and that assure the sustainability of these sectors.

20. Average audiences and theatre markets in excess of 50% consistently across the country.

21. Constructive and mutually-respectful working relationships between government and funding agencies on the one hand and civil society structures and practitioners on the other.

22. Support for initiatives that use existing infrastructure (school and church halls, homes of individuals, etc.) for rehearsal and performance space.

23. Artistic directors of the national circuit venues and companies to meet and plan national/regional tours by the companies.

24. Tertiary institutions to audition and host companies for one-year on graduation to learn the practicalities of running an independent company.

25. Theatres/companies to have resident designers, etc. to provide work/opportunities for new lighting, costume, stage designers i.e. those in technical fields.

26. A research publication documenting development of theatre and profiling new entrants.

27. Annual playwriting competitions in all languages, indigenous languages in particular.

28. All subsidised venues and venues to have translation/surtitle facilities.

29. Ongoing masterclasses be provided for actors to learn from local and international people who have excelled.

South Africa is not short of creative theatre talent. World-class theatre productions are produced with regularity, despite, rather than because of the "theatre system". The theatre sector has numerous committed, passionate individuals who are prepared to work long hours for little reward. There is, however, a disjuncture between those who create on the one hand, and, on the other, those responsible for policy and funding related to the theatre sector.

Theatre has different economies of scale to other creative industries such as publishing, visual art, craft and music. As with health, education and security, the theatre economy comprises commercial, subsidised and mixed economy elements. The potential for theatre to serve the full range of South Africa's population – rather than primarily an urban elite with disposable income – is dependent on policy makers realising its potential and the different and unique conditions under which theatre is created and distributed, and thus devising and implementing appropriate policy and funding strategies to realise this potential.

Authors List

KATLEGO CHALE is lecturer for Arts Administration, Theatre, History, Speech, Sounds, Physical Theatre and Stage Combat at the Tshwane University of Technology (TUT), South Africa

KHAYELIHLE DOM GUMEDE is a writer and a director at The Market Theatre, Johannesburg, South Africa

JOACHIM FIEBACH was a professor at the Department of Theatre at the Freie Universität Berlin, Germany

THERESA FREY is a Master Student at the University of Hildesheim and a theatre maker, Germany

HENNING FÜLLE is a dramaturge and researcher at the University of Hildesheim, Germany

YVETTE HARDIE is a theatre maker and the president of ASSITEJ, the International Association of Theatre for Children and Young People, Cape Town, South Africa

JULIUS HEINICKE is professor for applied cultural studies at the Coburg University of Applied sciences and Arts, Germany

ROLF C. HEMKE is dramaturge, the festival director of the Kunstfest Weimar and a PhD student at the Department of Cultural Policy at the University of Hildesheim, Germany

PETRA JEROMA is a Master Student at the University of Hildesheim and theatre maker, Germany

OBAKENG KGWASI is a PhD Candiate at the Ambrose Ally University, Ekpoma, Nigeria

JOHANNA KRAFT is a Master Student at the University of Hildesheim and theatre maker, Germany

ISA LANGE is the spokesperson of the University of Hildesheim, Germany

JANINE LEWIS is associate professor and the Head of Department of Entertainment Technology at the Tshwane University of Technology (TUT), South Africa

REFILWE MADUMO is a theatre practitioner, actress and registered for MTech Drama at the Tshwane University of Technology (TUT), South Africa

MOTSUMI MAKHENE is a cultural practitioner and arts and culture policy analyst, South Africa

ONGEZWA MBELE is a PhD Candidate at the Drama Department of the University of Cape Town (UCT), South Africa

SEFAKO BETHUEL MOHLOMI is a Chairperson at the North West Cultural Policy Reading Group, South Africa

MONTSHIWA K. MOSHOUNYANE is a lecturer at the University of Free State, South Africa

NONDUMISO LWAZI MSIMANGA is a former a lecturer at the University of Witswatersrand School of Arts, free-lance arts journalist, and currently Artistic Director at the Olive Tree Theatre in Alexandra Township, South Africa.

LEBOGANG L. NAWA is a former Post-Doctoral Researcher at the Tshwane University of Technology (TUT) and now Director of privately self-owned Segarona Culture Institute, South Africa

CALVIN RATLADI is an MTech Drama student at the Tshwane University of Technology (TUT), producer, director, writer, actor/performer, choreographer, fieldworker and arts administrator, South Africa

WOLFGANG SCHNEIDER is chair holder of the UNESCO Chair in Cultural Policy for the Arts in Development and professor for cultural policy at the University of Hildesheim, Germany